IMAGES
of America

POCATELLO

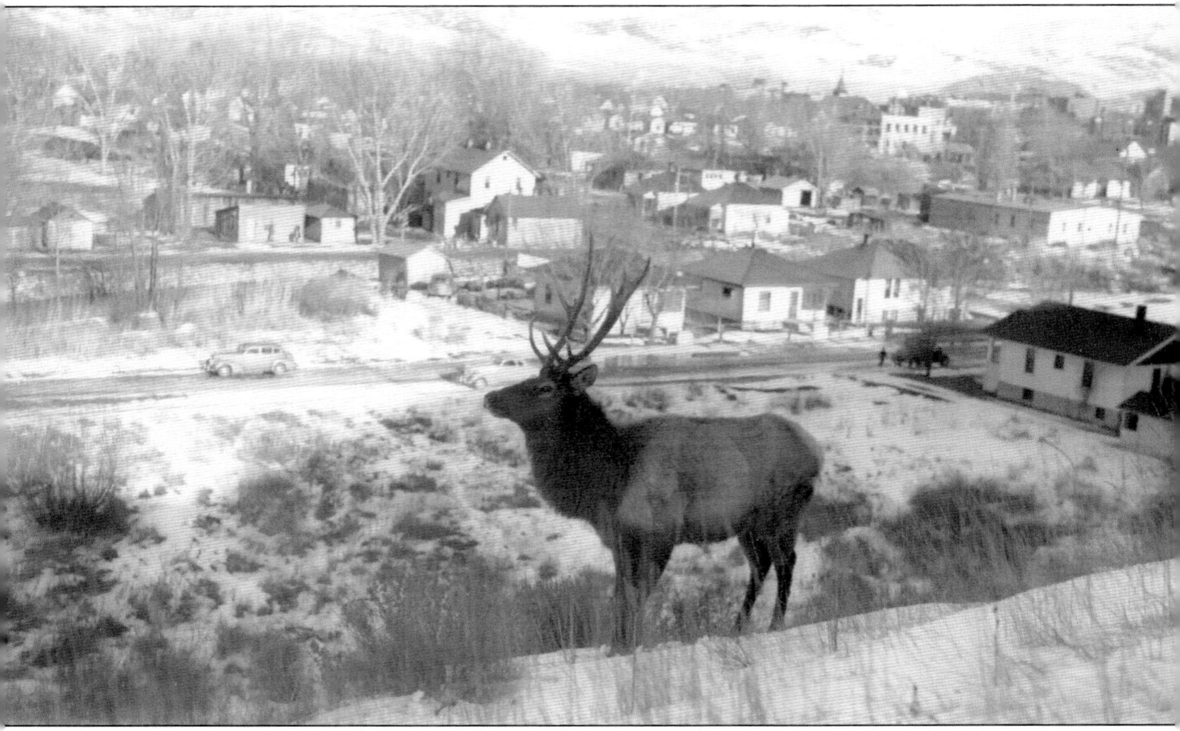

This c. 1940 photograph of an elk along the West Bench area of Pocatello reflects both the urban and rural nature of Pocatello. Even today, wildlife is a common sight both in and around the city, although sighting some wildlife, like elk, tends to be rather rare. (Bannock County Historical Society.)

On the Cover: This 1938 photograph of West Center Street looks east. A variety of retail outlets are visible in this shot of downtown Pocatello. Many of these buildings still stand today. (Bannock County Historical Society.)

IMAGES
of America

POCATELLO

Walter P. Mallette and Lance J. Holladay

ARCADIA
PUBLISHING

ISBN 978-0-7385-9645-7

Published by Arcadia Publishing
Charleston, South Carolina

Printed in the United States of America

Library of Congress Control Number: 2012945459

For all general information, please contact Arcadia Publishing:
Telephone 843-853-2070
Fax 843-853-0044
E-mail sales@arcadiapublishing.com
For customer service and orders:
Toll-Free 1-888-313-2665

Visit us on the Internet at www.arcadiapublishing.com

To all those who call Pocatello their home.

Contents

ACKNOWLEDGMENTS

This book is the product of a collaboration of two authors. We found out about our common love of Pocatello history through a social media forum. Despite the fact that we graduated from different high schools, we found that our shared interest in Pocatello's history bonded us in a way that reflects the best of the city.

This book would not have been possible without the help of many people who were kind enough to grant us access to resources that would not have been available to us otherwise. To this end, we wish to thank Tabatha Butler and her staff at the Bannock County Historical Society (BCHS); Robin Stanger at the Department of Special Collections, Idaho State University (ISU); Kenneth Swanson at the Idaho Military History Museum (IMHM); Daisy Njoku, Stephanie Christensen, and Gina Rappaport at the National Anthropological Archives, Smithsonian Institution (NAA); the archives staff at the Idaho State Historical Society (ISHS); and Cindy Brightenburg at the Harold B. Lee Library, Brigham Young University (BYU). Our thanks also go to Herman Garcia for access to his Bistline photograph collection, Alison Gwinn May for access to her family's photograph collection, and Steven Cluff and Paul Leffler for access to their photograph collections and information. We also wish to thank Amy Kline, our editor at Arcadia Publishing, for her suggestions, endless patience, and understanding while we were making our way through the writing of this book.

We also offer our sincere thanks and appreciation to our families and friends, whose love and support made the journey a rewarding experience. We could not have undertaken this task without their support, and for that, we are most grateful. Finally, we wish to thank the people of Pocatello, past and present, for this is their story, and we hope that we did justice to them in this book.

Introduction

Pocatello, well known in the area as Gate City, is located in the Portneuf Valley where it opens into the Snake River Plain. It was a "Gateway to the Northwest" during the freight wagon and stagecoach era, again as a railroad junction, and even now, as a junction for Interstate Highways 15 and 86. Named in honor of a Northwestern Shoshoni tribal chief, the city of Pocatello is situated in Southeastern Idaho along the banks of the Portneuf River.

The first inhabitants of this area were Bannock and Shoshoni Indians, and the first outsiders who came to the Portneuf Valley were traders led by Capt. Nathaniel Wyeth, who established Fort Hall on June 15, 1834. Originally a military post, Fort Hall instead served as a trading post and way station for wagon trains traveling on the Oregon Trail.

In the early 1860s, what is now the city of Pocatello was nothing more than a couple of stage stops along a freight wagon and stagecoach road through the Portneuf Valley, adjacent to the Fort Hall location. The wagon roads that led from Fort Hall were, in places, little more than wagon wheel ruts. This route, which has also been referred to as "Idaho's Gold Road," made the movement of people and supplies possible between Salt Lake City, Utah, and gold-mining towns in Montana, then still part of the Idaho Territory. This trail through the valley was originally used as a branch of the Oregon Trail, with the main route actually passing north, near Fort Hall. In 1868, this area in the Portneuf Valley became part of the Fort Hall Indian Reservation.

The transcontinental railroad arrived in 1869 with all of its potential. The discovery of gold in Montana encouraged the establishment of a rail line from the mines to Salt Lake City, threading through the Portneuf Valley. But the Bannock and Shoshoni did not make this easy. The uprising by the nearby Nez Perce tribes at the time, which threatened to involve the Bannock and Shoshoni, added to complications. After protracted negotiations between the government and local chiefs, a narrow right-of-way was granted through the reservation for the Union Pacific Railroad on July 18, 1881. Later on, in 1882, the Pacific Hotel and Station was built along the rail line, becoming the first of many railroad-related structures in the new settlement of Pocatello Junction.

Narrow-gauge railroad tracks were laid by the Utah & Northern Railroad (originally the Utah Northern Railroad), north through Southeast Idaho and the Portneuf Valley towards Montana. These tracks were changed to standard gauge between Pocatello and McCammon, Idaho, later in 1882, with the entire line between Pocatello and Silver Bow, Montana, converted to standard gauge later on. Soon, railroad shops and related structures were set up along the tracks. The Oregon Short Line Railroad laid standard-gauge tracks west toward Boise and Oregon. They also had shops and equipment in the Portneuf Valley. In due course, this collection of shops, huts, tents, and shacks became known as Pocatello Junction.

Pocatello Junction received a boost in 1887 when the railroad-related facilities at Eagle Rock, Idaho, (later renamed Idaho Falls) were transferred to the facilities already in place in Pocatello Junction. Workers from the Eagle Rock facility arrived, along with their families. This migration led to a construction boom, which in turn led to further migration. Continued growth led to Pocatello's incorporation as a townsite by a special act of Congress on September 1, 1888. Pocatello became a village the following year, on April 29, 1889, and a "city of the second class" in 1892.

From that point forward, Pocatello grew rapidly. From an estimated 3,000 people residing in the town in 1892, Pocatello had 4,046 residents listed in the 1900 census, 9,112 residents in the 1910 census, and an estimated 16,000 residents by 1915. The main facilities for the Utah Northern and

Oregon Short Line Railroads west of Omaha were located in Pocatello. Because of this activity, Pocatello became the second-largest city in Idaho, after Boise.

Another major factor in the growth of Pocatello was the Academy of Idaho. The academy was established in 1901 as a college preparatory and industrial school, and in a noteworthy development for the time, was open to all social strata. From an original enrollment of 40 students, the Academy of Idaho grew to 295 students by 1910. Renamed the Idaho Technical Institute (1915), the University of Idaho, Southern Branch (1927), and Idaho State College (1947), Idaho State University (1962) continues to play an important role in Pocatello.

With its growing importance as a commercial center for the Southeastern Idaho region, Pocatello soon generated enough wealth to encourage the establishment of cultural venues. Theaters, to be supplanted in due course by cinemas, were able to attract top-level talent to perform at the city's stages. This legacy has continued in Pocatello to this day, with many cultural events still held in the city, and public art featured in both the downtown area and the Idaho State University campus.

One by-product of the rapid growth of railroad operations was the influx of various ethnic and racial groups that were hired to work in the rail shops and trains and who also came to work in other businesses in the city. This influx of Greeks, Italians, Chinese, Japanese, and Mexicans, along with immigrants from other countries, as well as African Americans migrating from the South, created a highly diverse population within the city limits. These immigrants lived in a city that already had a population of Bannock and Shoshoni. This diversity was not initially welcomed by all; in due course, measures were undertaken to limit certain groups from residing within the downtown area—the so-called "West Side." These residents were relegated to areas of the "East Side" of the city—opposite the railroad tracks. While this discrimination was deeply felt by the residents of the East Side, increased diversity made Pocatello a more cosmopolitan city, enriching the community.

While Pocatello was able to remain relatively prosperous during the 1920s, there were signs of trouble. The fall of commodity prices after World War I caused hardship in rural Idaho, which led to a lower level of consumption in Pocatello itself, and the Wall Street Crash of 1929 only made the situation worse. Soon, railroad traffic, the lifeblood of the Pocatello economy, dropped off, causing rumors of layoffs to spring up. With the coming of the Roosevelt administration in 1933, the situation changed for the better. Such programs as the Works Progress Administration (WPA) and the Civilian Conservation Corps (CCC) left their mark on Pocatello, both in terms of structures (such as the Center Street underpass and the Pocatello High School gym) and the opportunities to earn a living that were granted to residents who were otherwise left with few.

World War II affected Pocatello deeply, both those who went off to fight overseas, as well as those who did their part on the home front. Pocatello became an important player in the war effort, with both an Army Air Force training facility and the Naval Ordnance Plant. The railroad, which transported troops and supplies, also assumed a greater importance during the war. This meant that Pocatello's importance as a railroad facility also increased during the war.

The post–World War II economic boom in the United States benefitted Pocatello in numerous ways. The railroads benefitted from increased prosperity in the country, which in the case of Pocatello led to increased employment and higher wages. The influx of veterans brought housing development as well as higher enrollment at the University of Idaho, Southern Branch (Idaho State College). These events propelled Pocatello to a level of prosperity it had not seen before.

Unfortunately, the prosperity of the postwar years did not last. The major shift from railroads to airplanes and automobiles for transporting both passengers and commercial goods led to a reduction in the workforce. And Pocatello was not spared. The overall economy of the city took a significant hit, the aftershocks of which continue to be felt to this day. However, the city shows slow but steady growth, and the people of Pocatello continue to have pride in their city and their heritage, and a number of businesses, industries, and institutions, such as Idaho State University, continue to give Pocatello a place in the world.

One

Early Pocatello

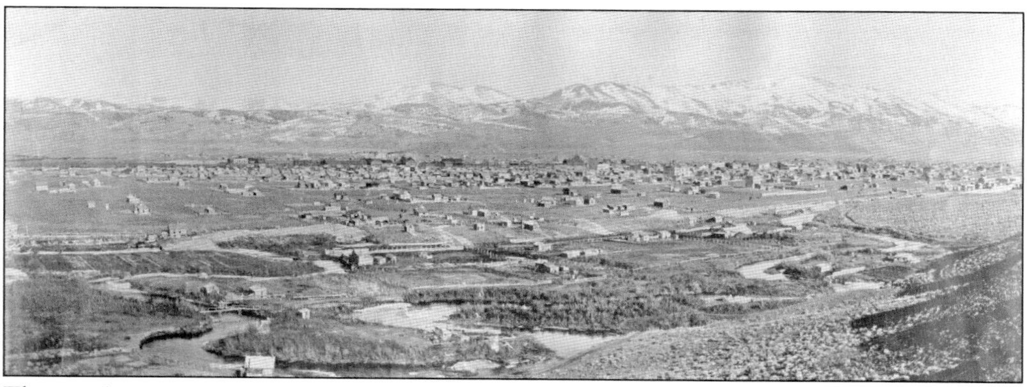

This 1895 panoramic photograph shows early Pocatello. The Oregon Short Line depot and the Pacific Hotel are in the center of the photograph, with the beginnings of the downtown area on the right. At this time, the town had not grown much beyond these points, save for some agricultural activity on the banks of the Portneuf River. (BCHS.)

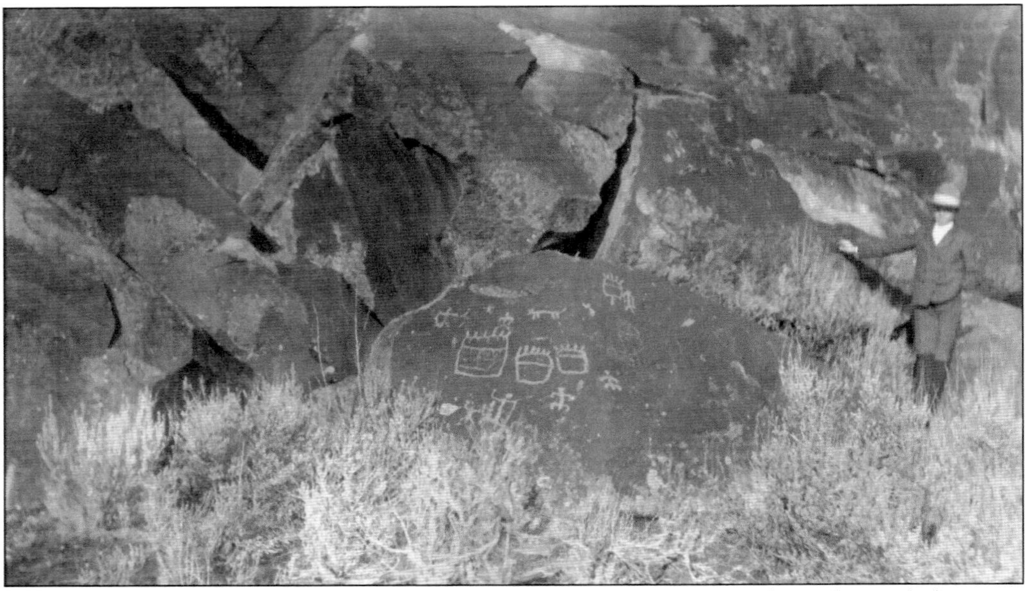

The earliest inhabitants of the Pocatello Basin were the native Bannock and Shoshoni. Their carvings could be found on the faces of boulders along what is now the area east of South Second Avenue and the Portneuf River, on the southern edge of Pocatello. The young man shown here is Paul Bistline. (Bistline.)

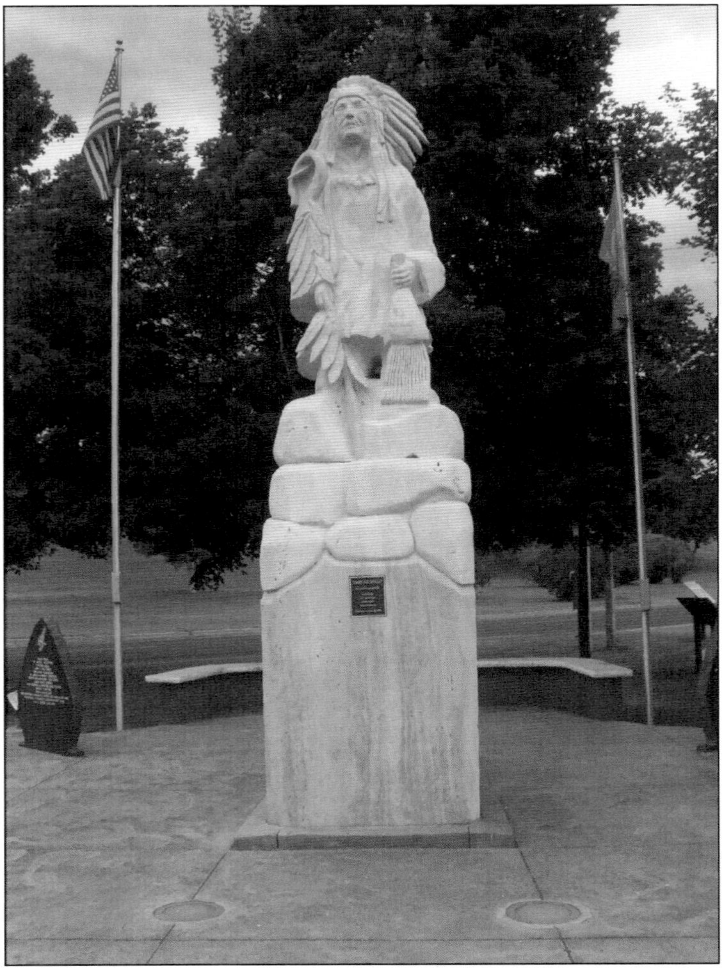

Chief Pocatello is commemorated by this statue, located on South Fifth Avenue on the southern outskirts of the city. This would have to be considered an approximation of the likeness of Chief Pocatello, since no photographs of him have been verified to exist. (Walter Mallette.).

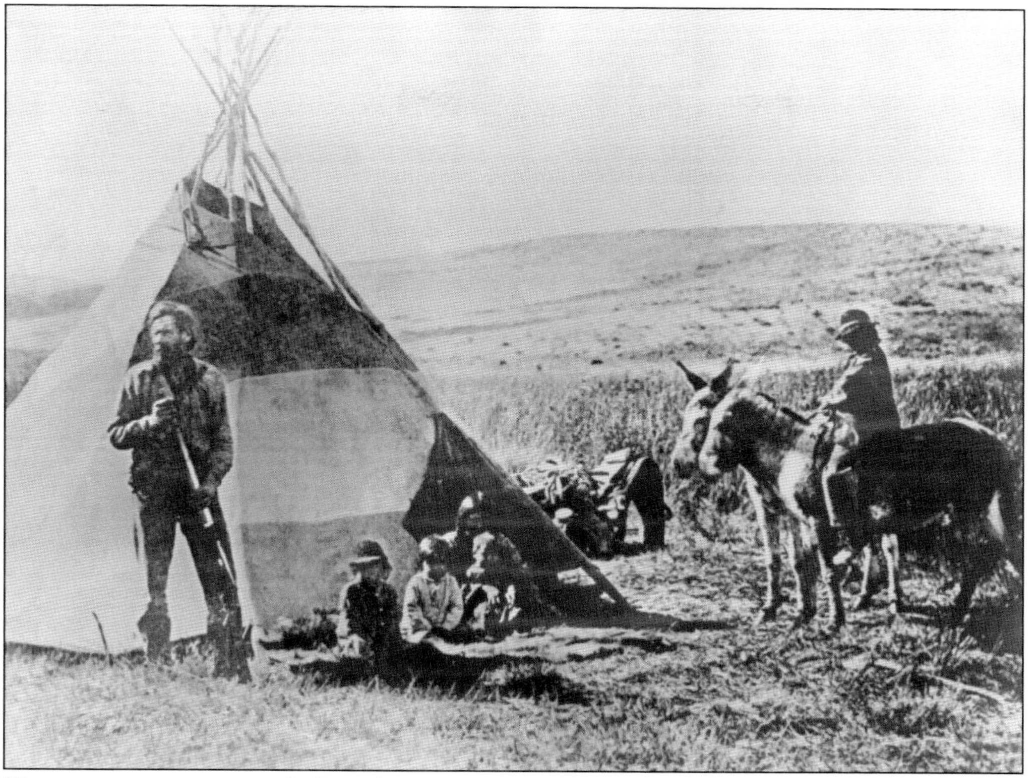

These teepees were erected when the Bannock and Shoshoni were moved to the Fort Hall Reservation. Teepees were seen on the outskirts of Pocatello Junction as late as 1886. (BCHS.)

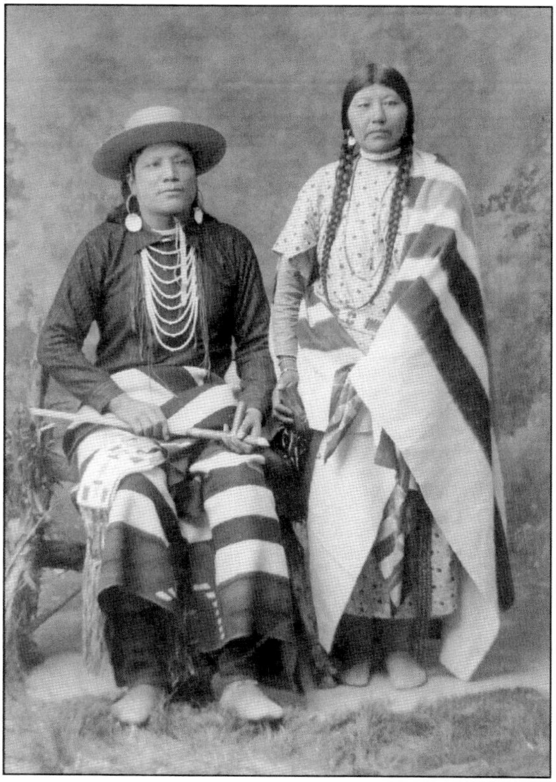

One of the major figures in the Bannock tribal structure on the Fort Hall Reservation was Pat Tyhee, seen here with his wife in a Benedicte Wrensted studio photograph. Tyhee's legacy lives on in Pocatello with a street and an elementary school named in his honor. (BCHS.)

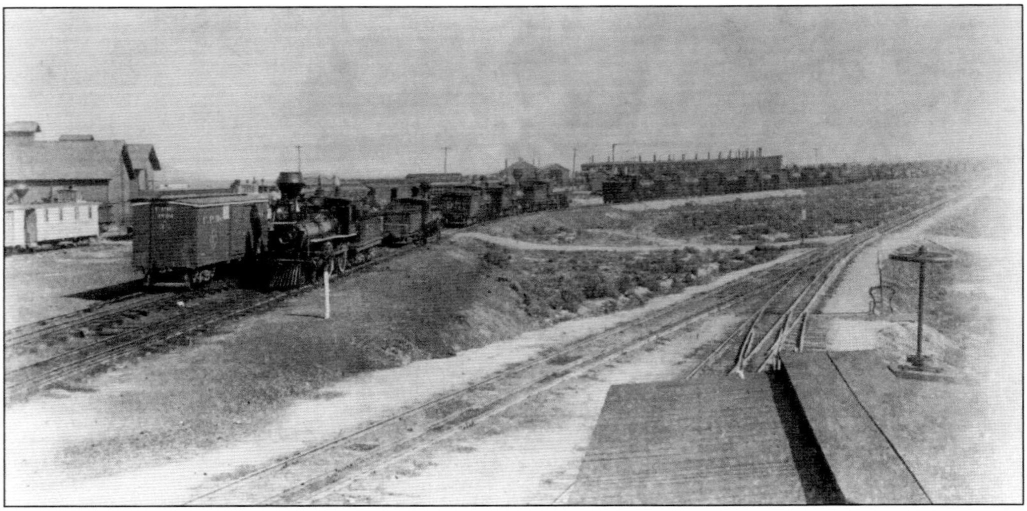

Railroad facilities are visible in one of the earliest photographs of Pocatello known to exist, taken either in 1885 or 1886. At this time, both the Oregon Short Line (OSL) and the Utah & Northern Railroads (both owned by Union Pacific) had buildings and equipment in Pocatello. The OSL took over operations in the area from the Utah & Northern Railroad, and the narrow-gauge rails were widened to standard gauge. (BCHS.)

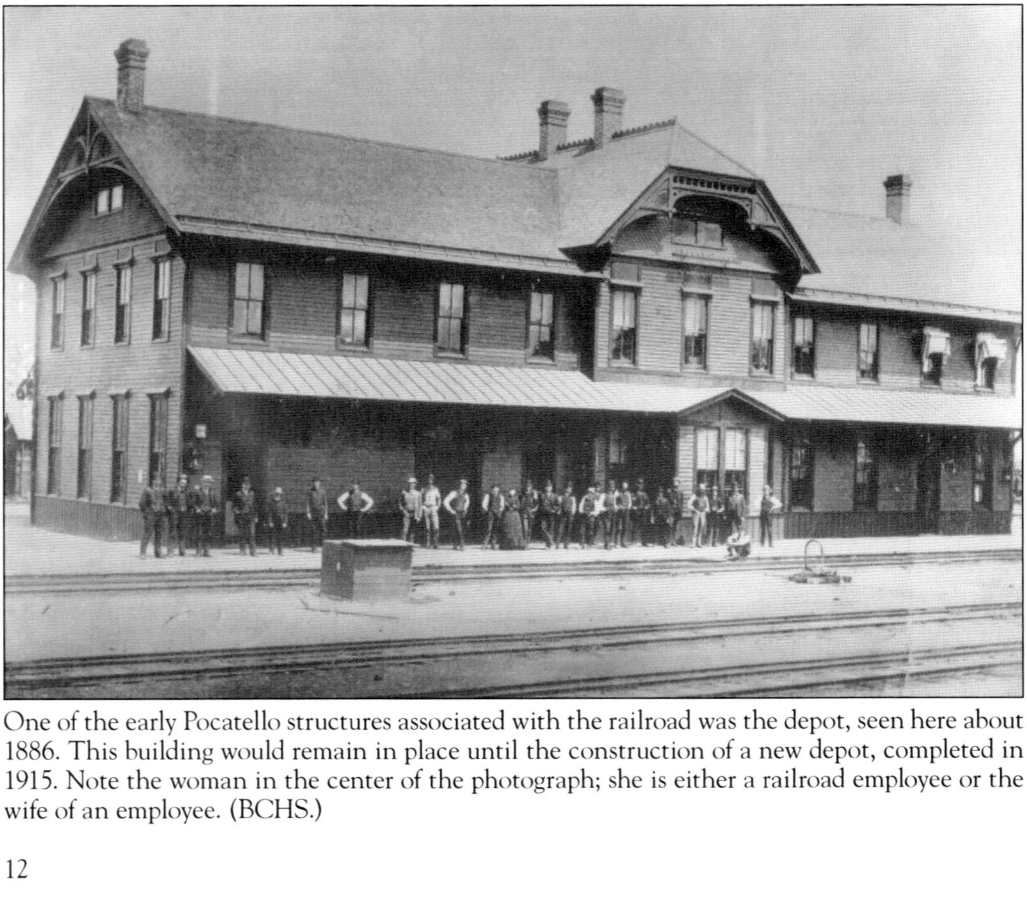

One of the early Pocatello structures associated with the railroad was the depot, seen here about 1886. This building would remain in place until the construction of a new depot, completed in 1915. Note the woman in the center of the photograph; she is either a railroad employee or the wife of an employee. (BCHS.)

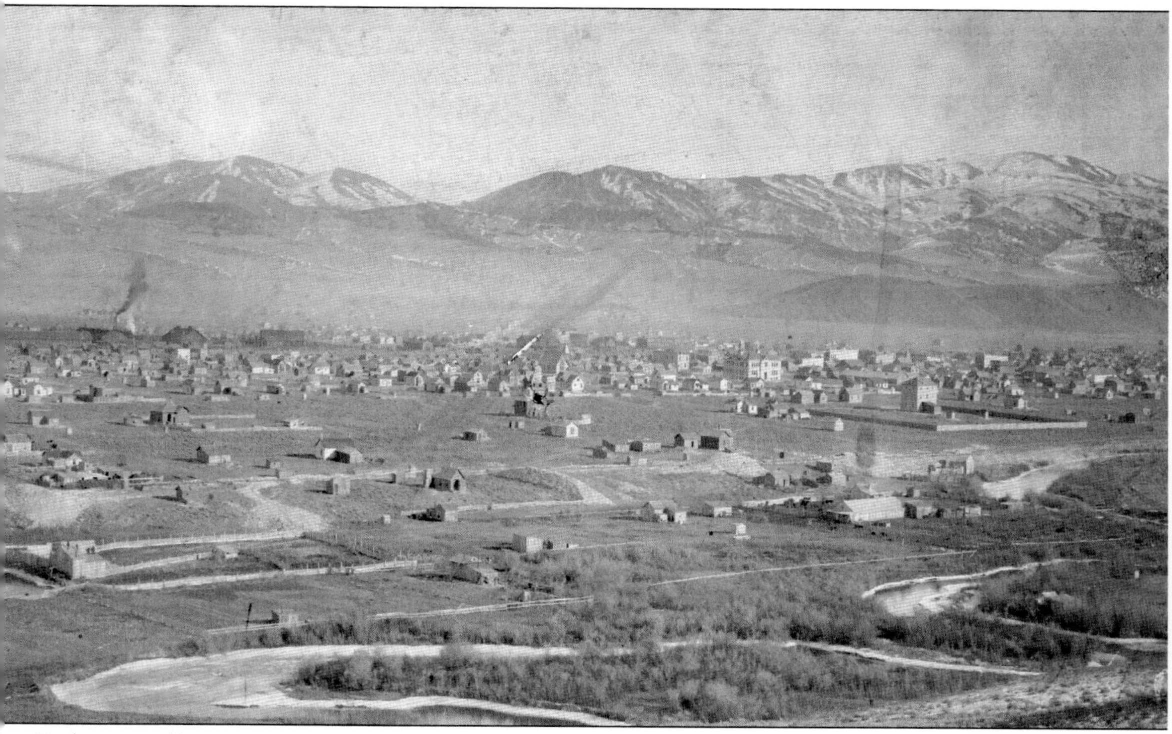

Early Pocatello soon became a popular destination for photographers seeking to chronicle the Intermountain West. This 1891 photograph shows the town from the northwest. The Portneuf River can be seen in the foreground, with the town in mid-background. The structures associated with the railroad are at the left center, with the West Side School (later Pocatello High School) towards the right. (ISU.)

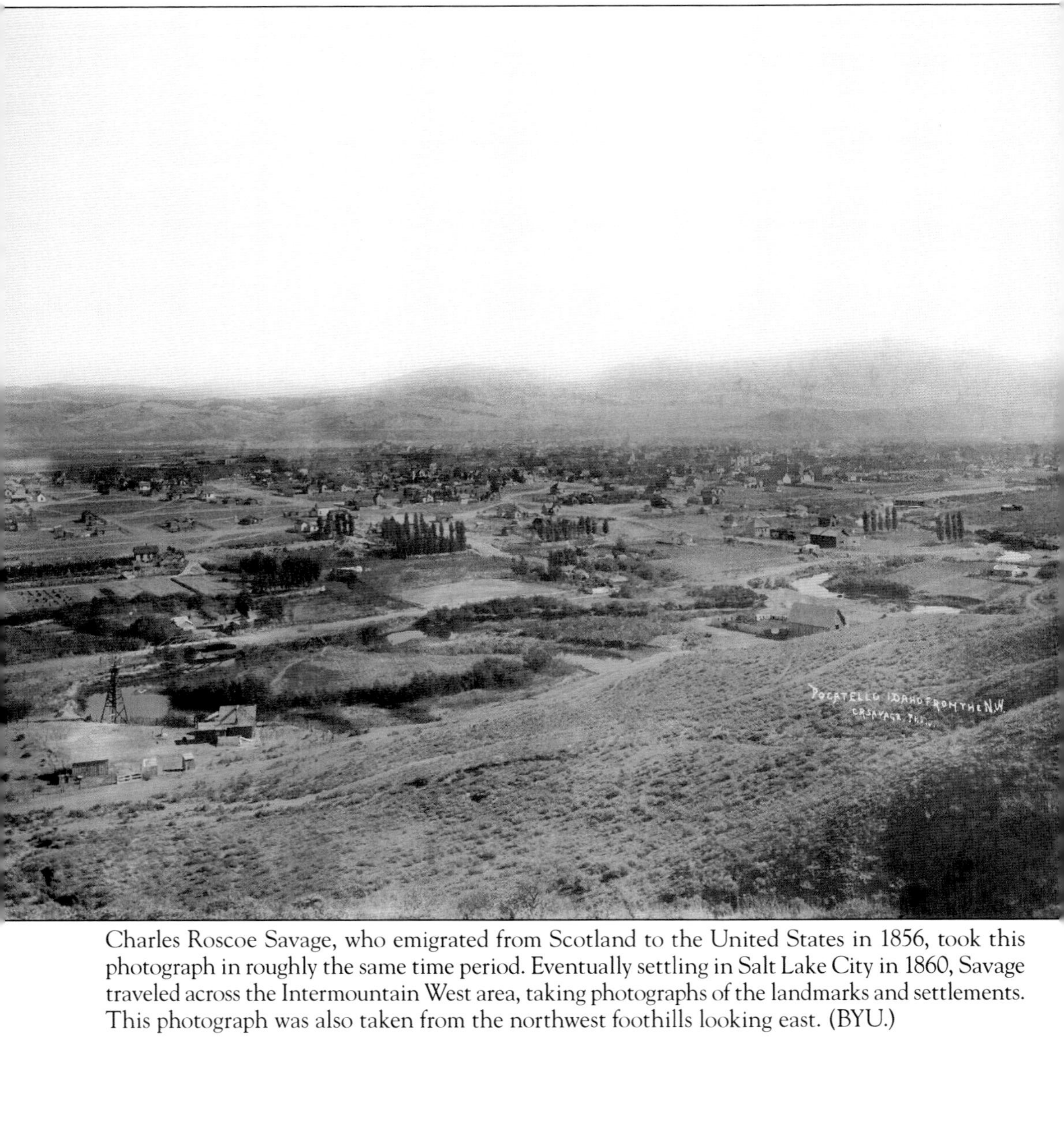

Charles Roscoe Savage, who emigrated from Scotland to the United States in 1856, took this photograph in roughly the same time period. Eventually settling in Salt Lake City in 1860, Savage traveled across the Intermountain West area, taking photographs of the landmarks and settlements. This photograph was also taken from the northwest foothills looking east. (BYU.)

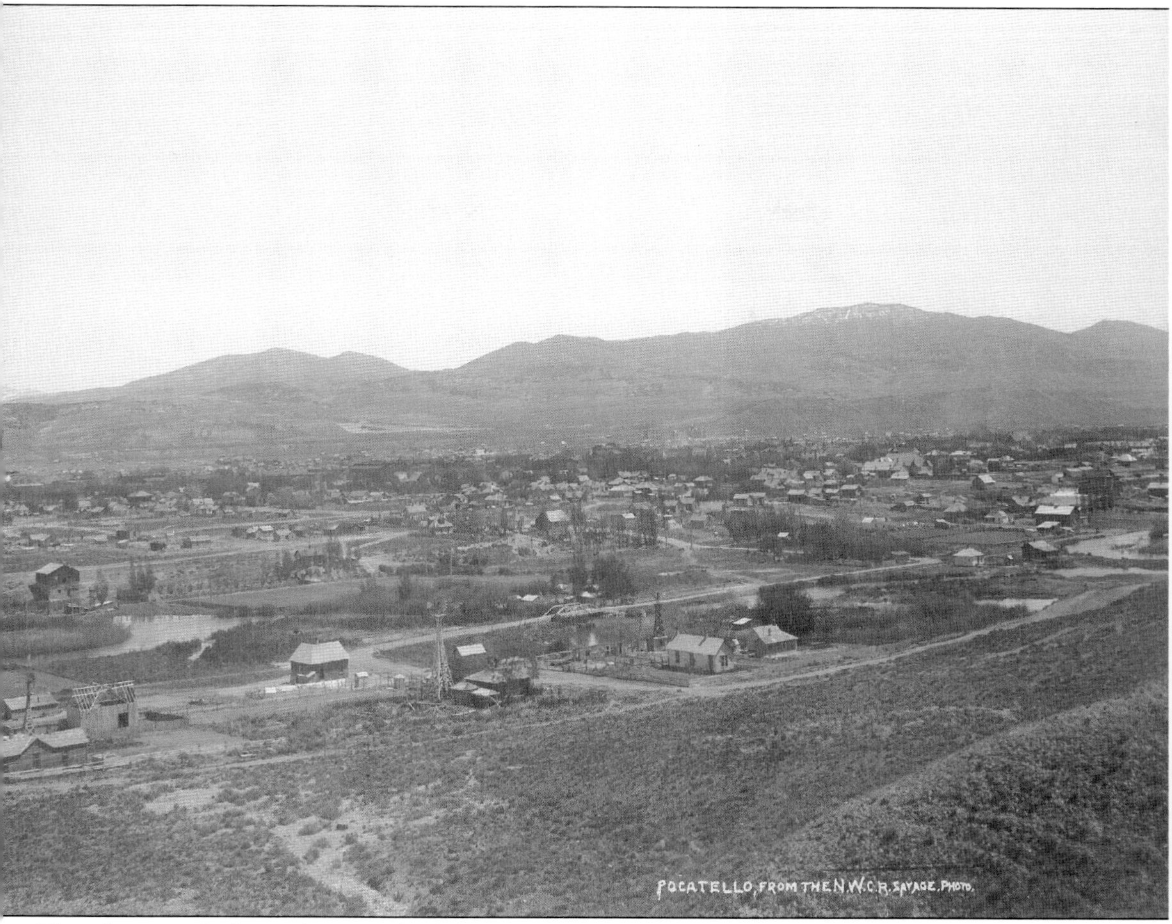

This photograph shows the growth of the town from the previous two panoramic photographs. The expansion of the railroad facilities, including the construction of the powerhouse with its smokestack, is visible. The downtown area has grown as well, and the East Side of Pocatello is beginning to take shape. The structures associated with the Academy of Idaho (later Idaho State University) can be seen in the right background, which means this photograph was taken no earlier than 1901. (Photograph by C.R. Savage; BYU.)

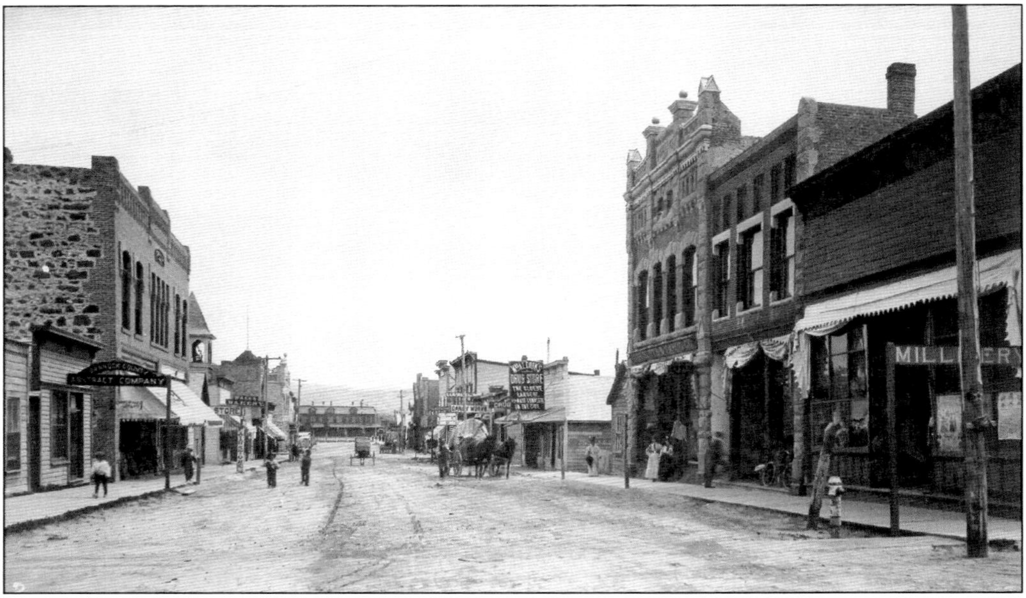

This view of Center Street in 1890 shows predominantly wooden structures with the beginnings of stone and brick structures. The streets would remain unpaved until well into the 1910s. The railroad's Pacific Hotel can be seen in the center background. Mrs. A.L. (Sarah) Cook, whose drugstore can be seen on the right side of the street, played a prominent role in early Pocatello. (ISHS.)

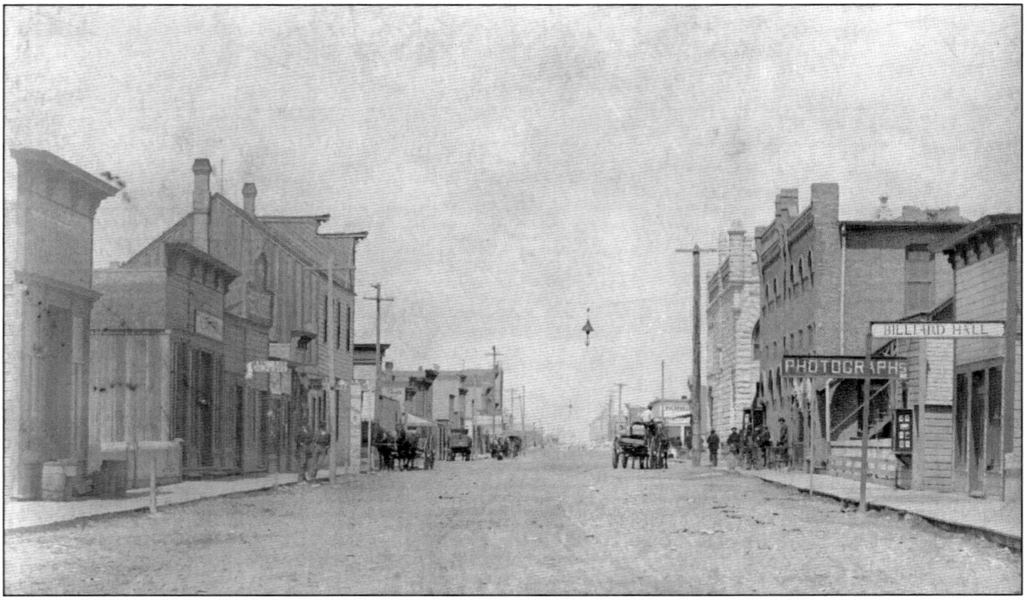

This c. 1892 view of Cleveland Street (later renamed Main Street) provides yet another glimpse of early Pocatello. Note the mixture of wooden and brick buildings in the downtown area, which would be a feature of the downtown until well into the early portion of the 20th century. Of special note here is the Chung Lee Laundry on the left, which shows how a minority presence was seen in Pocatello even at this early stage; and the photography studio on the right, which was probably owned by J.J. McEvoy at this time. The studio would later be bought by Benedicte Wrensted. (BCHS.)

Among the most important of early Pocatello residents were Doctors William (1868–1948) and Minnie Howard (1872–1965). Residents of Kansas prior to moving to Pocatello, the Howards were both trained physicians, having received their medical degrees from the University of Kansas Medical School. Prior to setting up a medical practice in Pocatello, the Howards had a practice in Cuba, Kansas. They moved to Pocatello in 1902, setting up a joint practice in the city. This photograph was presumably taken early in their marriage, before their move to Pocatello. (BCHS.)

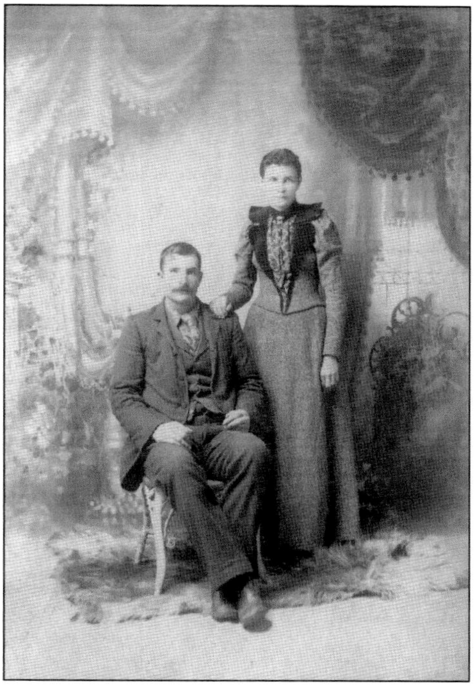

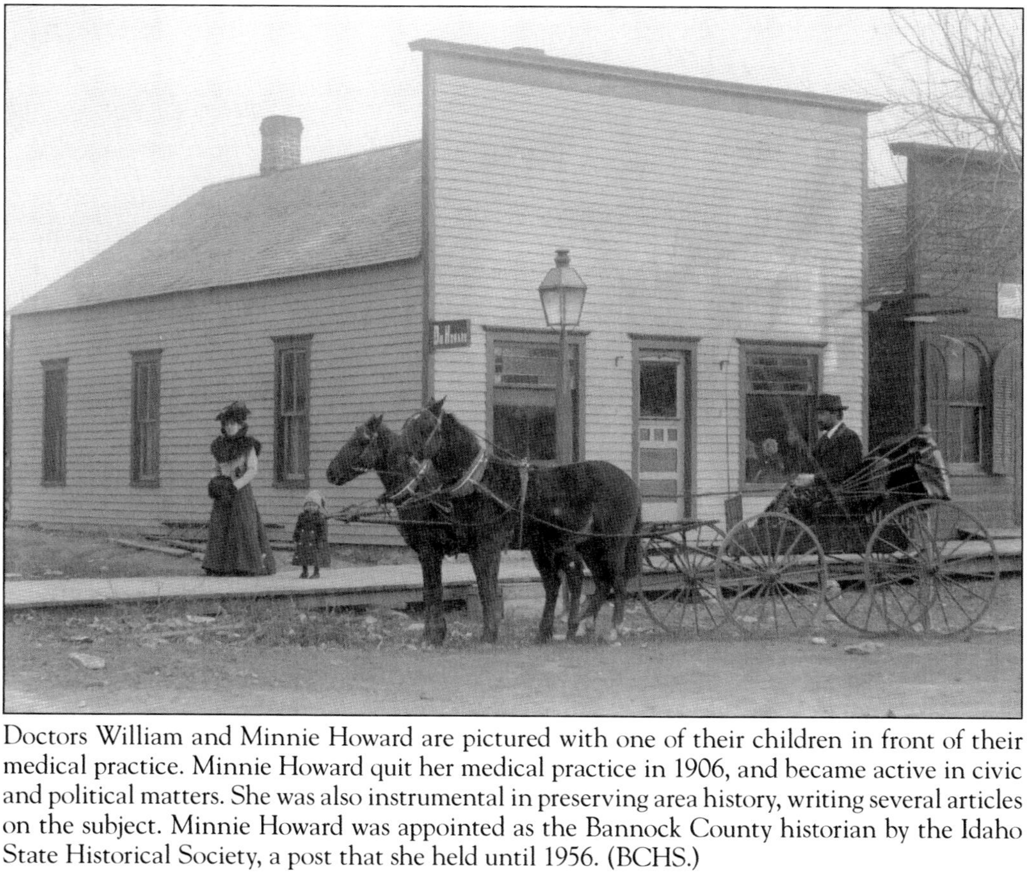

Doctors William and Minnie Howard are pictured with one of their children in front of their medical practice. Minnie Howard quit her medical practice in 1906, and became active in civic and political matters. She was also instrumental in preserving area history, writing several articles on the subject. Minnie Howard was appointed as the Bannock County historian by the Idaho State Historical Society, a post that she held until 1956. (BCHS.)

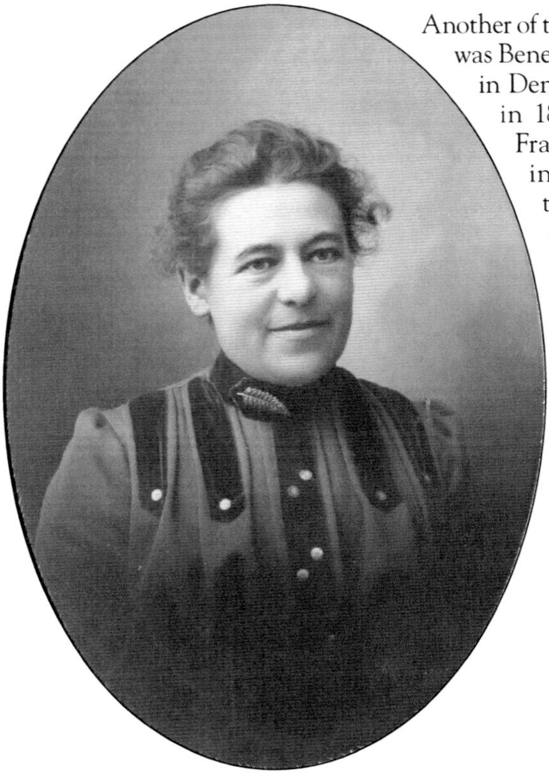

Another of the early prominent figures in Pocatello history was Benedicte Wrensted (1859–1949). Originally born in Denmark, she immigrated to the United States in 1894, originally intent on settling in San Francisco. She eventually settled in Pocatello in 1895, setting up her photography studio there, which she ran until 1912. It is mainly due to her that a photographic record of early Pocatello life remains, as well as a record of the Bannock and Shoshoni during their time of resettlement to Fort Hall. Wrensted left Pocatello for Southern California in 1912, where she would live until her death in 1949. (BCHS.)

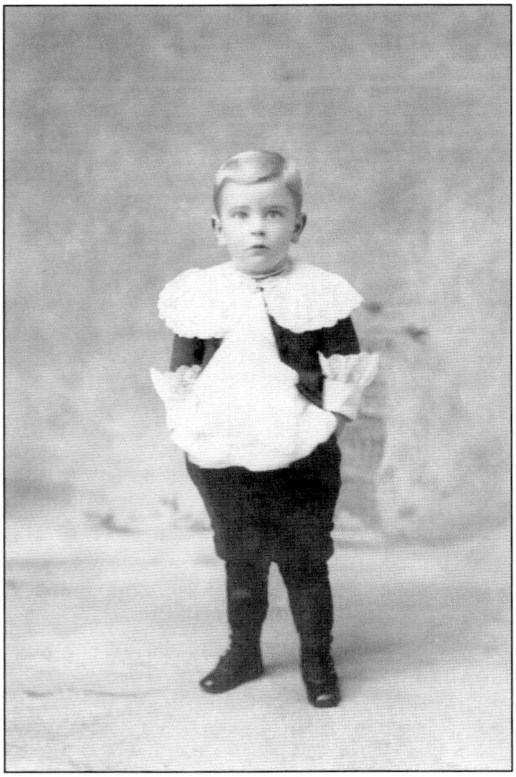

One of the services offered by Wrensted was studio portrait photography, which provided a steady stream of customers. This boy was one of many Pocatellans who posed for Wrensted's camera. (BCHS.)

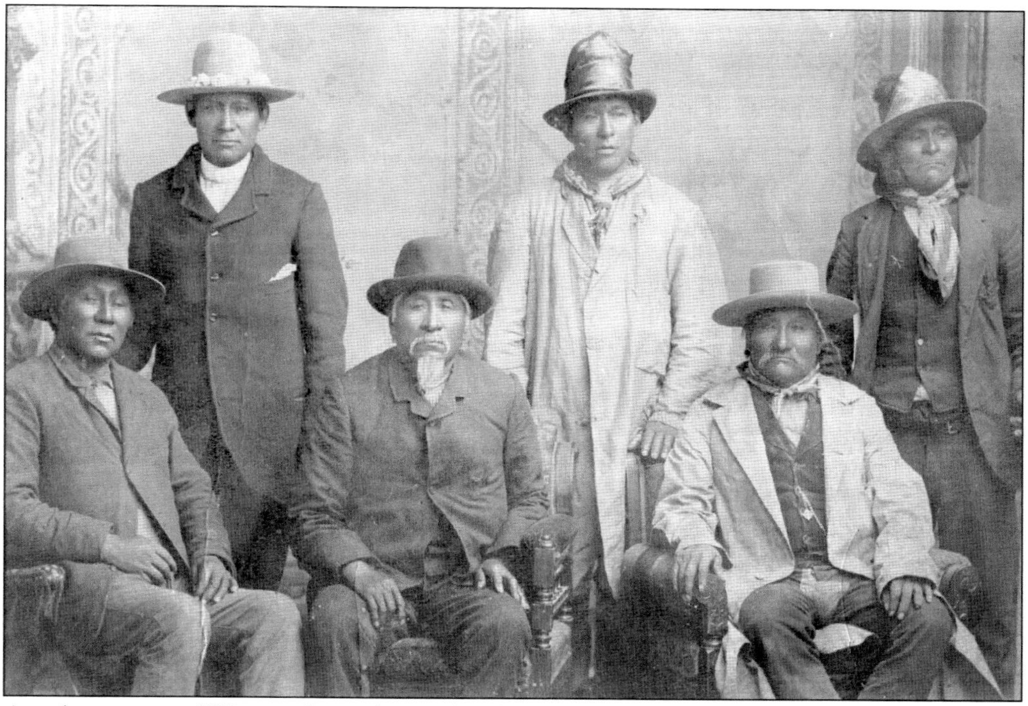

Another aspect of Wrensted's work was the chronicling of the native Bannock and Shoshoni tribe members, who were being placed into the Fort Hall Indian Reservation at this time by the federal government. Wrensted allowed the tribe members to dress in whatever garb they chose, making her photographs unique for this period. This group of six tribe members was photographed in Wrensted's studio sometime in the 1900s. (BCHS.)

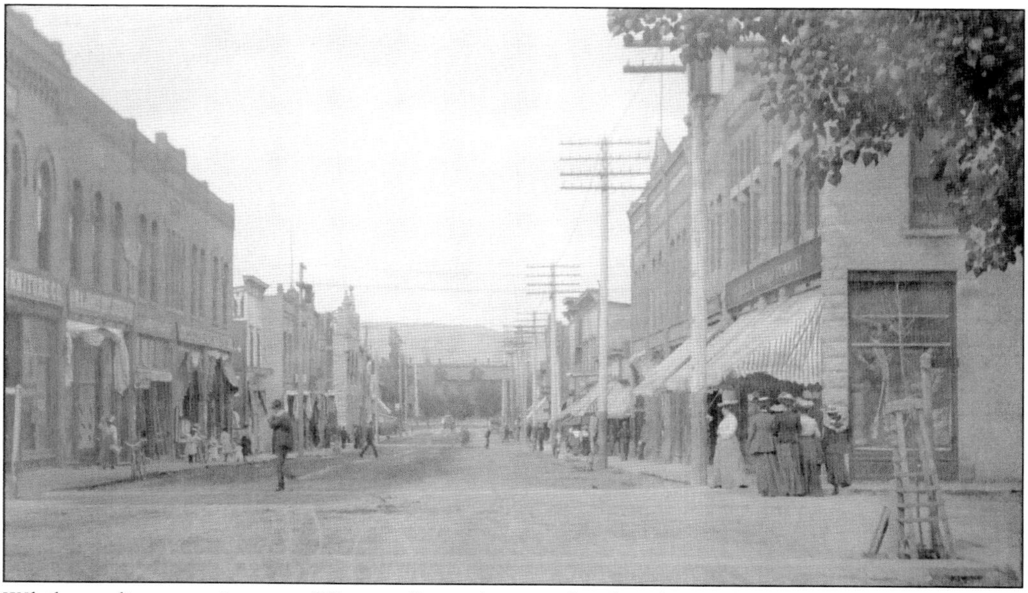

While studio portraits were Wrensted's stock in trade, she also took photographs of Pocatello streets during its growth phase early in the 20th century. This view of West Center Street, looking eastwards, would have been taken in the early 1900s. The railroad's Pacific Hotel can be seen in the background. (BCHS.)

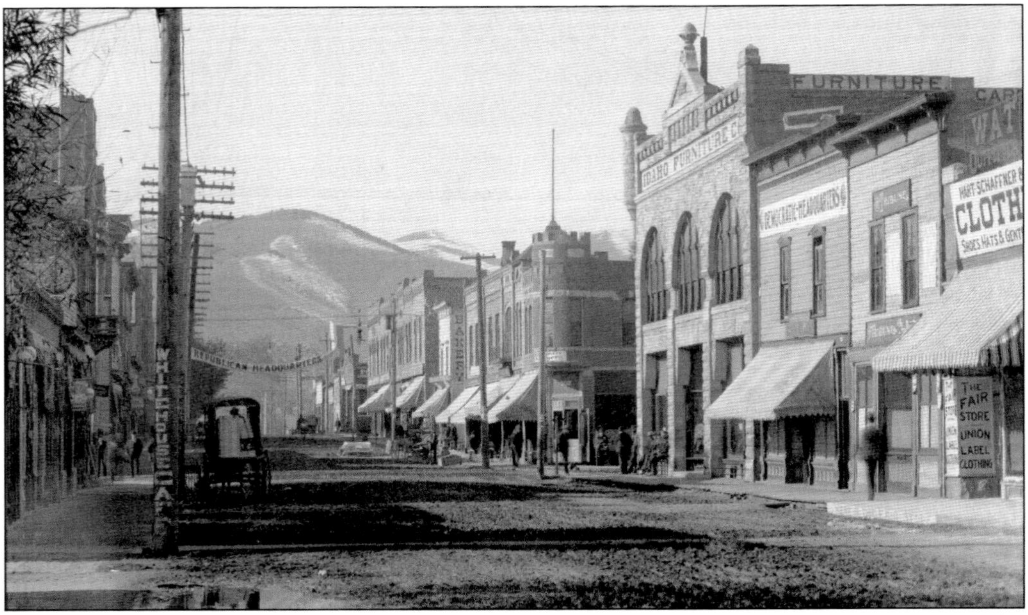

This view of West Center Street, taken between 1900 and 1909, now looking westwards, provides another glimpse into early Pocatello. The Idaho Furniture Company Building is located on what is now Center and Main Streets and is still standing today. Unpaved streets were a typical feature of early Pocatello. Note the Democratic and Republican Party headquarters in close proximity, which indicates that this was an election year. (BCHS.)

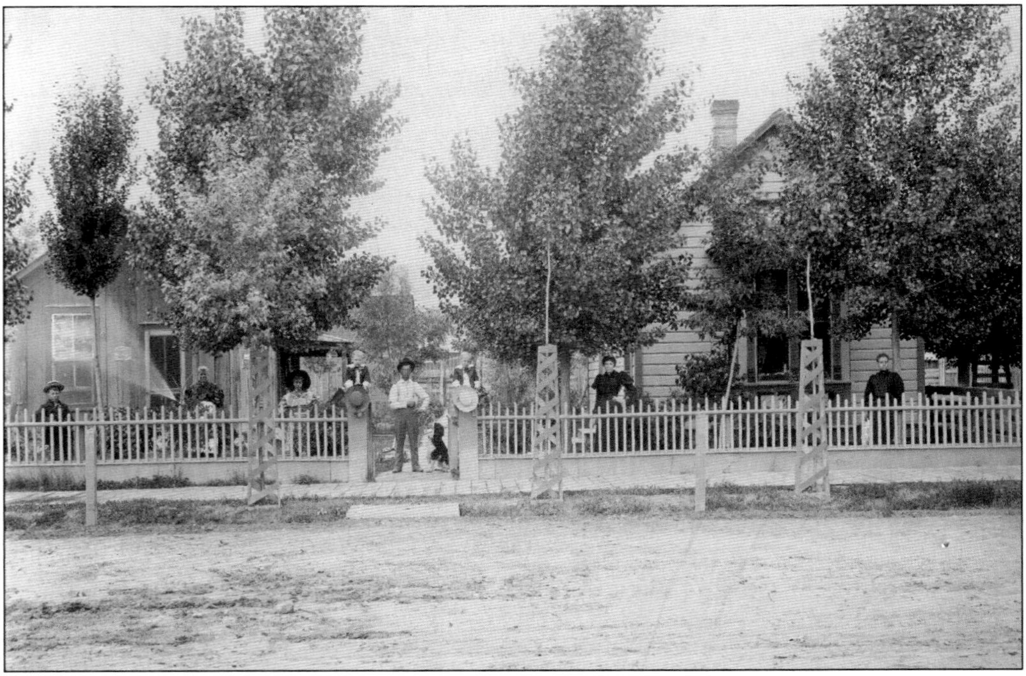

This 1892 photograph shows the Joseph Edgley home at 829 North Harrison Avenue, typical of those built in Pocatello during the transition from railroad junction to a town. As indicated by their dress and the size of their homes, the owners of these residences enjoyed a measure of prosperity. (BCHS.)

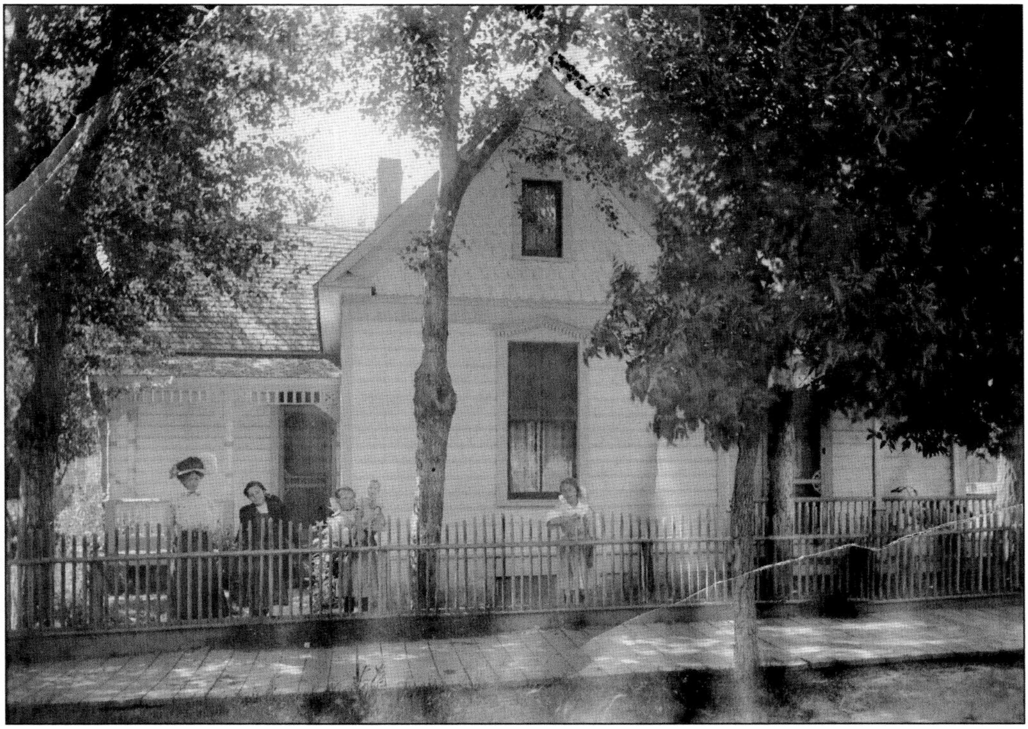

The Thomas Barrett home at 536 West Lander Street provides yet another glimpse of how Pocatello transformed itself at the turn of the 20th century. (BCHS.)

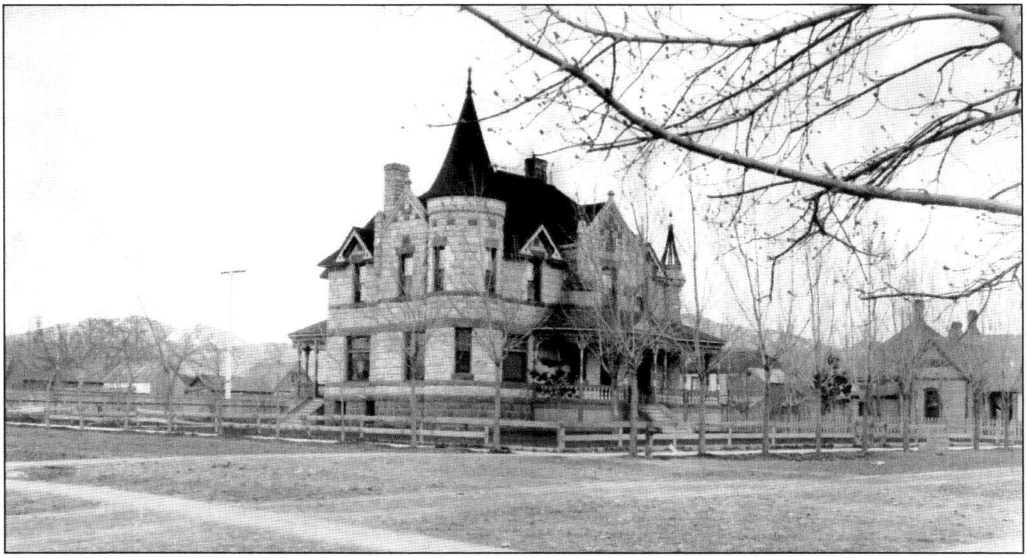

One of the most important homes in the history of Pocatello and one of the most ornate of the early Pocatello period was the Standrod home on North Garfield Avenue, pictured here in the mid-1900s. A local landmark, it can be found on numerous panoramic photographs of the era. Drew W. Standrod was a judge in Pocatello from 1895 until 1899, when he returned to private practice. As well as being a lawyer, he was also was a financier and served as a bank president. His wife, Emma Standrod, was the founder and head of the local chapter of the Daughters of the American Revolution, and was also involved in historic preservation. (Bistline.)

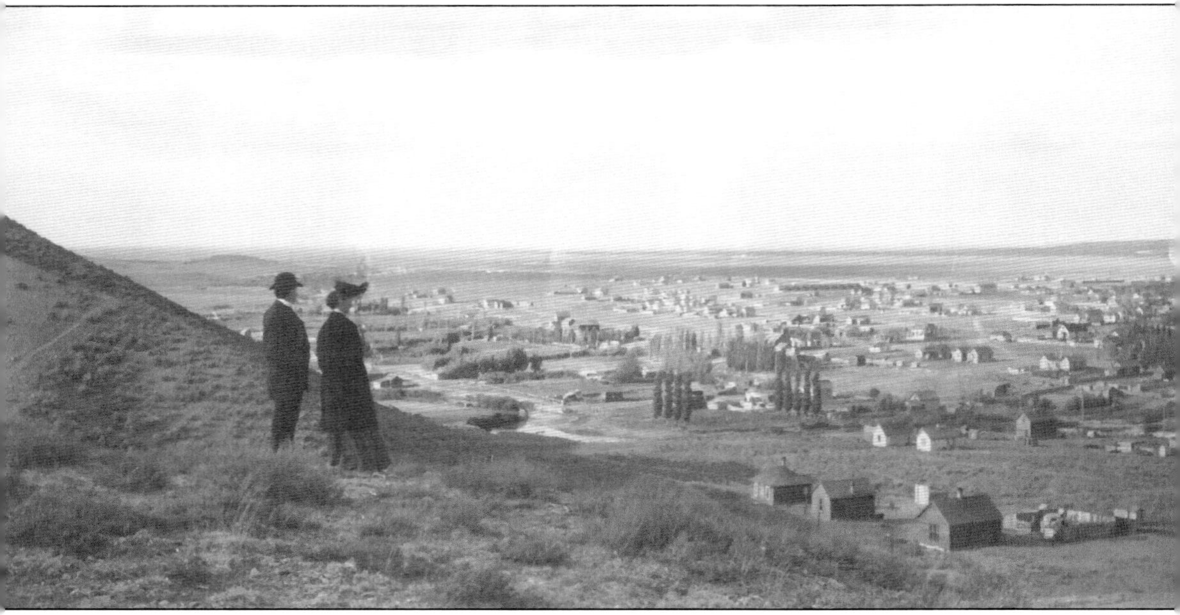

This c. 1900 photograph shows northwestern Pocatello. A couple, perched on the heights along the West Side, looks out on a growing town. (BCHS.)

Two

A City Develops

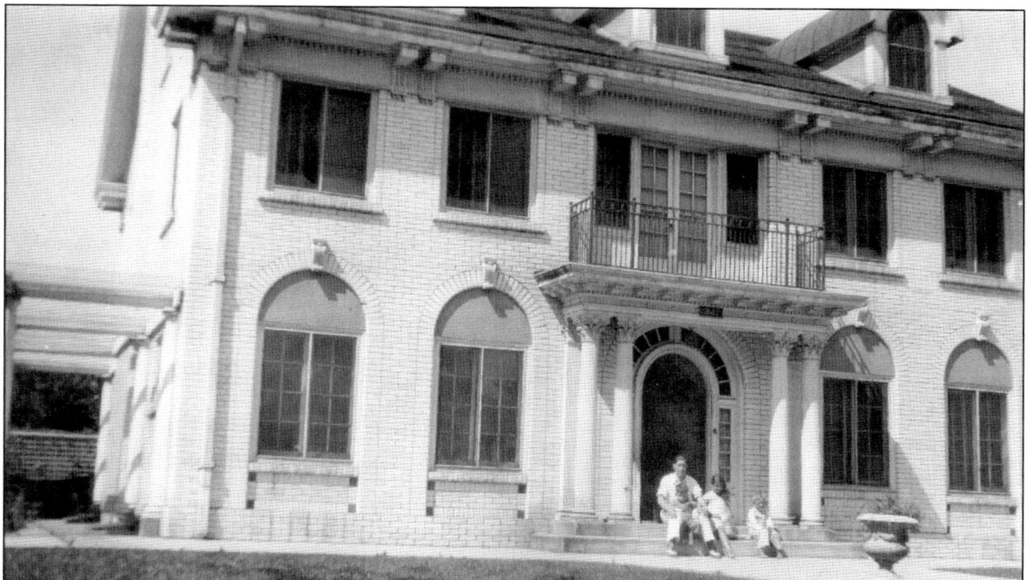

As Pocatello continued to grow and prosper in the first half of the 20th century, the city continued to change in appearance, and began to show a permanence that was not foreseen during its Pocatello Junction days. This development is visible in this shot of the Servel family house at 341 South 7th Avenue, taken in the 1930s. Sitting on the front steps of the house are, from left to right, Pierre (holding Joe), Julie, and Xavier "Bud" Servel. The Servel house is now owned by Idaho State University, and serves as the residence of the university president. (Photo courtesy of Alison Gwinn May)

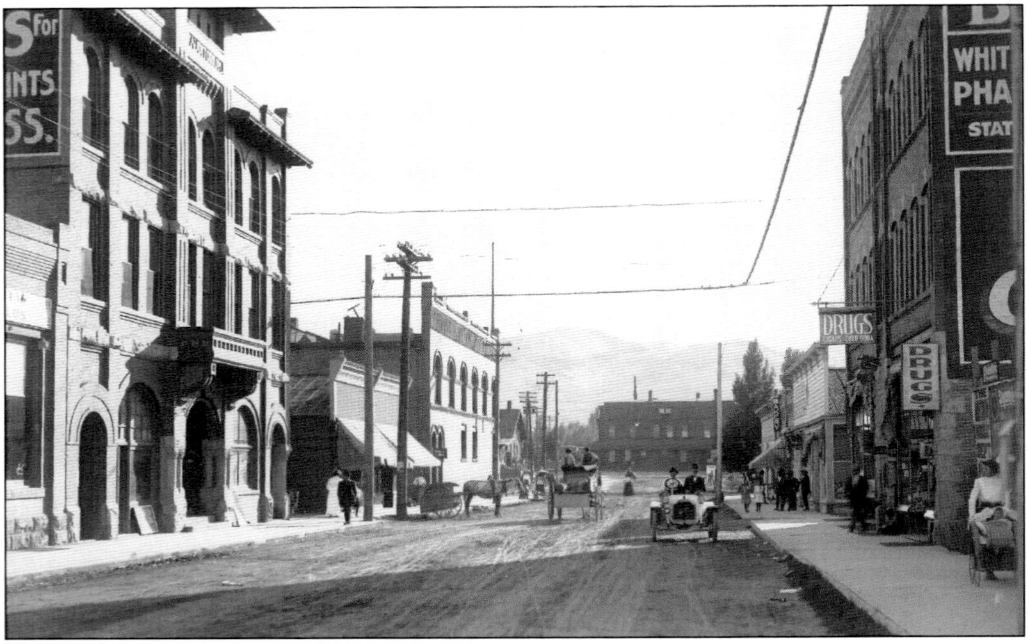

As Pocatello transitioned from a railroad junction to a city, the look of the downtown area began to change. This view of East Center Street, taken in 1910, provides a glimpse of downtown between the era of Pocatello as a frontier post and a city. There are permanent, stone buildings in evidence, replacing wooden structures previously in place. However, the streets have not yet been paved, and a crossing over the railroad tracks seen in the background is not yet in place. This lack of a secure crossing would prove to be a danger to passersby, and be subject to remedy within a year. The prominent brick building on the left is the Auditorium Theater. (BCHS.)

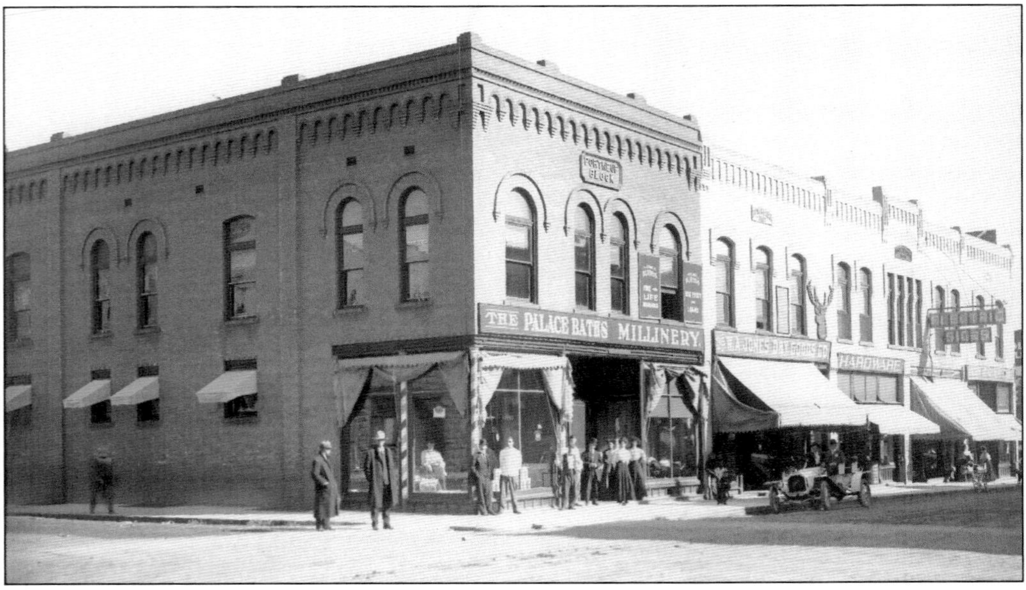

This view of West Center Street at Arthur Avenue, taken at about the same time as the image above, also shows the downtown area in transition. The Portneuf Building at the corner of the street was another of the more permanent structures that gradually replaced the frontier-era wooden structures in the downtown area. (BCHS.)

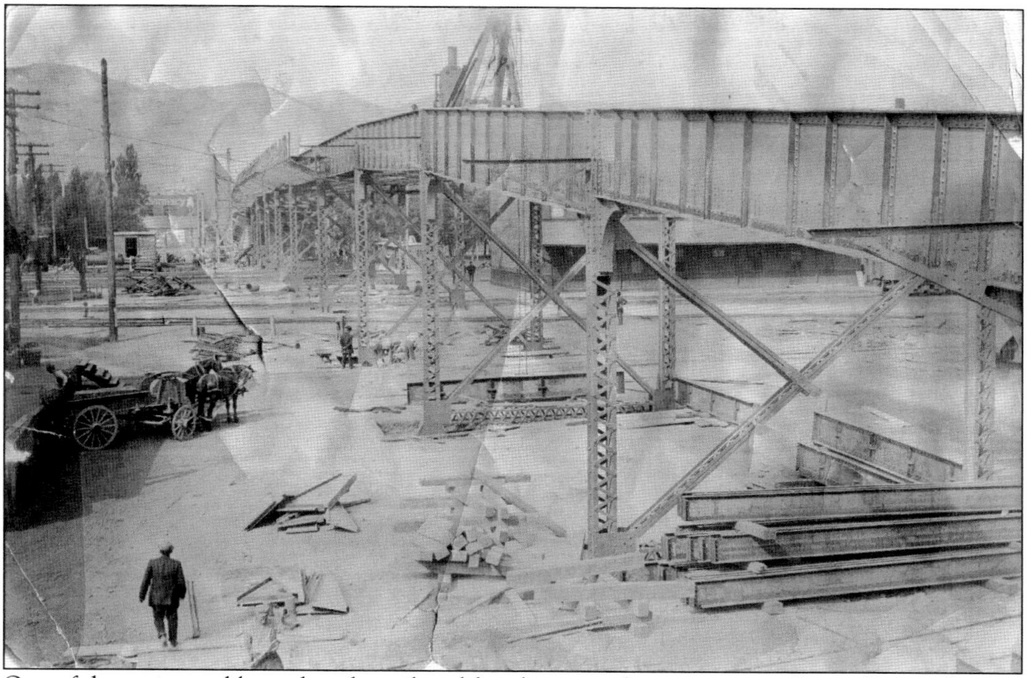

One of the major problems that the railroad faced in its early operations in Pocatello was the foot crossing, a well-worn path traversing the tracks at Center Street. Prior to 1911, pedestrians who needed to get from one side of the city to the other were obligated to cross the railroad tracks. This led to fatal accidents, mainly due to pedestrians being struck by oncoming trains. To deal with this situation, a viaduct was constructed over the tracks at Center Street. The south end of the Pacific Hotel had to be dismantled, shortening it to make room for the viaduct. This 1911 photograph shows the viaduct in the final stages of construction. (BCHS.)

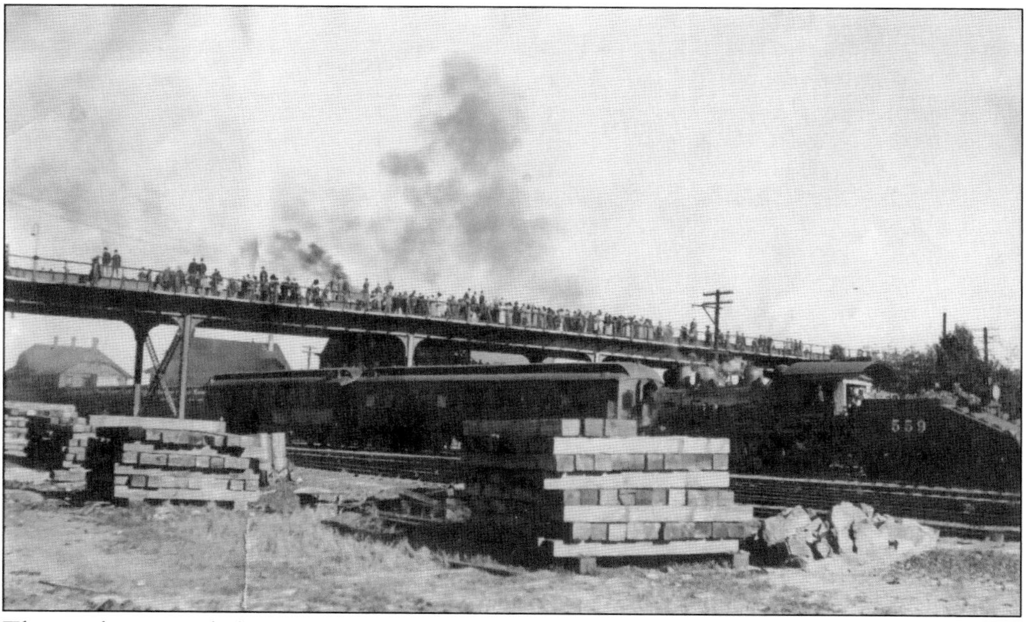

The viaduct was dedicated on October 6, 1911. A crowd gathers to witness the opening ceremonies. (BCHS.)

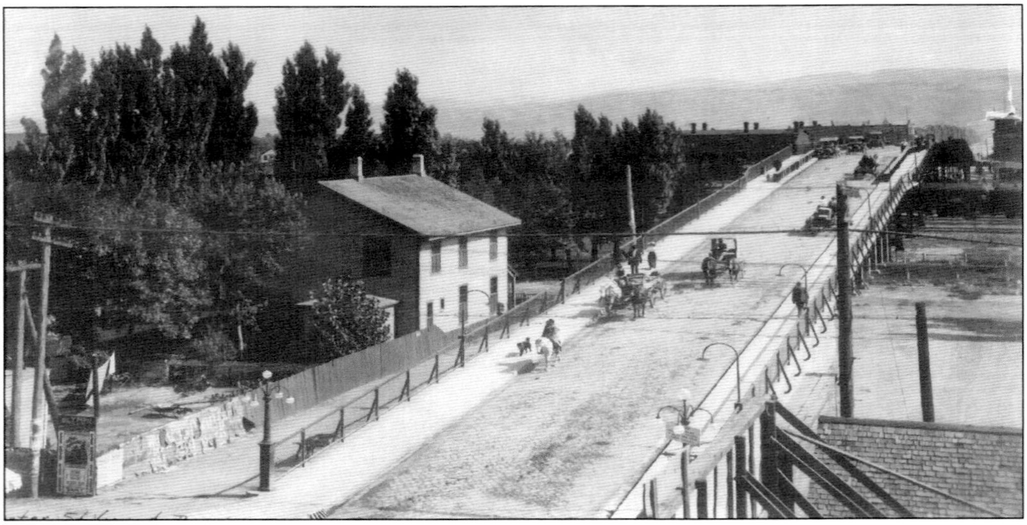

The installation of the Center Street viaduct not only remedied a safety issue, it also provided easier access to and from Pocatello's downtown area, which helped contribute to the city's growth. This 1916 photograph gives some indication of the transformation of the city at this time. Along with the usual horse-drawn wagons, a number of automobiles are visible crossing the viaduct. This would be a more common sight as time went on. (BCHS.)

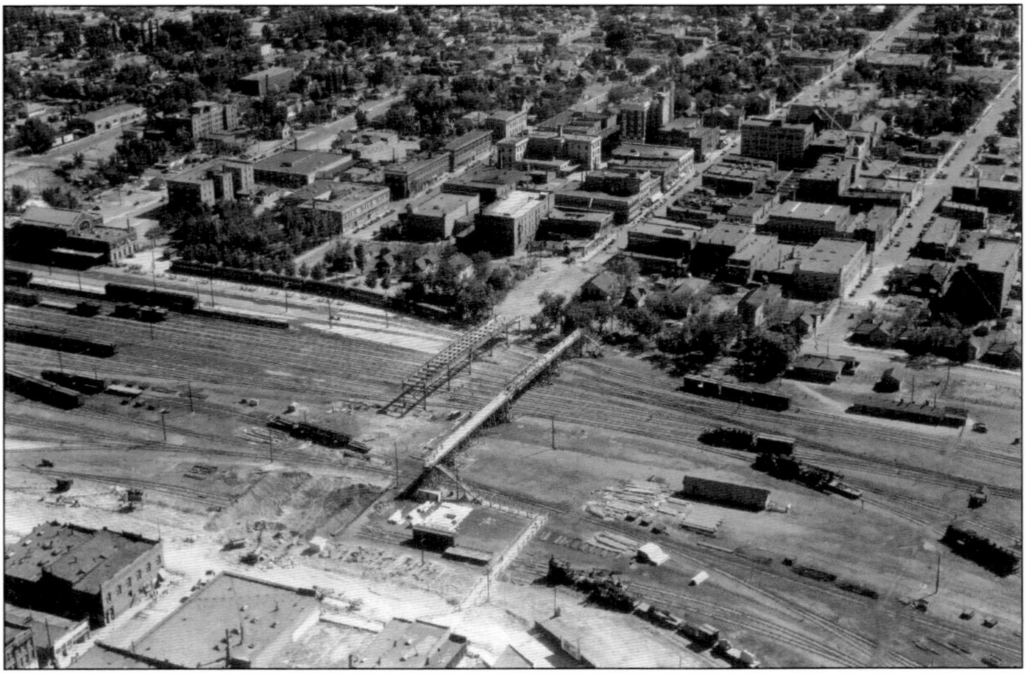

To avoid bypassing several businesses on East Center Street and First Avenue, the east end of the viaduct was constructed with ramps onto First Avenue, rather than sloping it down onto Center Street. These narrow ramps required a tight, 90-degree turn, later making it a difficult route to travel by automobile or truck. To remedy this dangerous situation, the viaduct was removed in favor of an underpass structure in the mid-1930s. This aerial photograph, taken either in 1934 or 1935, shows the remains of the viaduct being dismantled and a temporary wooden structure in place over the railroad tracks. Note the initial excavation work for the underpass. (BCHS.)

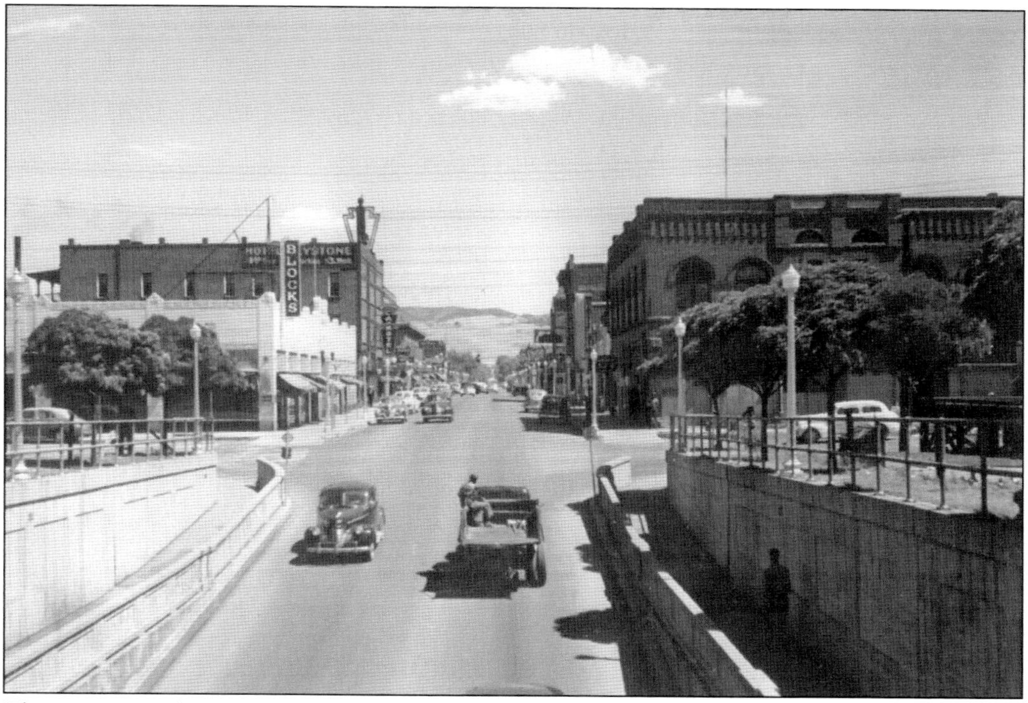

This is a view of East Center Street, looking towards First Avenue and the East Side business district, taken sometime in the latter part of the 1930s. The view from atop the underpass shows what motorists would have seen once they emerged from the underpass. The Blocks department store is visible on the left. (ISU.)

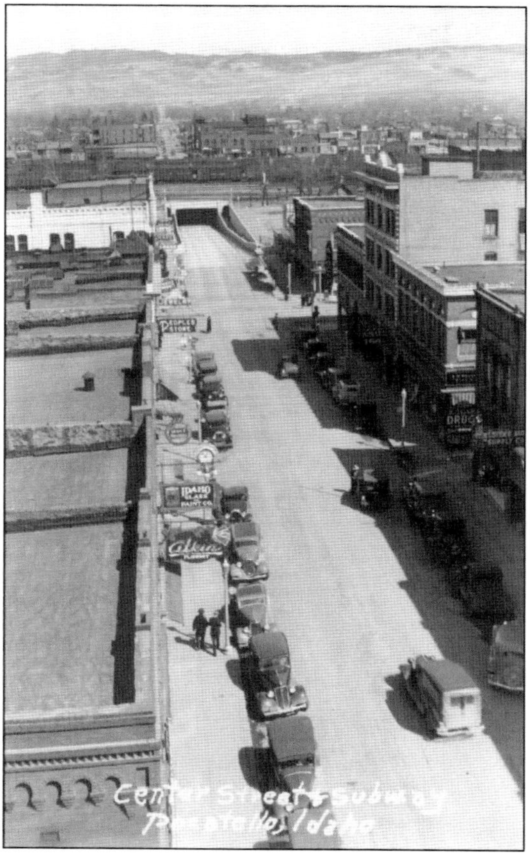

This photograph of the Center Street underpass was taken from the downtown area and shows Center Street as it approaches Main Street. The retail outlets on Center Street at the time included the People's Store, Molinelli Jewelers, and the Blocks department store. (ISU.)

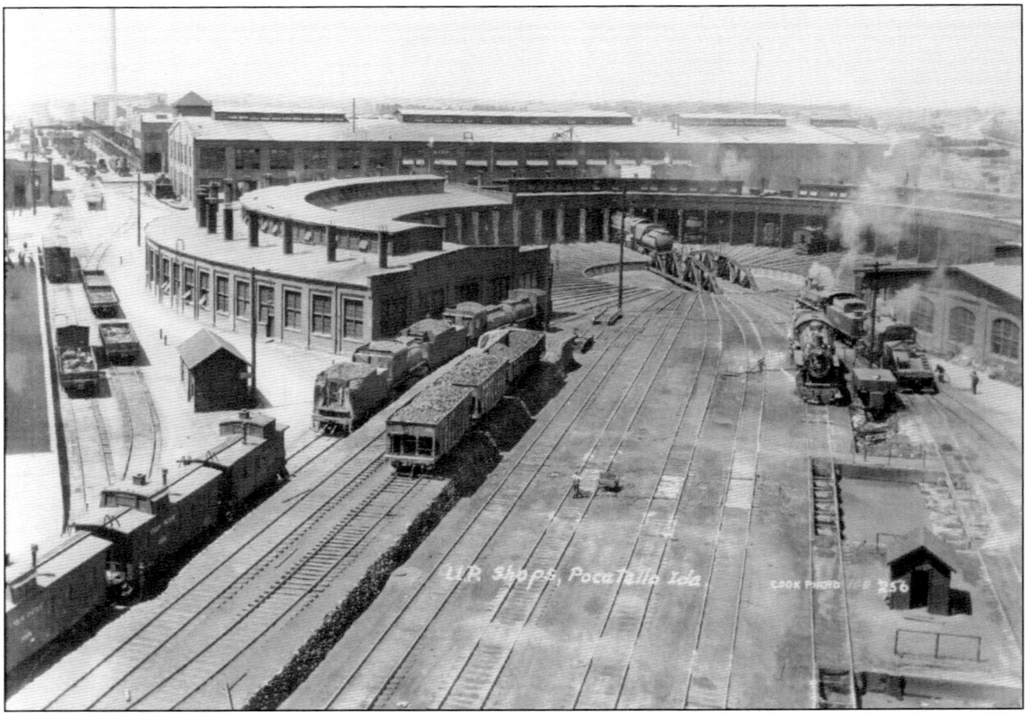

Railroad operations in Pocatello continued to expand (and the economy along with it) in the first half of the 20th century. The importance that the Oregon Short Line Railroad (and later, the Union Pacific Railroad), attached to its operations in Pocatello can be gauged by the expanded roundhouse seen in this 1938 photograph. This roundhouse and turntable allowed for multiple locomotives to be serviced at a given time, streamlining operations and speeding up the turnaround time for the locomotive fleet. (BCHS.)

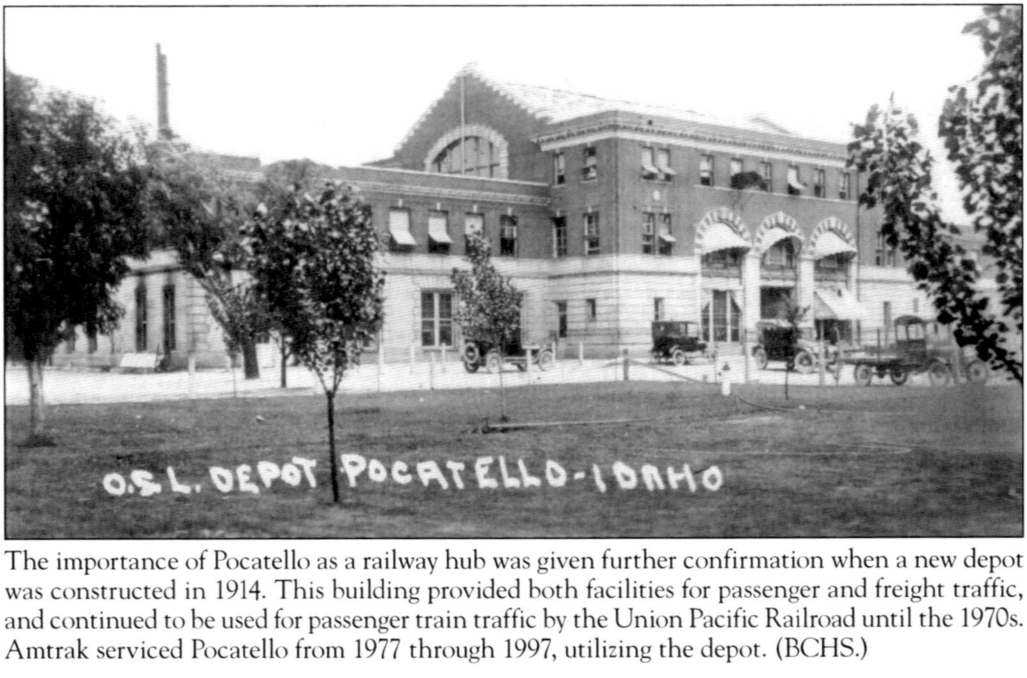

The importance of Pocatello as a railway hub was given further confirmation when a new depot was constructed in 1914. This building provided both facilities for passenger and freight traffic, and continued to be used for passenger train traffic by the Union Pacific Railroad until the 1970s. Amtrak serviced Pocatello from 1977 through 1997, utilizing the depot. (BCHS.)

This photograph of the depot building, taken at Christmastime, provides a glimpse of the interior of the passenger lobby. This scene was familiar to those who traveled by rail during the golden era of railroads. While the depot building still stands, rail passenger service has long since ceased at the Pocatello Depot. Union Pacific utilizes the building for offices. (BCHS.)

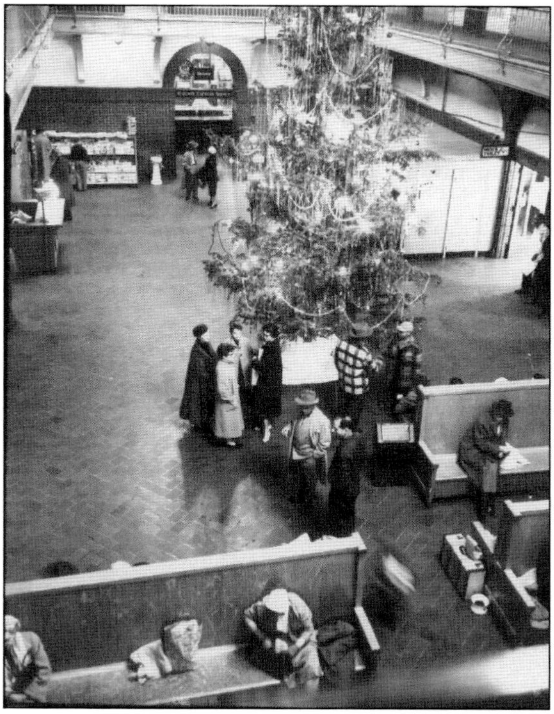

This grain elevator, next to the rail yard, was another gauge of the importance of the railroad to the region. This c. 1938 aerial photograph provides an idea of the size and scale of the elevators. The structure is still in place today. (BCHS.)

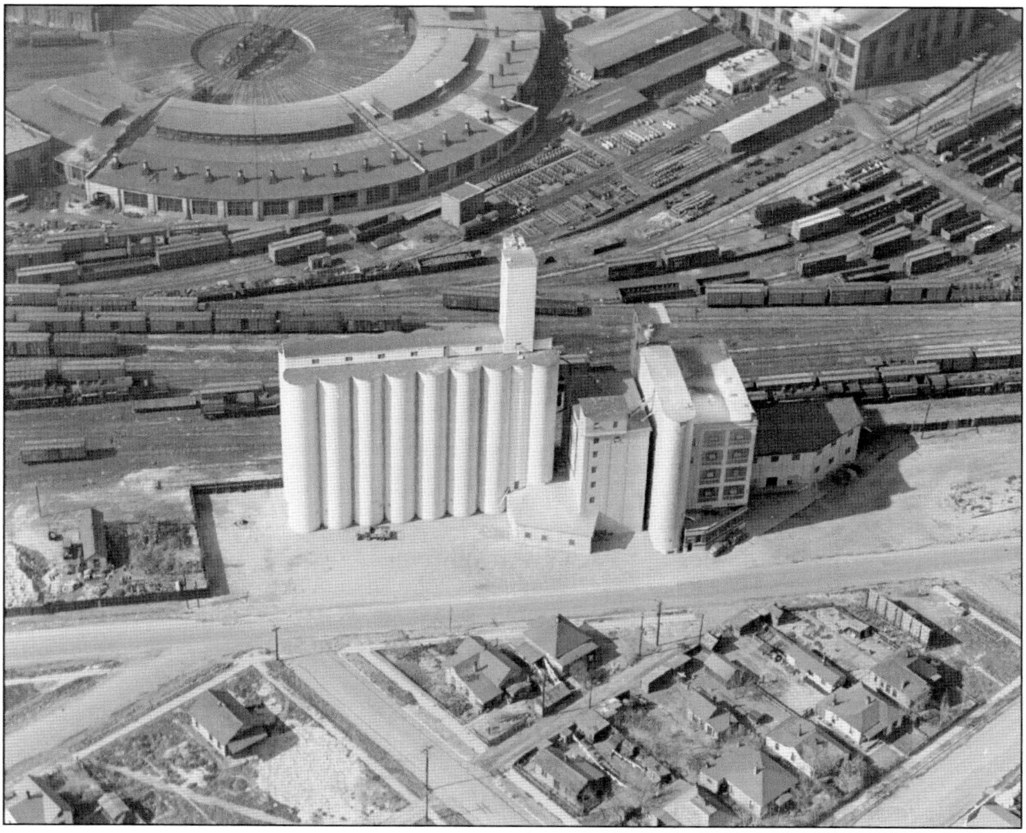

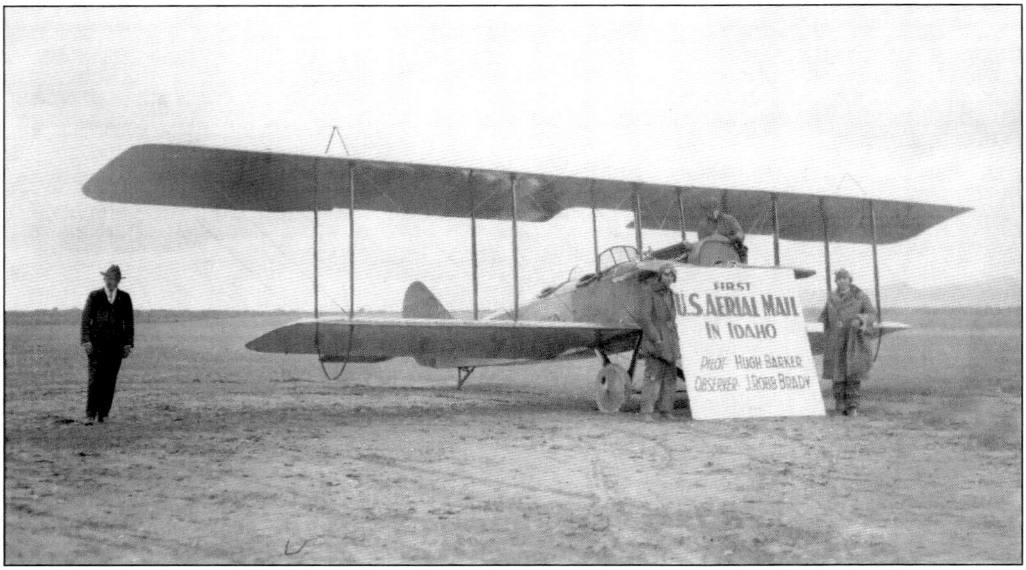

Pocatello came into the 20th century in earnest when it became a base for air service. As was the case with most cities in the United States, the first air service to Pocatello was airmail. As shown in this photograph, Pocatello became the first locale in Idaho to have airmail service. (BCHS.)

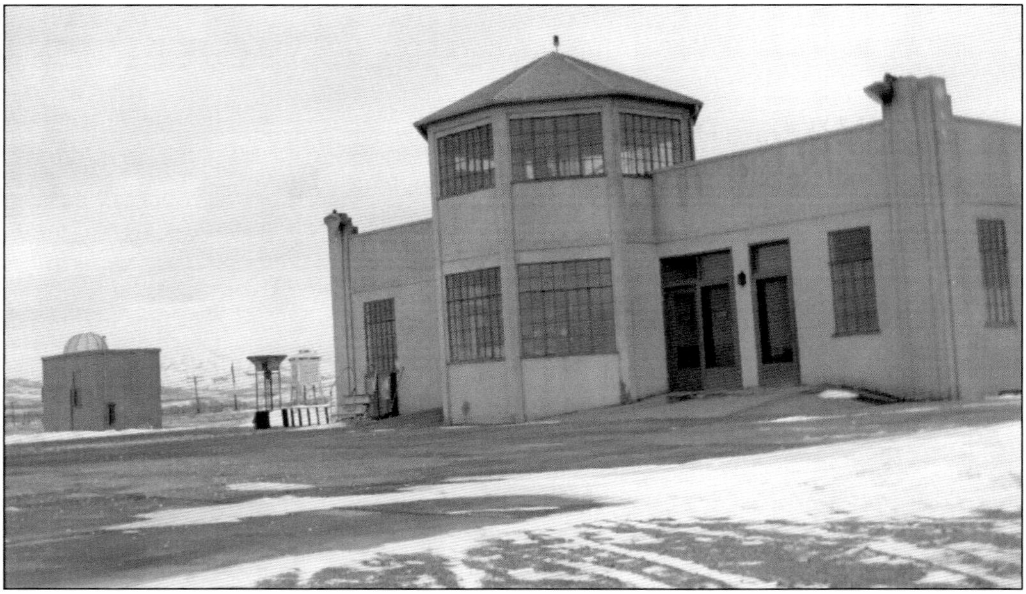

While there was air traffic into and out of Pocatello, the lack of facilities made landing and taking off a difficult process. The only airfield in the early days of air service was a hardened dirt field, with a bonfire to provide guidance for pilots getting ready to land. To remedy this situation, a site was selected for Pocatello's first real airstrip. Named McDougall Field in honor of a World War I flying ace from Pocatello who died in an air crash on Armistice Day 1928, the field was built with federal funds and constructed with labor provided by the WPA. McDougall Field was opened for flights in 1938. It was located east of the current airport site and across Highway 30 from the West Vaco facility (later operated by FMC). The primary east/west runway was later used as a drag racing strip. This photograph shows McDougall Field Terminal 1 shortly after construction was finished on the building. (ISU.)

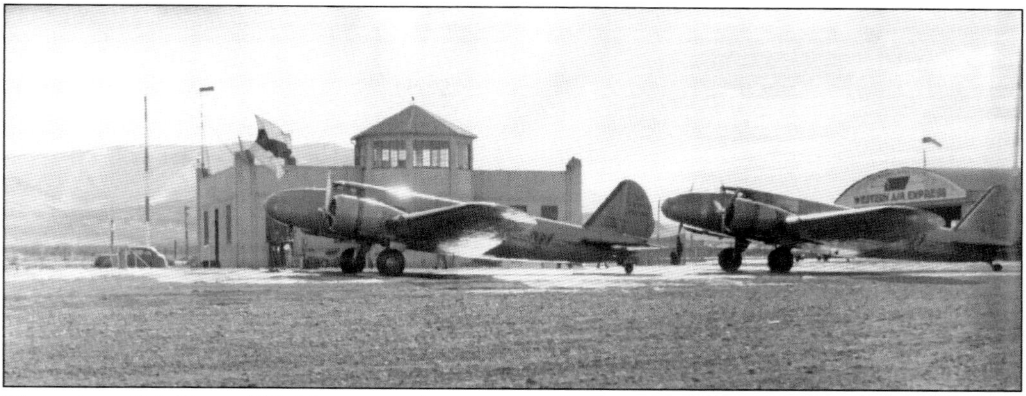

The value of McDougall Field to general aviation is illustrated in this photograph of Western Air Express Mainliners at the field on December 18, 1940. These aircraft were scheduled to land at Salt Lake City Airport, but fog over the airport prevented them from landing there. In this case, McDougall Field was used as a divert field for the aircraft. (ISU.)

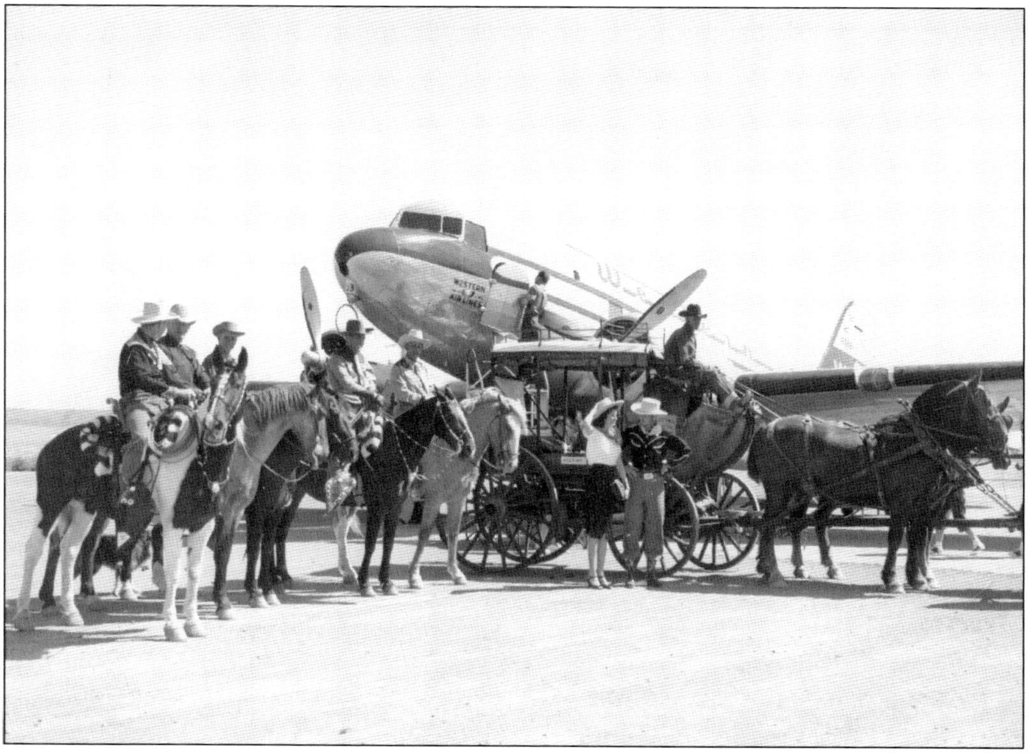

McDougall Field continued to provide air service after World War II and was the site of events such as Pocatello Air Age Day, which took place on May 19, 1956. In this publicity photograph, a group of cowboys greets a Western Air Lines DC-3. Even as Pocatello embraced modernity, it still had a foothold in its frontier past. (ISU.)

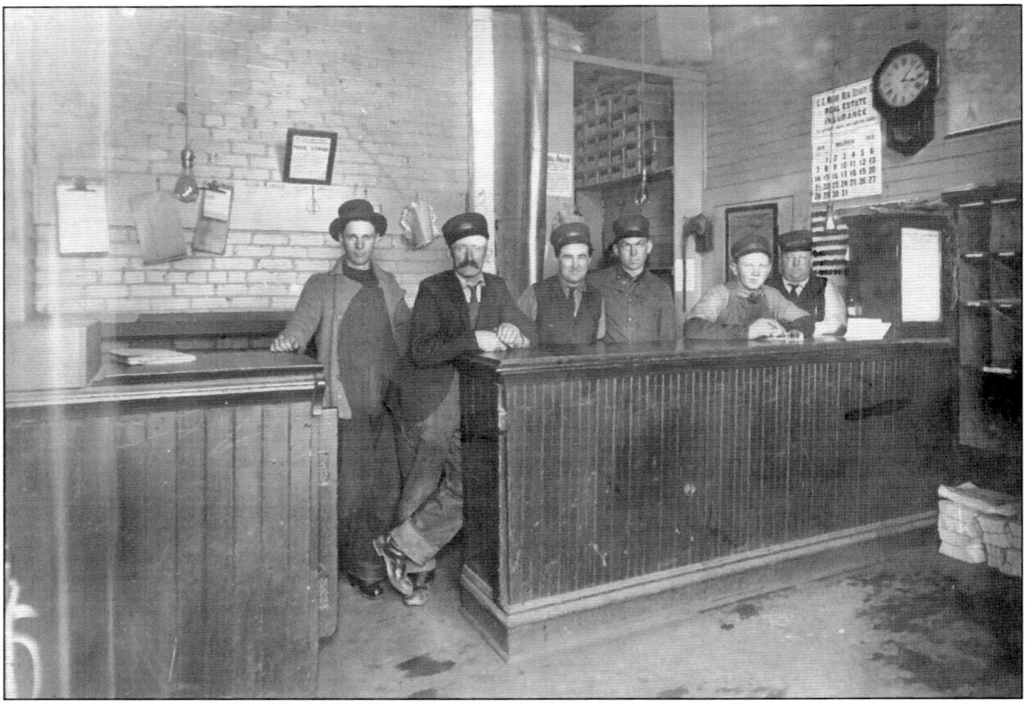

The railroad continued to be the largest employer in Pocatello in the first half of the 20th century. The railroad provided jobs in a number of areas within the rail yard, and one that had particular importance was that of baggage handler. The safe handling of passenger baggage was vital for repeat business. These men in the Pocatello baggage room, seen in either March or April 1915, are (from left to right) Jed Thomas, unidentified, Ed Wright, Lyman Shira, and two unidentified. Note the bandage around the head of the baggage handler next to Jed Thomas. (BCHS.)

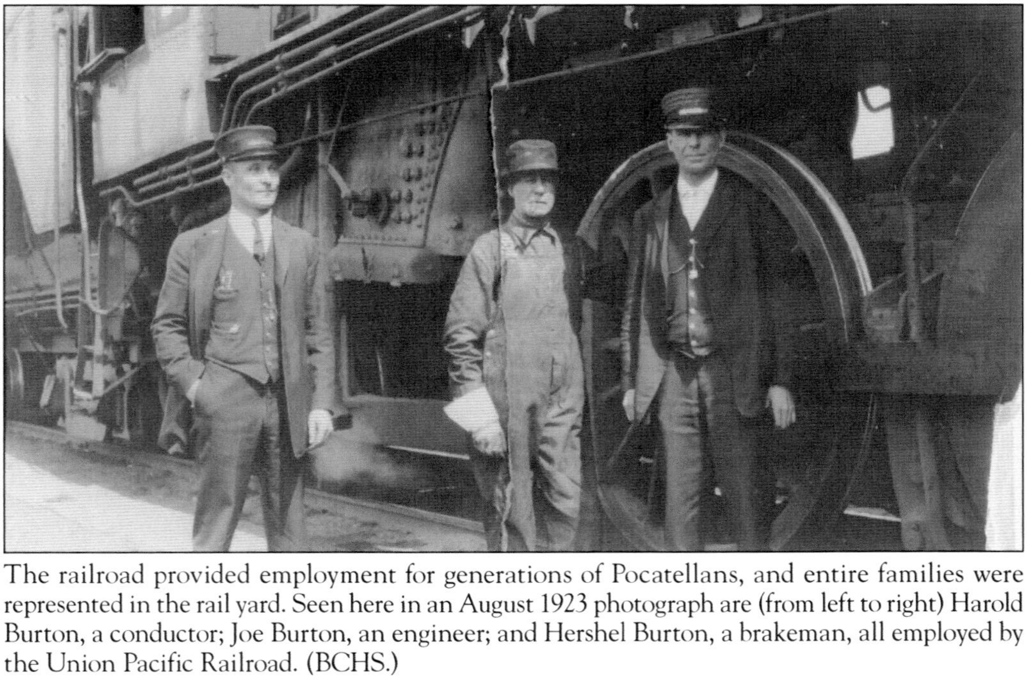

The railroad provided employment for generations of Pocatellans, and entire families were represented in the rail yard. Seen here in an August 1923 photograph are (from left to right) Harold Burton, a conductor; Joe Burton, an engineer; and Hershel Burton, a brakeman, all employed by the Union Pacific Railroad. (BCHS.)

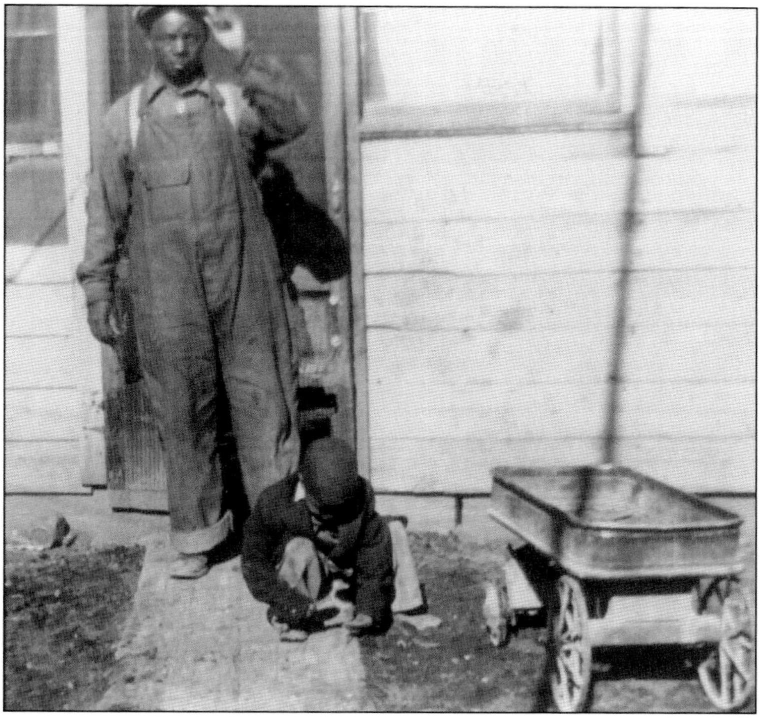

The railroad provided employment opportunities to many ethnic and racial groups who otherwise would not have been able to find a job. Such was the case for Sam Calahan, who came to Pocatello on Labor Day in 1925 and worked for both the Oregon Short Line Railroad and the Union Pacific Railroad. (BCHS.)

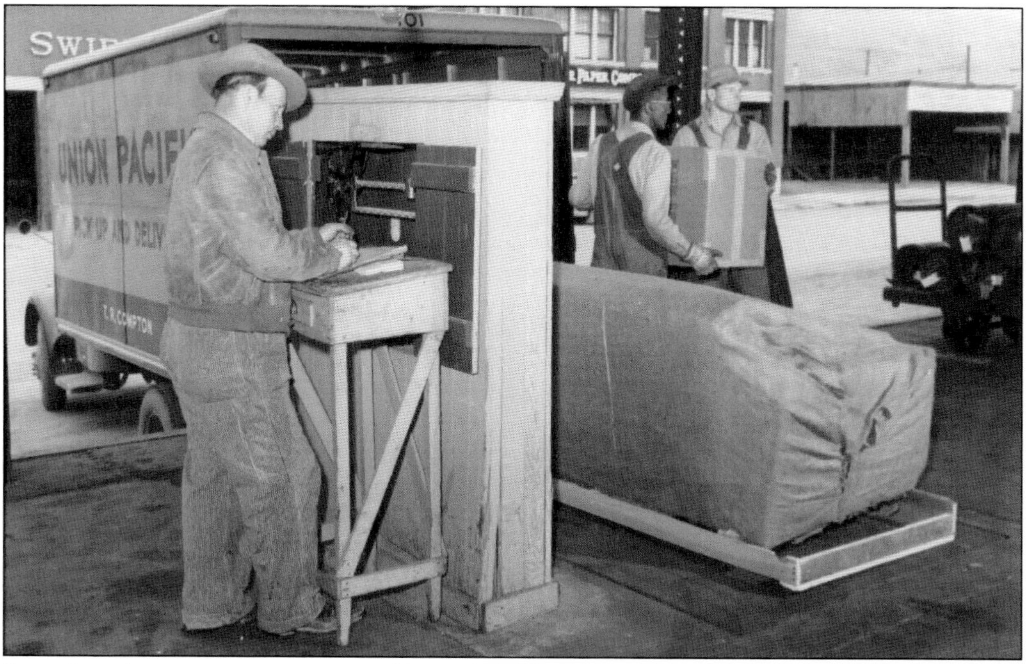

Even though minority groups were able to obtain employment with the railroad, positions were limited by policies in favor of white workers. Seen here in an early 1960s Union Pacific publicity photograph is an example of this policy, where a white supervisor is in charge of unloading operations. Note that a white worker is unloading a truck alongside an African American worker. This freight dock opened onto First Avenue on the East Side (shown) where trucks could load and unload. The West Side opened to the tracks for access to the rail cars. (BCHS.)

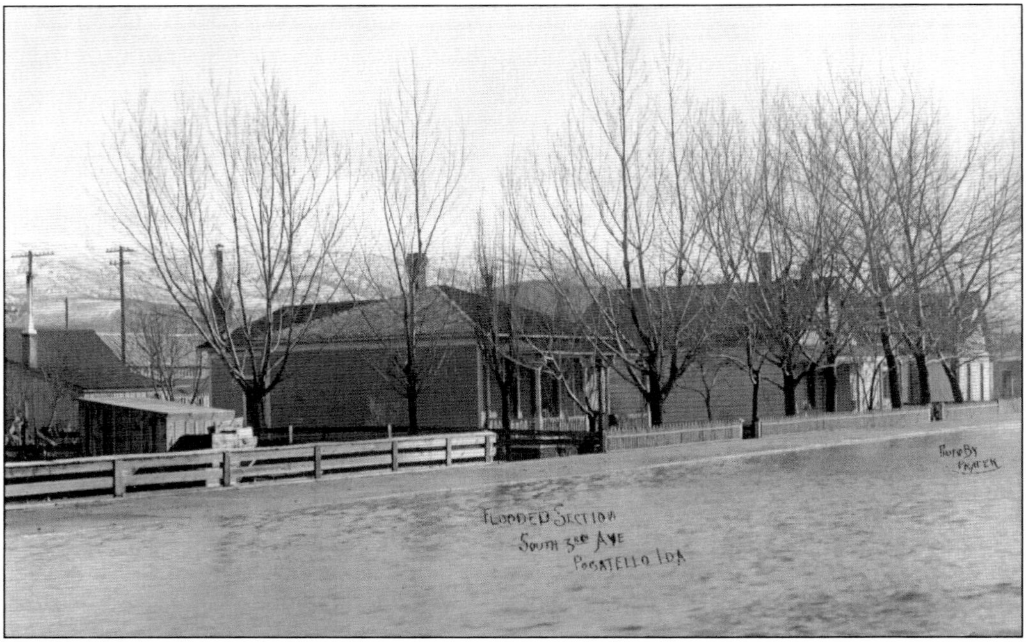

Until relatively recently, flooding of the Portneuf River posed a continuous problem for Pocatello residents. The valley basin was particularly susceptible to flooding. In 1911, Pocatello was hit with a massive flood, and the entire city was affected by the rising waters. In a photograph taken by Paul Bistline, the area around Third Avenue is being inundated by the floodwaters coming through the area. (Bistline.)

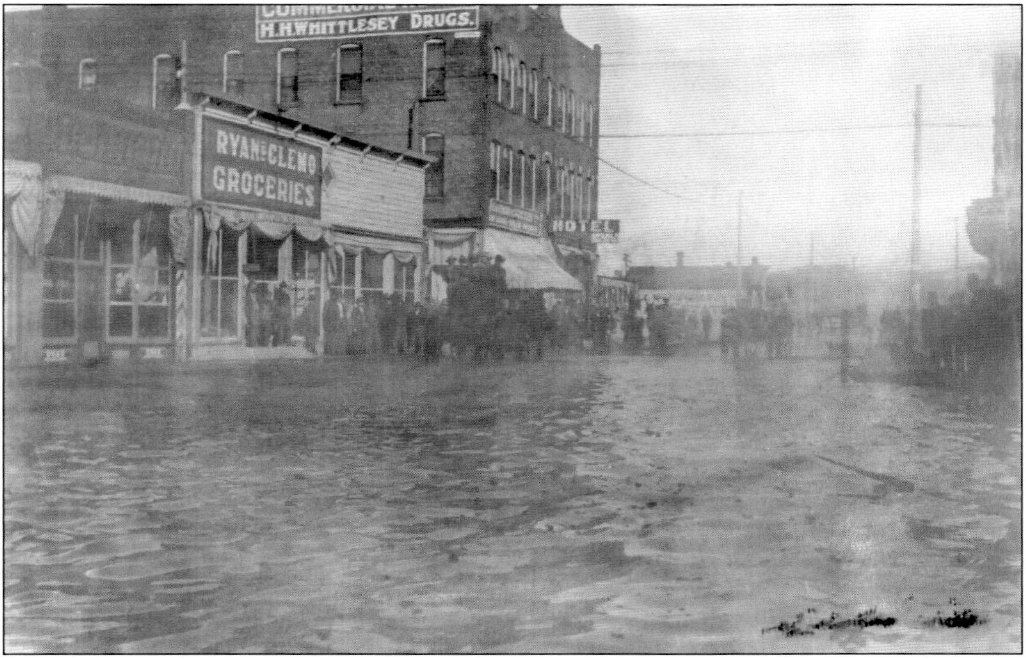

This photograph shows East Center Street between First and Second Avenues during the flood of 1911. (BCHS.)

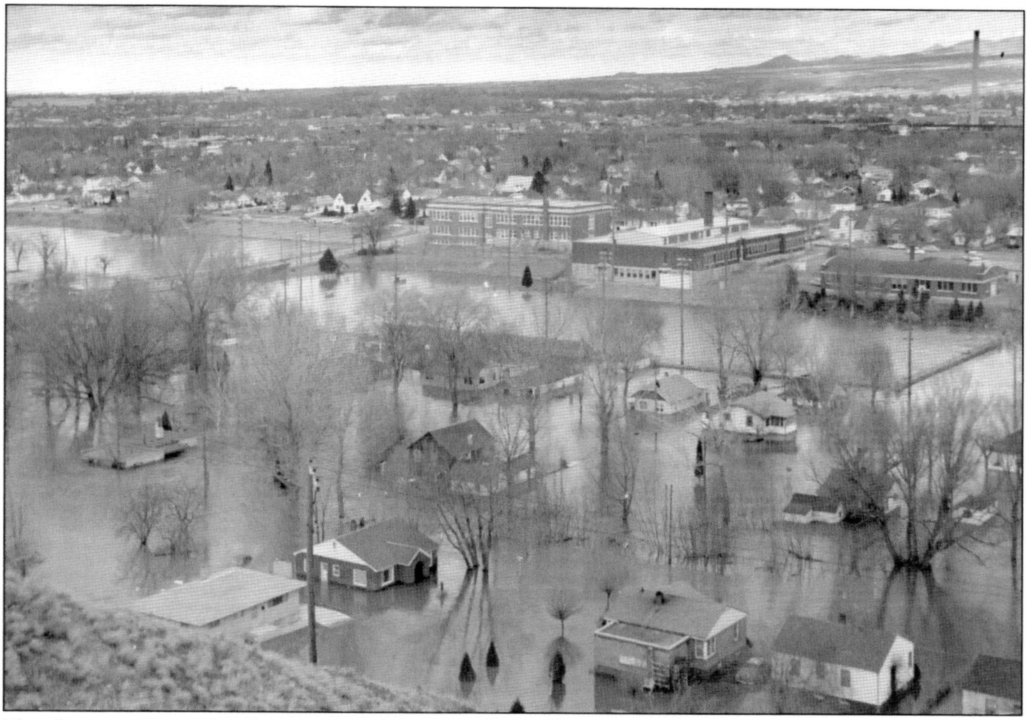

Flooding continued to be an issue for Pocatello well into the 20th century. This photograph of the downtown area in the midst of the 1961 flood gives some indication of the vulnerability that Pocatello faced when the Portneuf River flowed over its banks. (BCHS.)

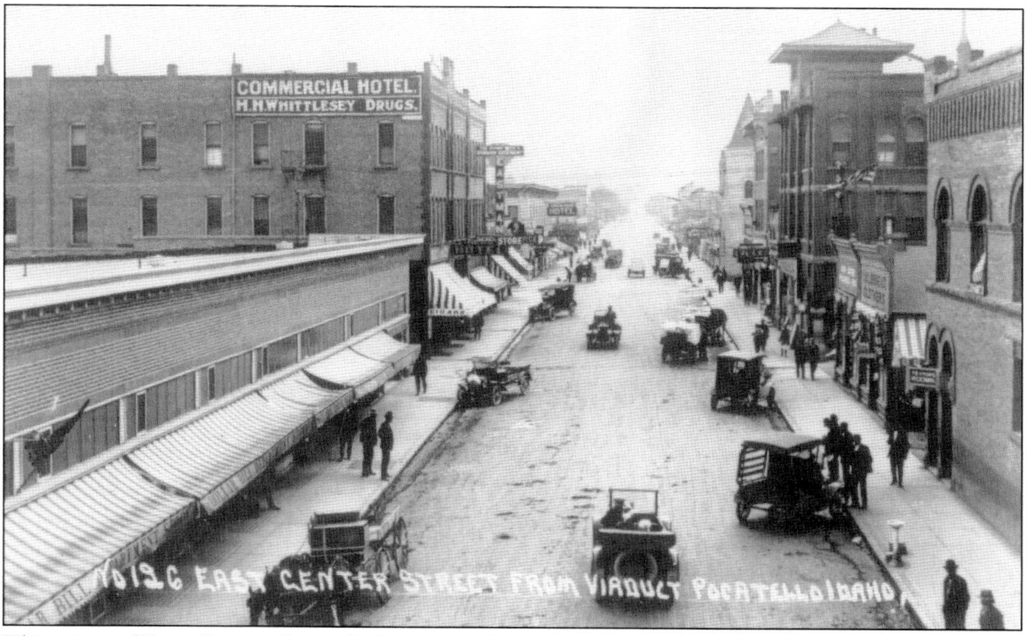

This view of East Center Street looking east from near the viaduct shows how quickly this area of downtown had grown by 1916. Note the Auditorium Theater, the taller, dark building on the right. Farther east, also on the right, is the Pocatello House, identified by its light colored stone and high peaked roof. (BCHS.)

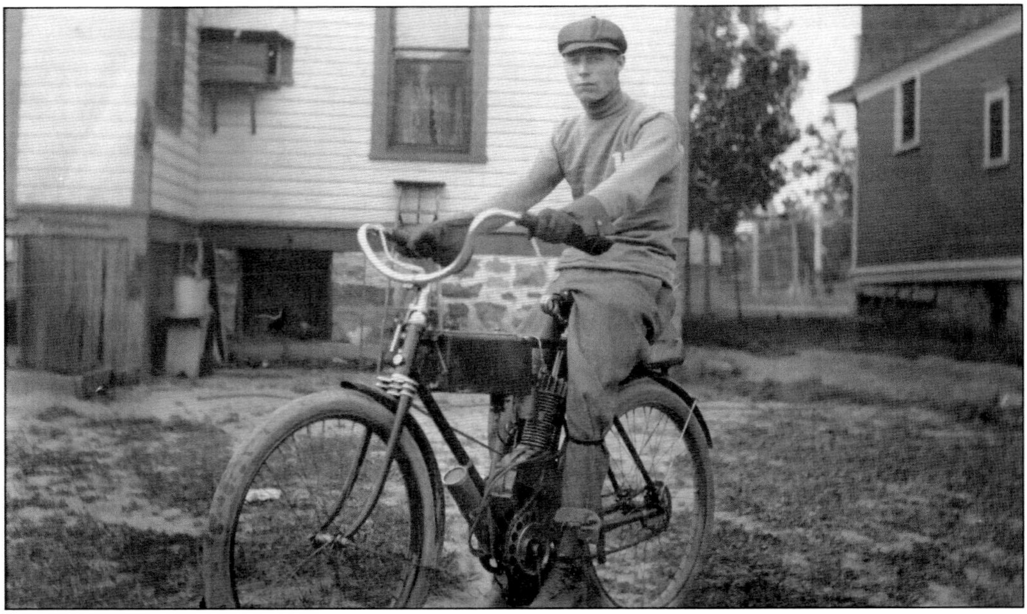

Probably taken before 1920, this photograph shows a young man sitting on an early motorcycle, in actuality more like a bicycle with a motor attached to it. The neighborhood pictured was typical of Pocatello in the early 20th century. (BCHS.)

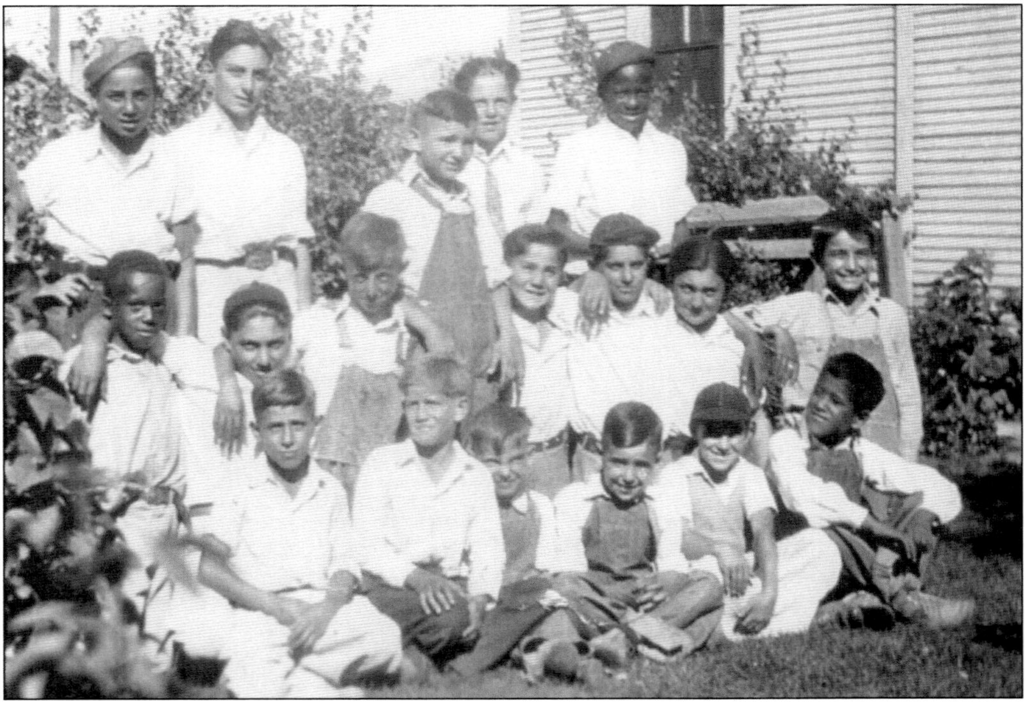

The diversity of the East Side of Pocatello is reflected in this photograph of a group of boys, probably in the mid-1930s. They are, from left to right, (first row) Gus Thiros, Ken Marchetti, Vern Peyron, Bob Peyron, Carmie Zaccardi, and Gaylord Devilla; (second row) Jake LaRue, Christ Harame, "Nick" Manfredo, Ted Thiros, Jim Scardino, unidentified, and Paul Dudaneke; (third row) John Dudaneke, Ted Harame, Maurie Peyron, Oriel Mitchell, and Bill "Boo" Birrell. (BCHS.)

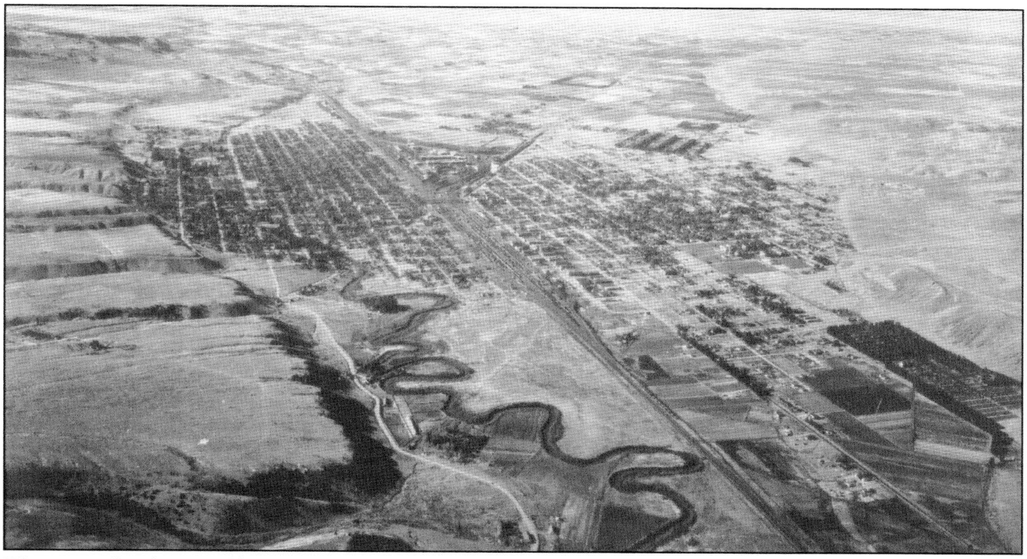

The growth of Pocatello was chronicled by aerial photography in the first half of the 20th century. This September 21, 1932, photograph shows Pocatello to the north. The Portneuf River is on the left, with the downtown area north of the river. The East Side of the city is expanding towards the foothills on the right and is gradually encircling the University of Idaho, Southern Branch campus off to the right-center. As of yet, there is no development visible north of the Union Pacific Railroad facilities; this would not really occur until after World War II. (BCHS.)

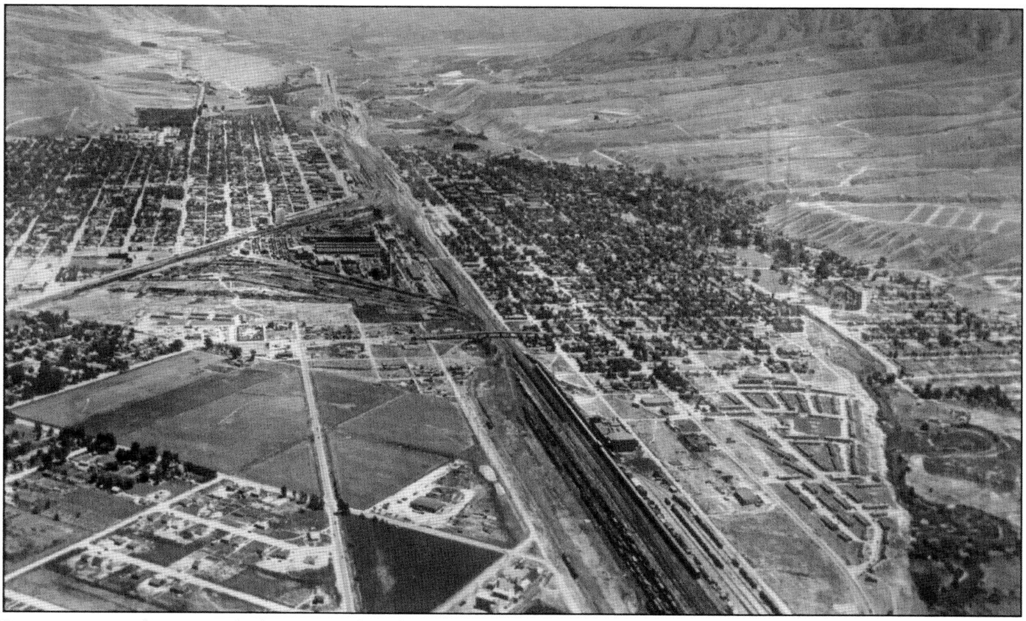

In contrast, this aerial photograph of Pocatello, taken sometime between 1948 and 1950, shows how the city grew in the aftermath of World War II. Looking south, the city has developed north of the downtown area. Here, neighborhoods are north of the Union Pacific railroad facilities (to the south in the photograph itself). The East Side has moved to the edge of the foothills and is about to completely encircle the Idaho State College campus. The West Side, seen surrounding the downtown area, is in the beginning phases of development, and is already encroaching on the west foothills of the city. (Paul Leffler.)

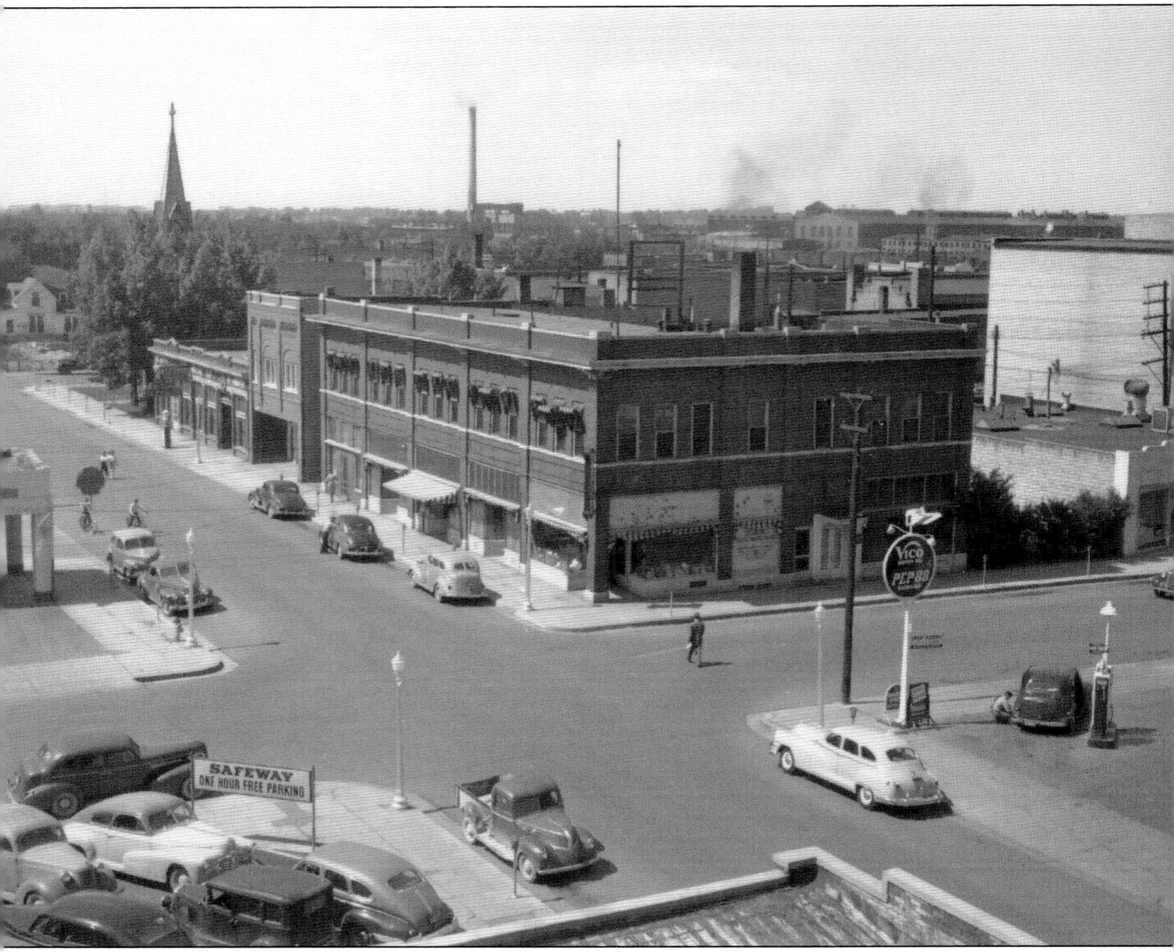

This 1946 photograph of the corner of Arthur Avenue and Clark Street shows downtown Pocatello in the post–World War II period. The prominent structure in the center is the Eagles Building. A two-story brick structure, it was completed in early 1916 at a cost of roughly $35,000. It was the new home and clubhouse of the Fraternal Order of Eagles. Many of the buildings constructed in Pocatello during this period were for the "secret and benevolent organizations" of the time, according to *Pocatello, Idaho's Potential Metropolis, 1915*. In the 1920s and 1930s, many dances were held in the hall on the second story. The building has housed many businesses and organizations over the years, including the Lynn Brothers' Benevolent Hospital and the Modern Barber Shop. The Pocatello Fire Department (at that time Station No. 1), to the left of the Eagles Building, was the first fire station in Pocatello. While no longer in use as a fire station, the structure still stands. Of particular interest is the Trinity Episcopal Church in the left background, which is one of the oldest-standing religious structures currently in the city. Pocatello High School is just out of view to the left. (Paul Leffler.)

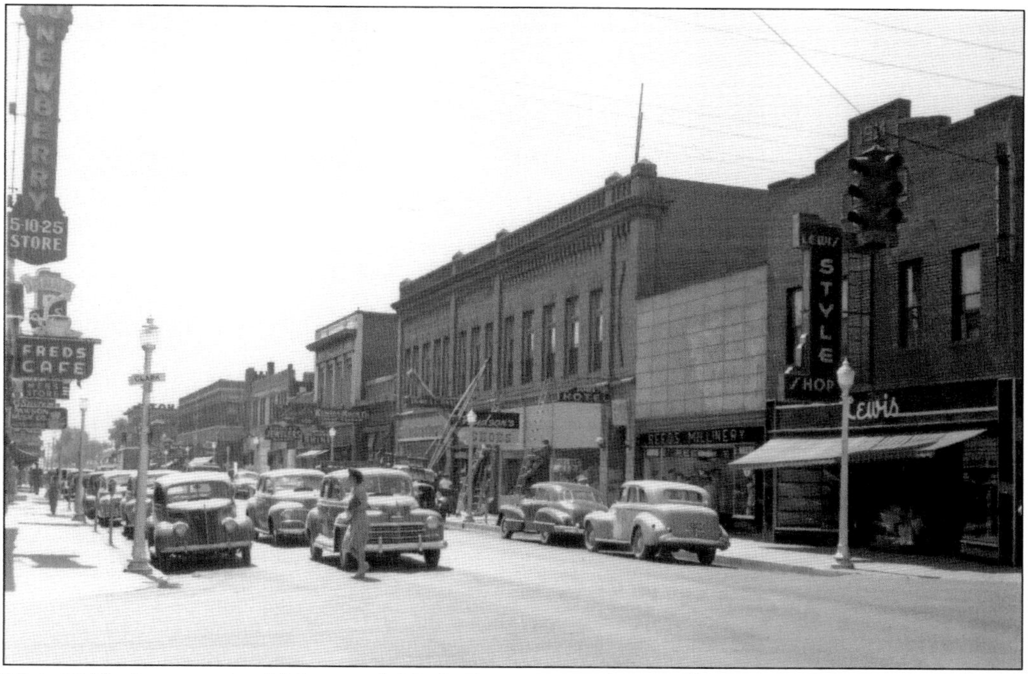

This 1948 photograph of Main and Clark Streets provides another view of post–World War II Pocatello. Prosperity is evident. Most of these buildings still stand today. However, only the bottom floor of the Ross Terrell building, seen here in the center, remains. The Lewis building, on the right, is now the site of a pizza parlor. (Paul Leffler.)

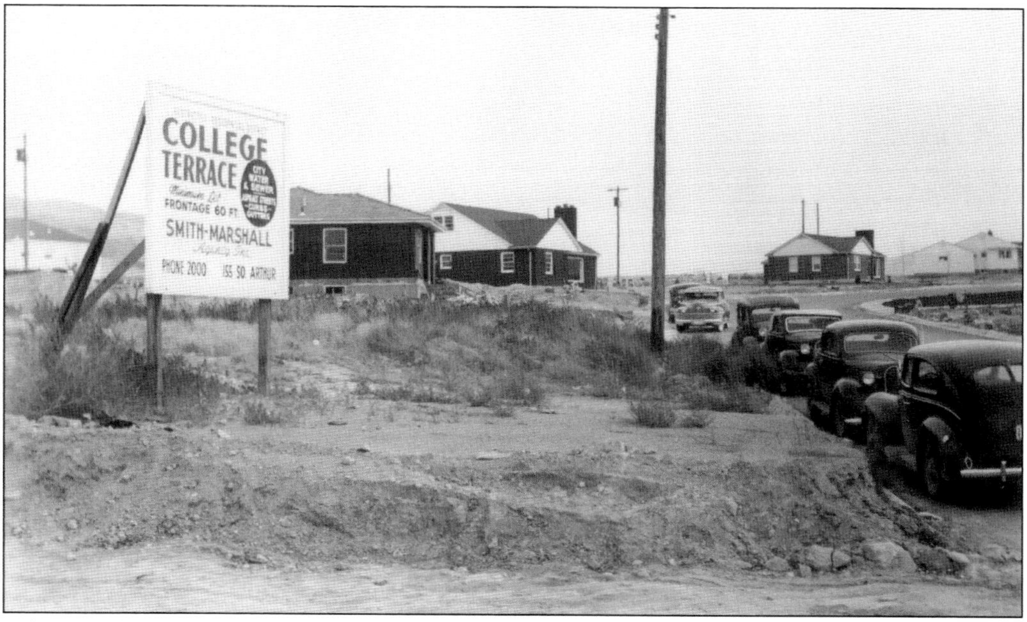

After World War II, a number of housing developments were constructed across the United States to accommodate returning servicemen and their families. Pocatello was no exception to this trend, with housing developments being built both on the north and south ends of the city. The College Terrace development, seen here in its finishing phases, was but one of these postwar housing developments. (BCHS.)

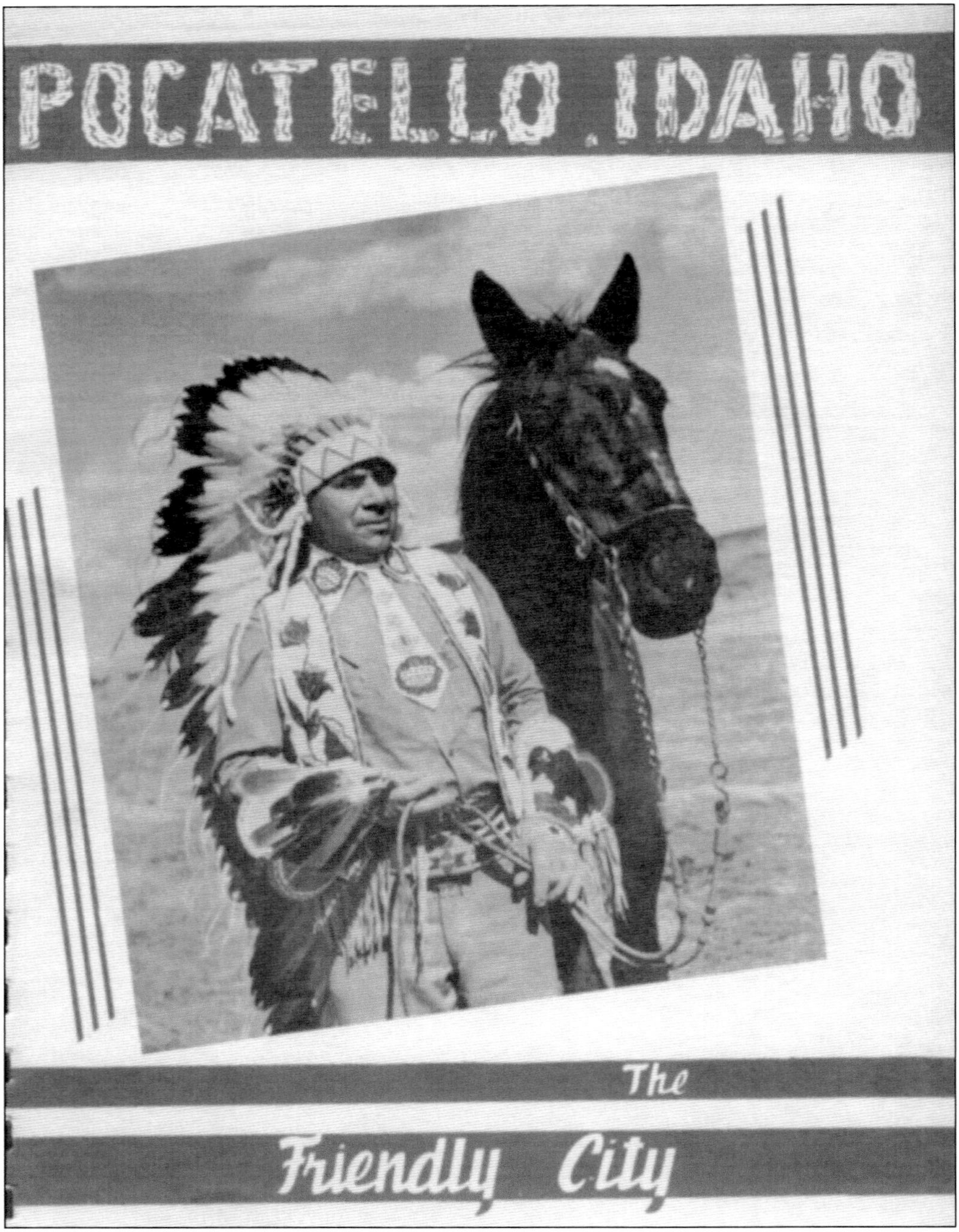

Even though Pocatello had made tremendous strides in its growth from a railroad junction to the major metropolis in the region, there was still a strong identification with the history of the region. This is clearly shown in this 1948 chamber of commerce guidebook, the cover of which features a native chief in what might (or might not) be traditional dress. (BCHS.)

Three

Civic Life

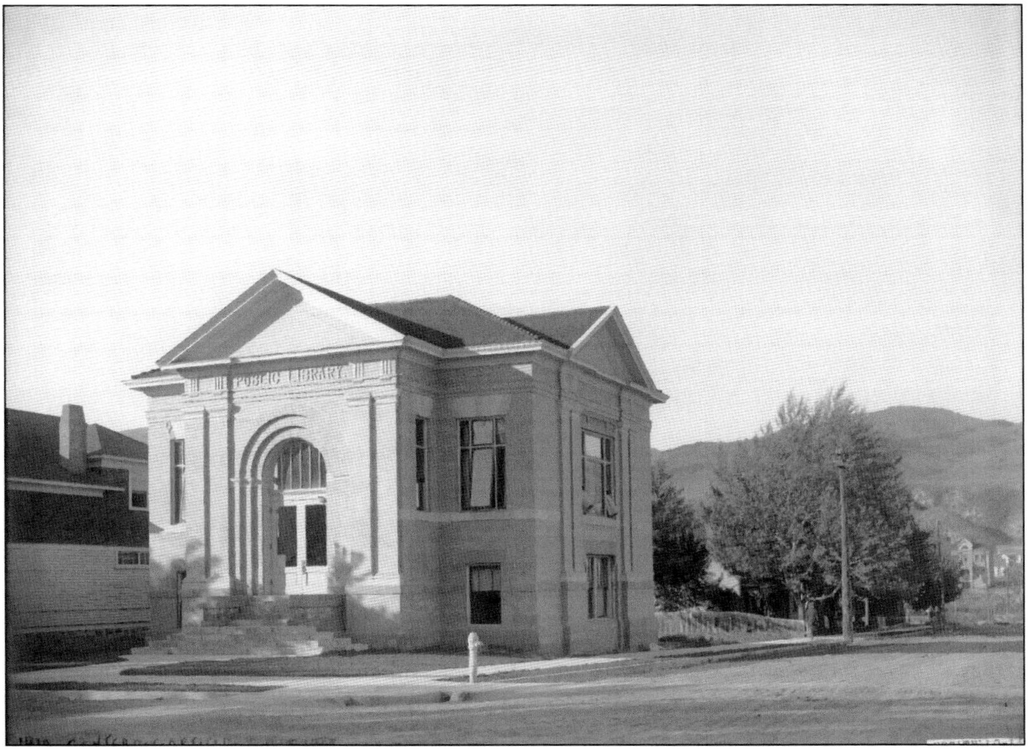

The Andrew Carnegie–financed main library in Pocatello, built in 1909, provided a source of information to the larger community for decades. This 1910 photograph shows the library building, on the corner of South Garfield Avenue and West Center Street, while it was still relatively new and the neighborhood around it had not yet been fully developed. The structure was later home to the Bannock County Historical Society Museum, and is now part of the current library building. (BCHS.)

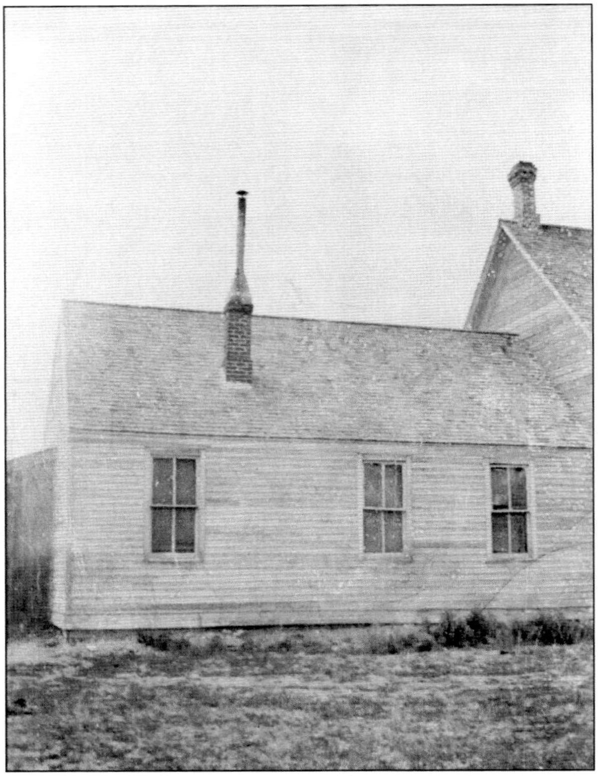

Pocatello has a long history of religious diversity. This photograph purports to show the first church built in the new town. There is no clear sign of denomination; it is possible that it was a nondenominational house of worship. (BCHS.)

One of the first permanent church structures in Pocatello was the First Ward building of the Church of Jesus Christ of Latter-Day Saints (LDS), also known as the Mormons. This church, located at the corner of Garfield and Center Streets, was built in the late 1880s. It featured a large painting by Minerva Teichert that depicted a pioneer scene. In this 1910 photograph, the neighborhood around the chapel is still relatively undeveloped, with a laundry being the closest structure to the church. Note the Railroad YMCA sign in the right background. (BCHS.)

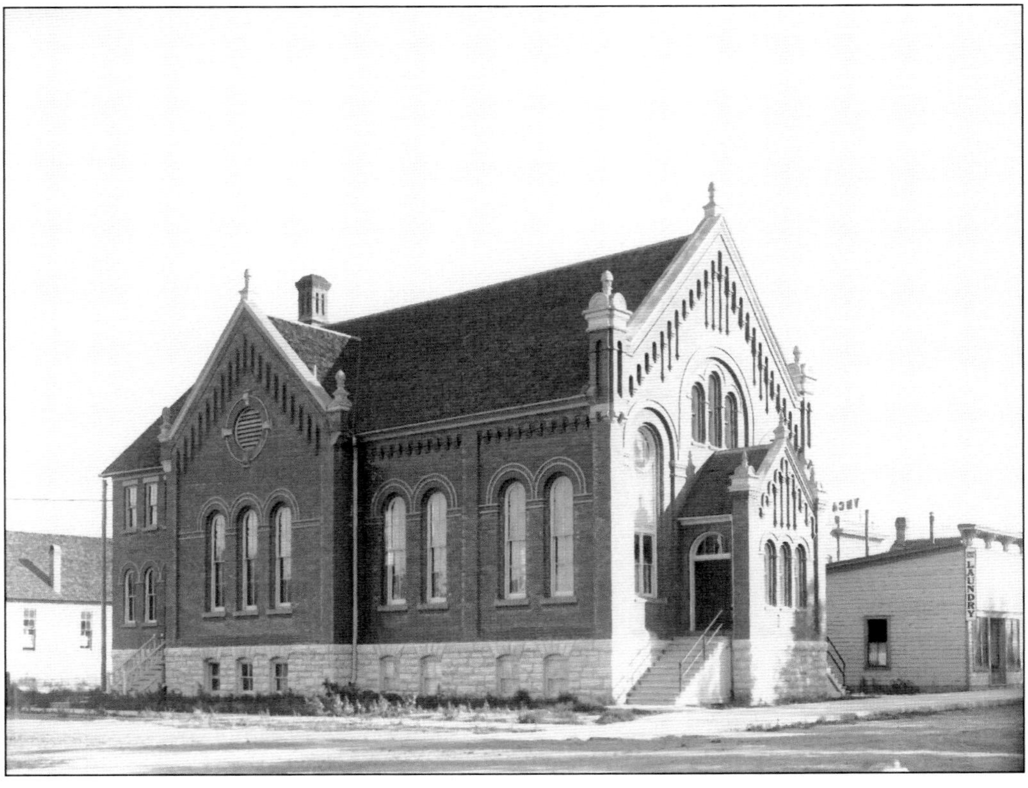

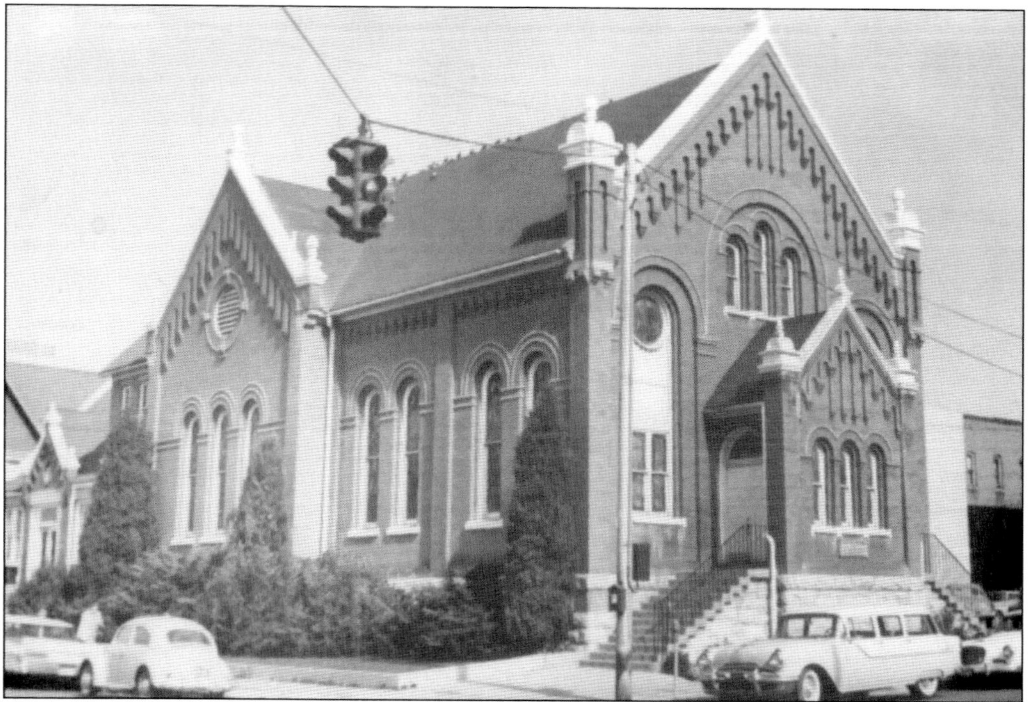

In this early 1960s photograph, the neighborhood around the First Ward Chapel had developed in the intervening period. The building was eventually torn down in 1962, and a parking lot for a nearby bank is now in its place. The painting was salvaged, and is now located in an LDS meetinghouse on Grant Avenue. (BCHS.)

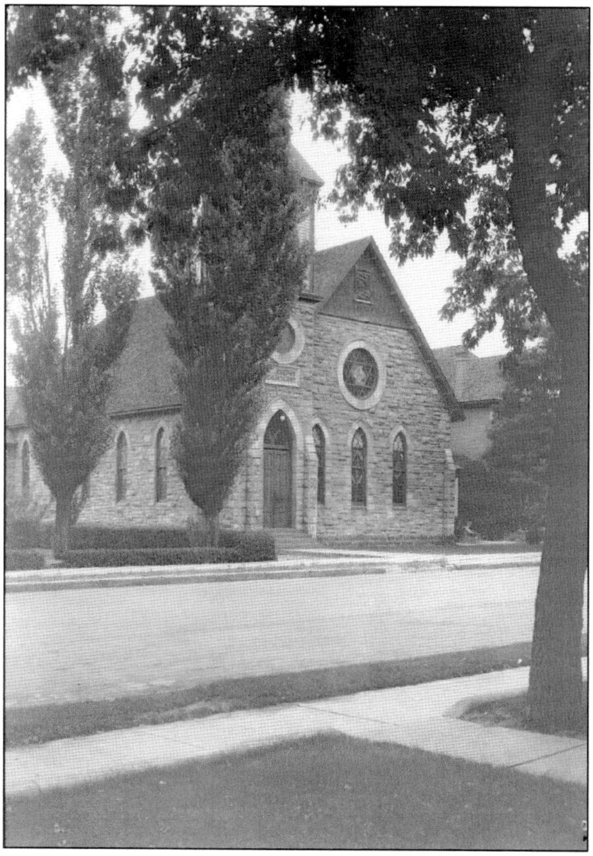

St. Joseph's Catholic Church was another early church in Pocatello. Completed in 1897, this sandstone structure located at 455 North Hayes Avenue is listed in the National Register of Historical Places. The stone was obtained from the nearby Fort Hall Reservation. The pews and stained glass windows were from Portland, Oregon. Over the next few years, more additions were made to the church, including a pipe organ and three large bells. (ISU.)

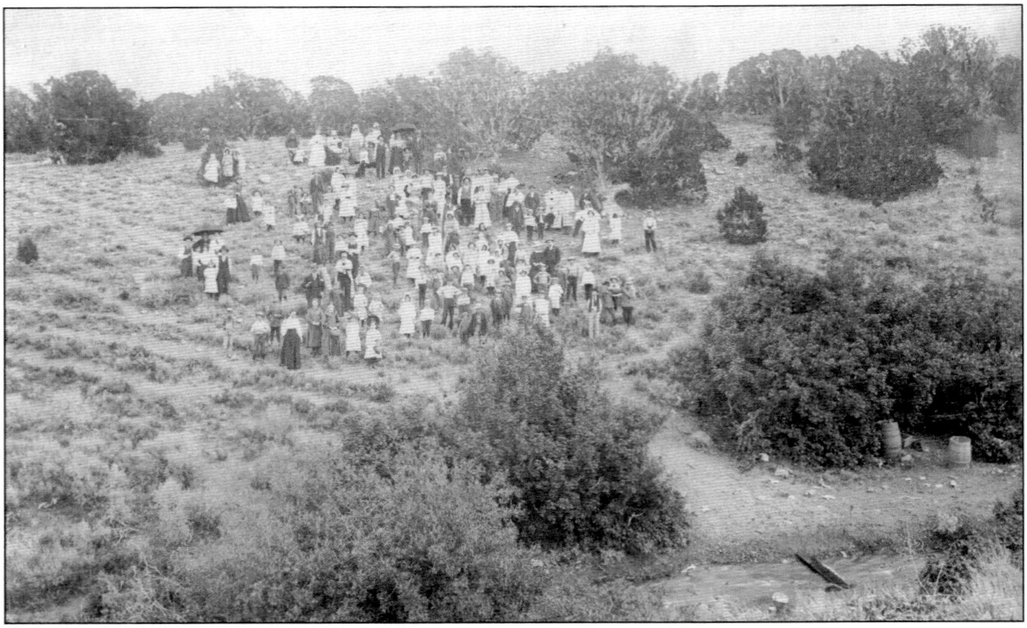

The churches in Pocatello provided activities, which built a sense of community within the group. One popular activity in the early days of Pocatello's existence was to hold picnics in the hills surrounding the fledgling town, as seen in this 1897 photograph of members of the LDS First Ward holding a Sunday school picnic in the City Creek area just outside of the then town limits. (BCHS.)

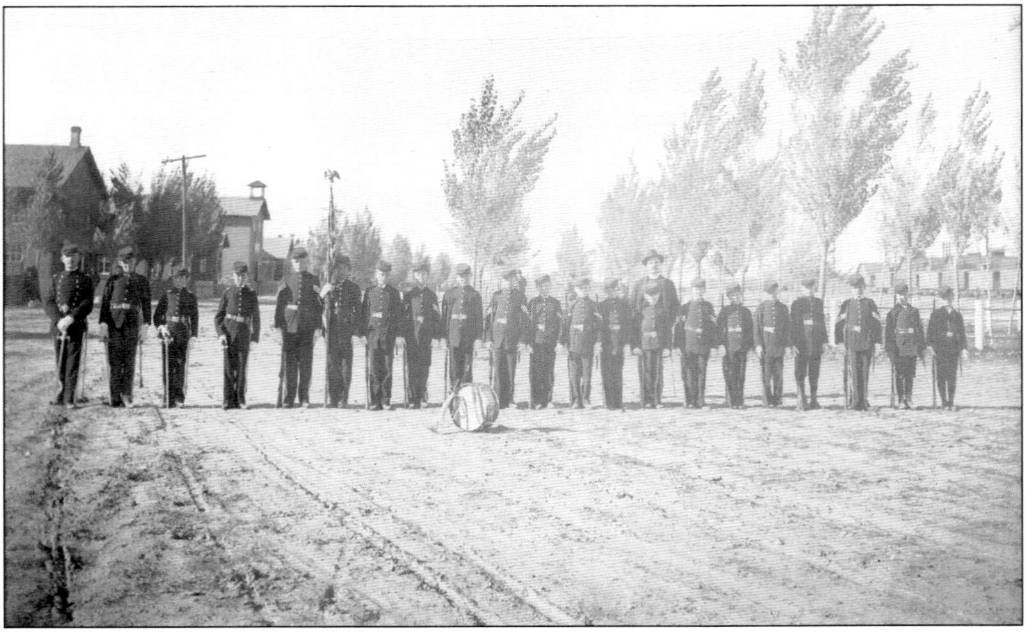

Another aspect of church life in Pocatello at the turn of the 20th century was in the area of youth activities. One such organization was the so-called "Boy's Brigade," which was run by Reverend Murphy of the Episcopalian Church in Pocatello. Particularly noteworthy here are the uniforms worn by the members of the "brigade," which are highly reminiscent of Civil War army uniforms. (BCHS.)

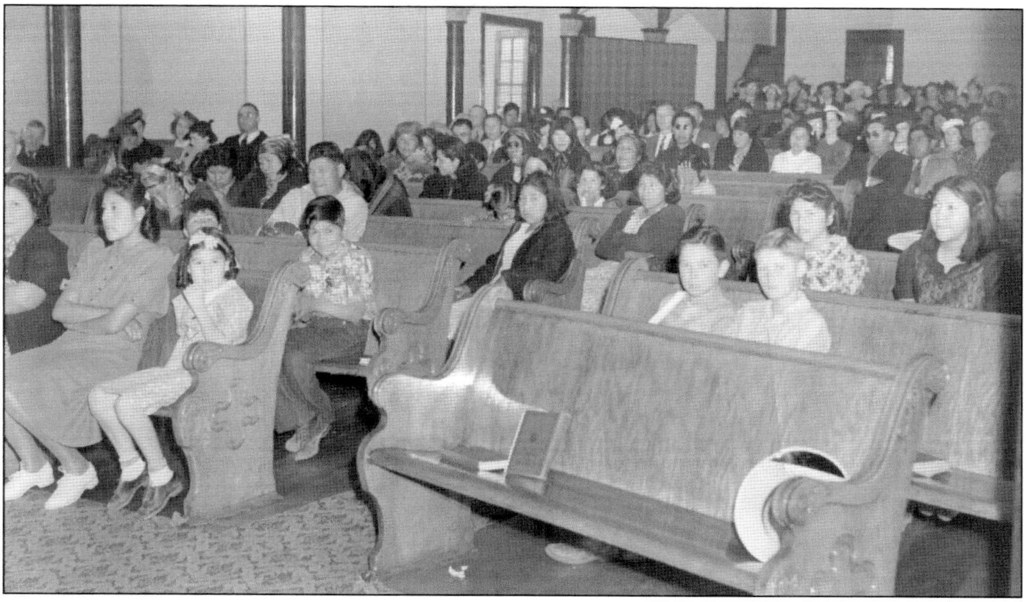

Pocatello churches have traditionally offered services for a diverse population. This photograph shows the services held on Indian Day at the Congregational church in Pocatello. These members of the Bannock and Shoshoni tribes are pictured in May 1939. (BCHS.)

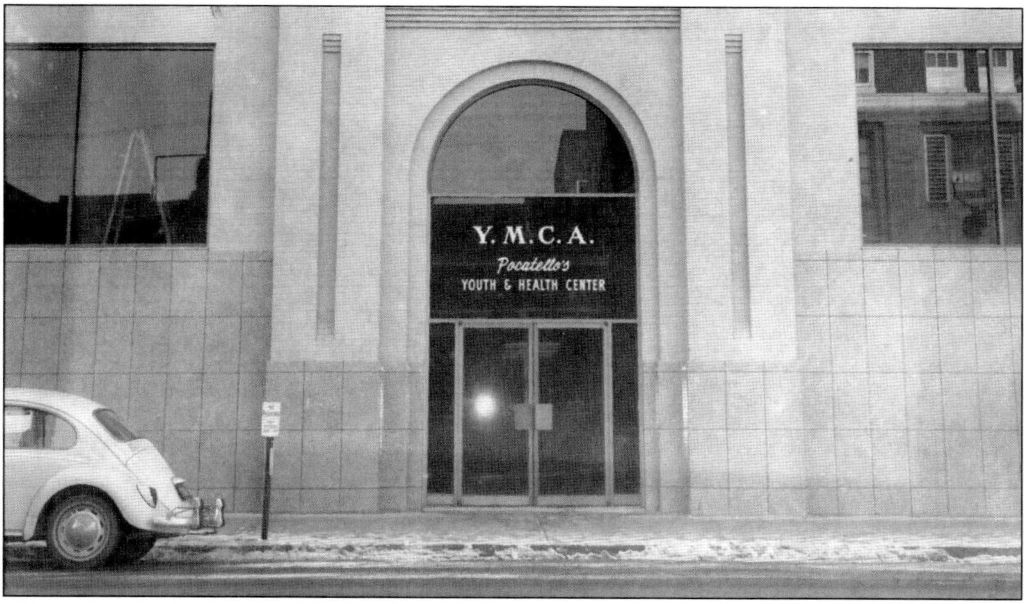

The railroad reached far beyond transportation and employment opportunities for the people of Pocatello. The importance of the railroad can be gauged by, among other things, the presence of this Railroad YMCA building at 133 North Arthur Avenue. Constructed in 1907, this edifice was the third home of the Pocatello Association, but the first constructed solely for its purposes. With such a large number of Oregon Short Line employees in the city, according to *Pocatello, Idaho's Potential Metropolis*, "it was only natural that some steps were taken for the welfare of these men." This railroad association operated the YMCA until the late 1930s, when the city took over its operation. The YMCA gradually became one of the main civic gathering places in the city, with many Pocatellans learning how to swim in the indoor pool. (BCHS.)

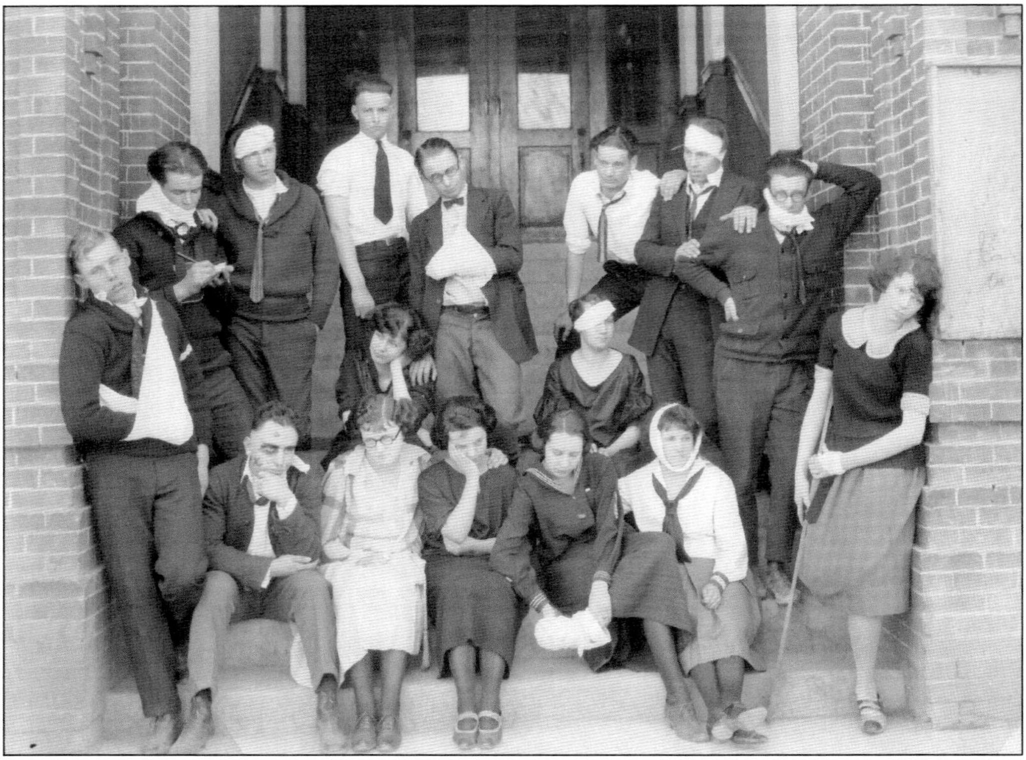

Another of the activities offered by the Railroad YMCA was instruction of first aid techniques. In this 1920s photograph, one group of first aid students is seen here after taking a course. It is obvious that a number of participants have gotten into their roles as injury cases. (BCHS.)

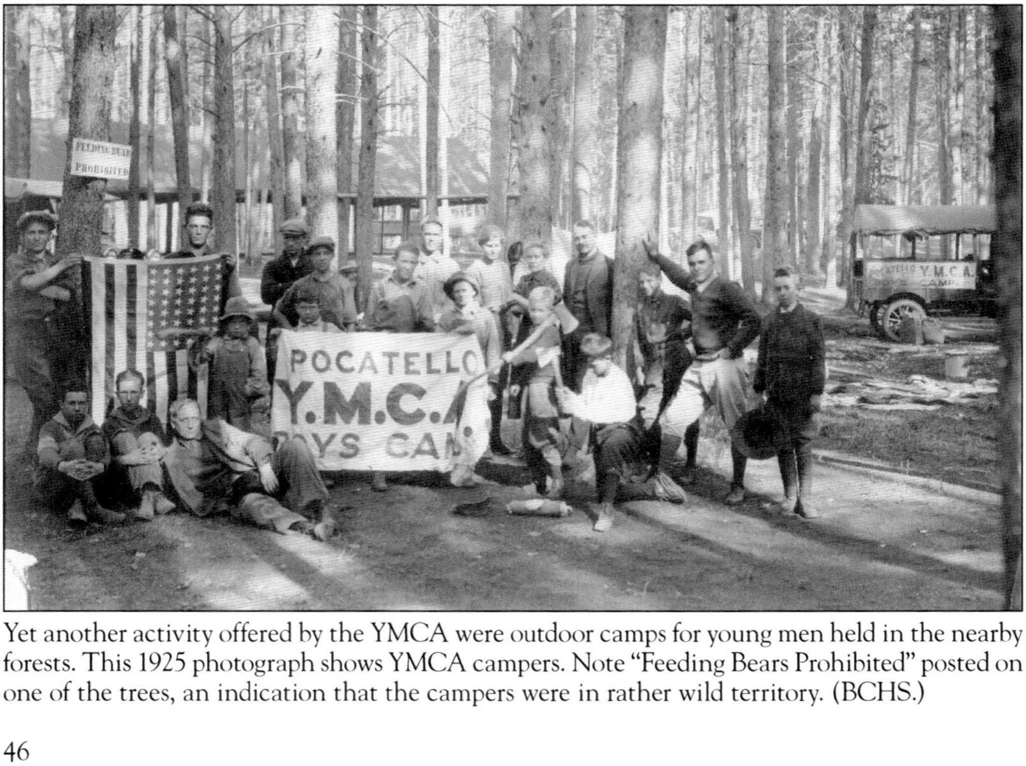

Yet another activity offered by the YMCA were outdoor camps for young men held in the nearby forests. This 1925 photograph shows YMCA campers. Note "Feeding Bears Prohibited" posted on one of the trees, an indication that the campers were in rather wild territory. (BCHS.)

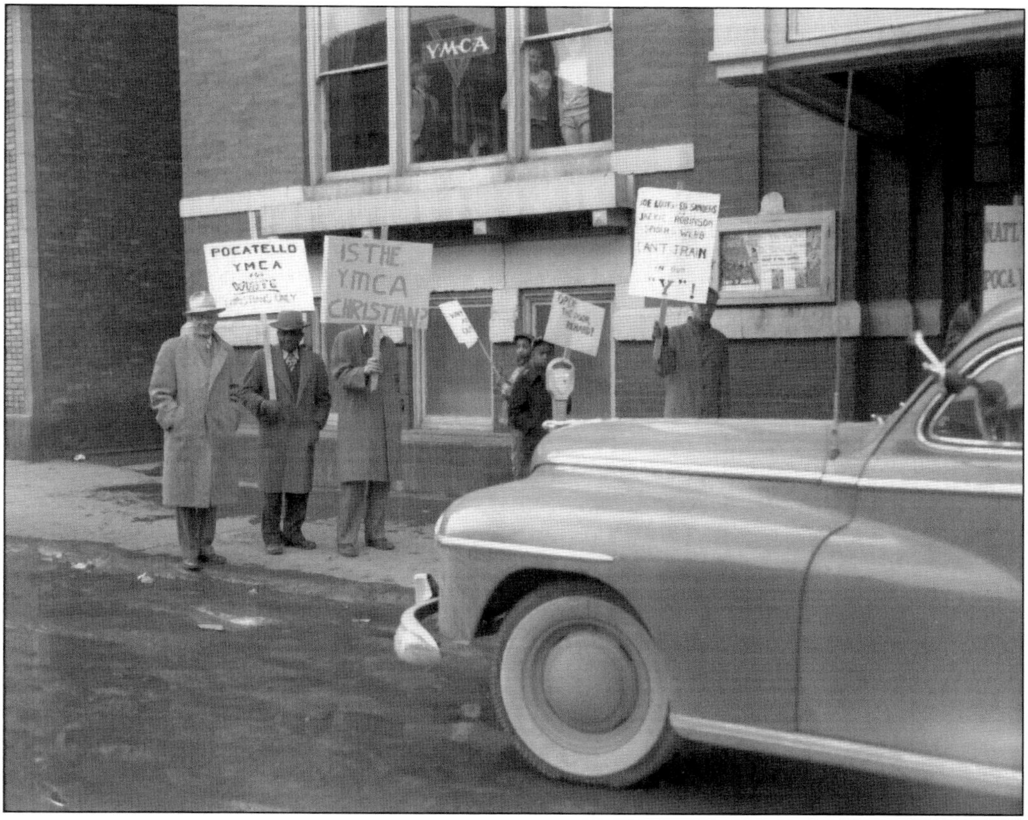

In keeping with norms that existed in the United States at the time, the YMCA in Pocatello allowed only certain ethnic and racial groups to use its facilities. This policy was eventually challenged, as this news photograph from about 1952 shows. This group of demonstrators is particularly notable for being composed of both African American and white persons, which was rare. The mention of Ed Sanders and "Spider" Webb on one of the demonstrator's placards refers to two African American boxers at Idaho State College who were noted members of the boxing team. (BCHS.)

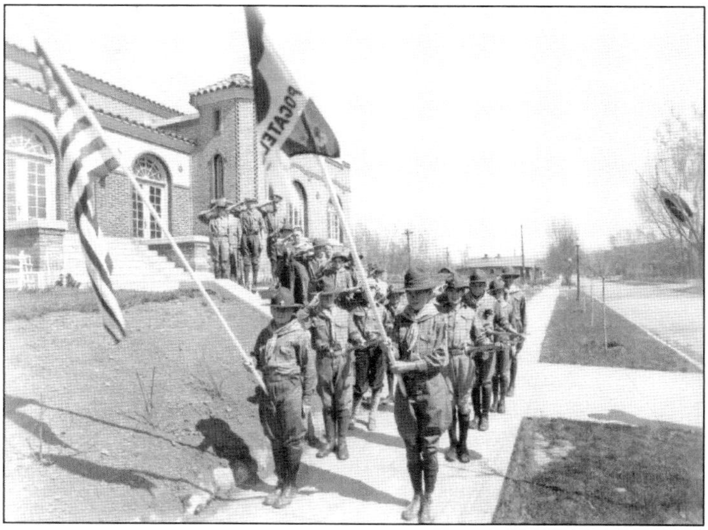

Another civic organization that had a strong presence in Pocatello was the Boy Scouts. In this May 11, 1929, photograph, members of Boy Scout Troop 3 have gathered before the Bannock County Memorial Building. (BCHS.)

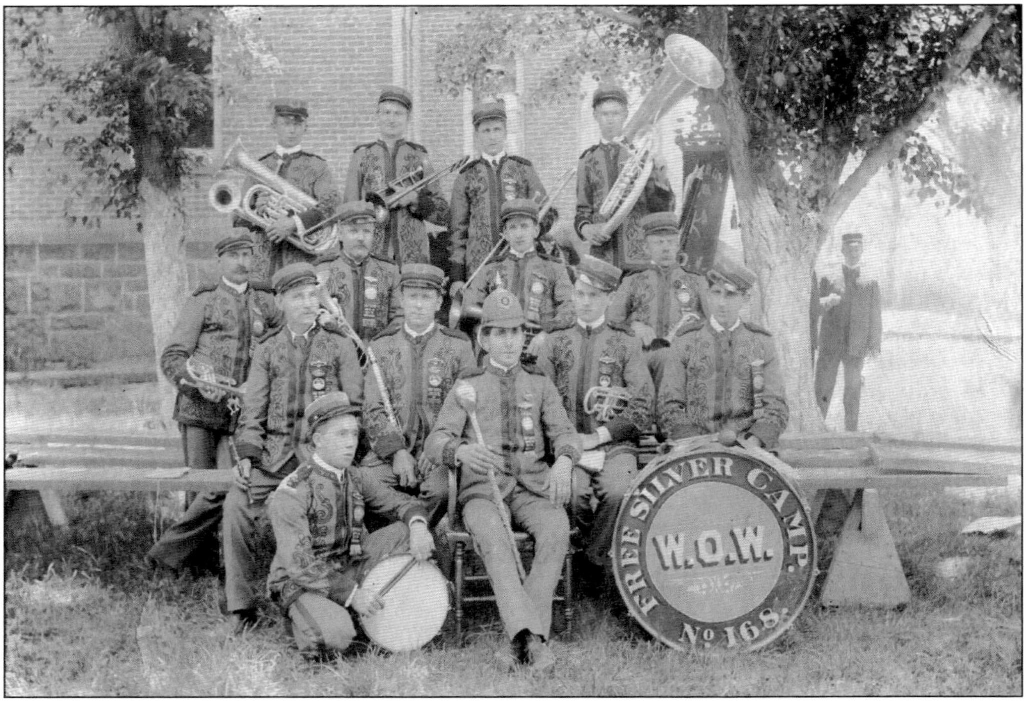

In the latter part of the 19th and early part of the 20th centuries, band music was a popular form of entertainment around the world. In Pocatello, a number of organizations mustered bands for civic and political functions. One such band was provided by the Woodmen of the World (WOW), a benevolent fraternal organization. This photograph of the WOW band was taken in the 1890s. Note that the band's drum is labeled Free Silver Camp. The Free Silver movement, which advocated for silver to be used as the means of backing the US dollar, was particularly popular in the Western states. (BCHS.)

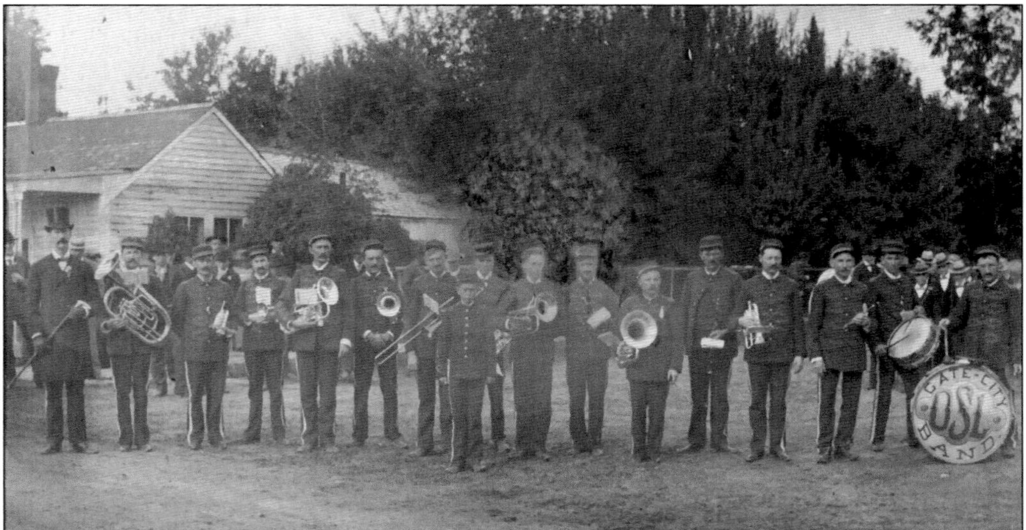

The Oregon Short Line Railroad was another entity that provided a band for gatherings and company functions. This photograph of the OSL Gate City Band was taken in Blackfoot in 1909, apparently during a tour of Eastern Idaho. (BCHS.)

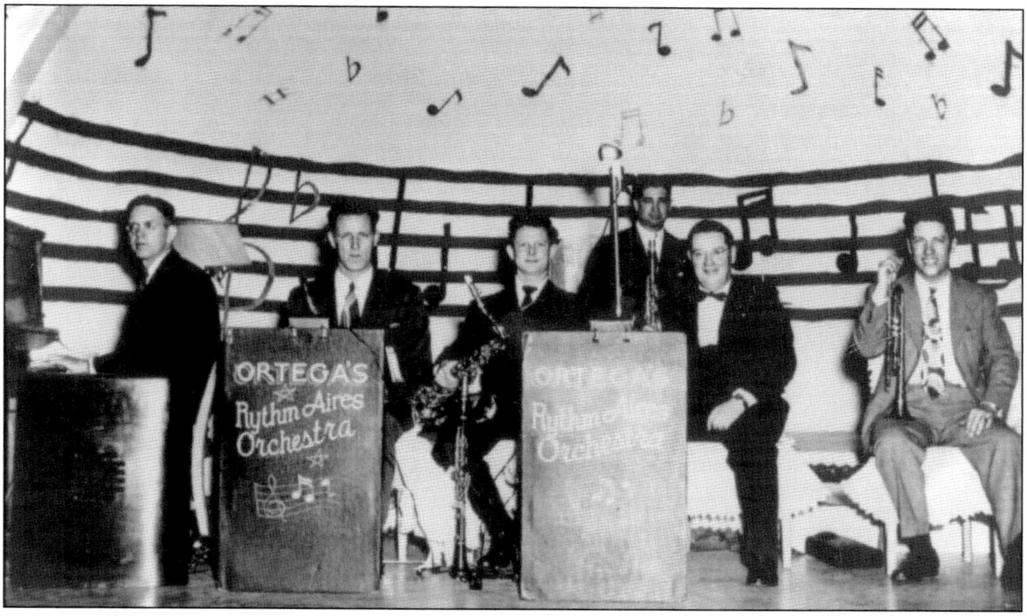

The railroad continued to play a role in bringing musical entertainment to the people of Pocatello and Southeastern Idaho in other ways. A Union Pacific Railroad yard clerk of Mexican heritage, Joe M. Ortega, founded a musical group, Ortega's Rhythm Aires Orchestra. This band, pictured in the late 1930s, played at numerous venues in Pocatello and Southeastern Idaho from the 1930s to the 1960s. (BCHS.)

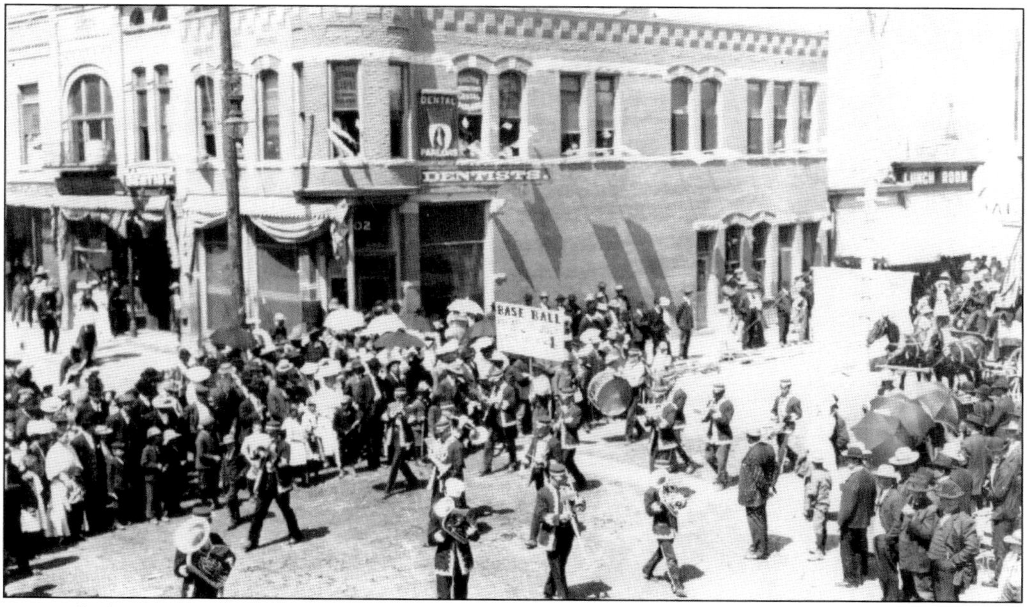

Pocatello has seen its share of marching bands perform on the Fourth of July. Here, a marching band performs at the Fourth of July parade in 1900 at the corner of Center and Main Streets in downtown Pocatello. (BCHS.)

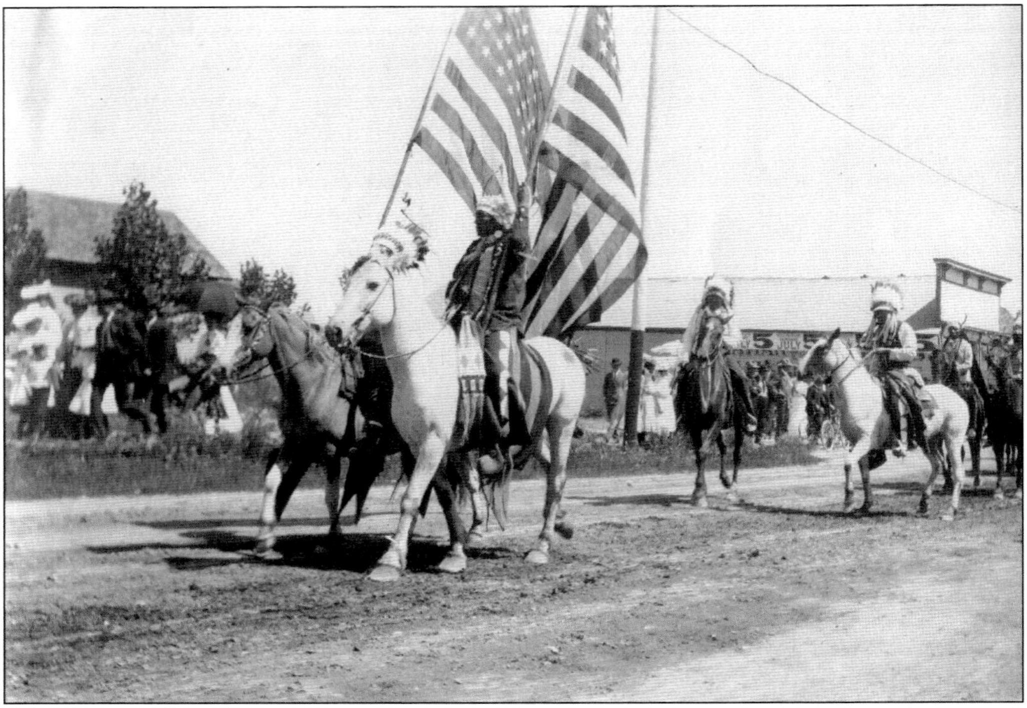

Among the most notable participants of Fourth of July parades in Pocatello were members of the Bannock-Shoshone tribes from nearby Fort Hall who had lost their lands in the Pocatello Valley during the settlement and expansion of the city itself. This photograph of Bannock-Shoshone tribesmen was taken at the 1906 parade. (BCHS.)

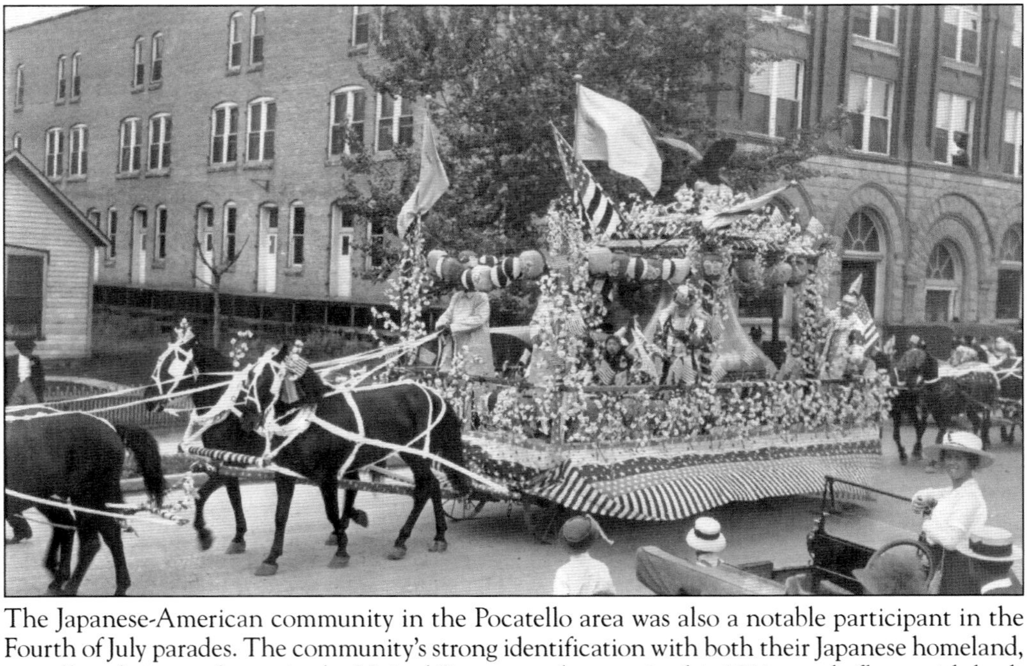

The Japanese-American community in the Pocatello area was also a notable participant in the Fourth of July parades. The community's strong identification with both their Japanese homeland, as well as their new home in the United States, can be seen in this 1914 parade float, with both Japanese and American cultural symbols present. (BCHS.)

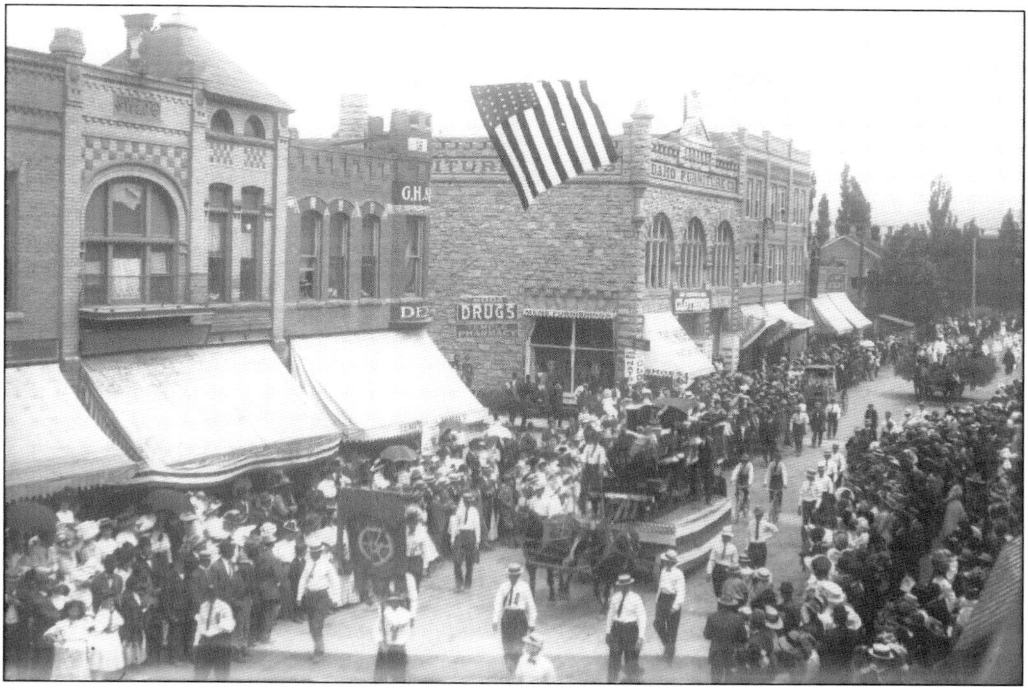

Civic organizations have also had a strong presence in Pocatello Fourth of July festivities. In this photograph of the 1914 parade, a group of Rotary members from the Pocatello lodge are seen parading up Center Street at Main Street. (BCHS.)

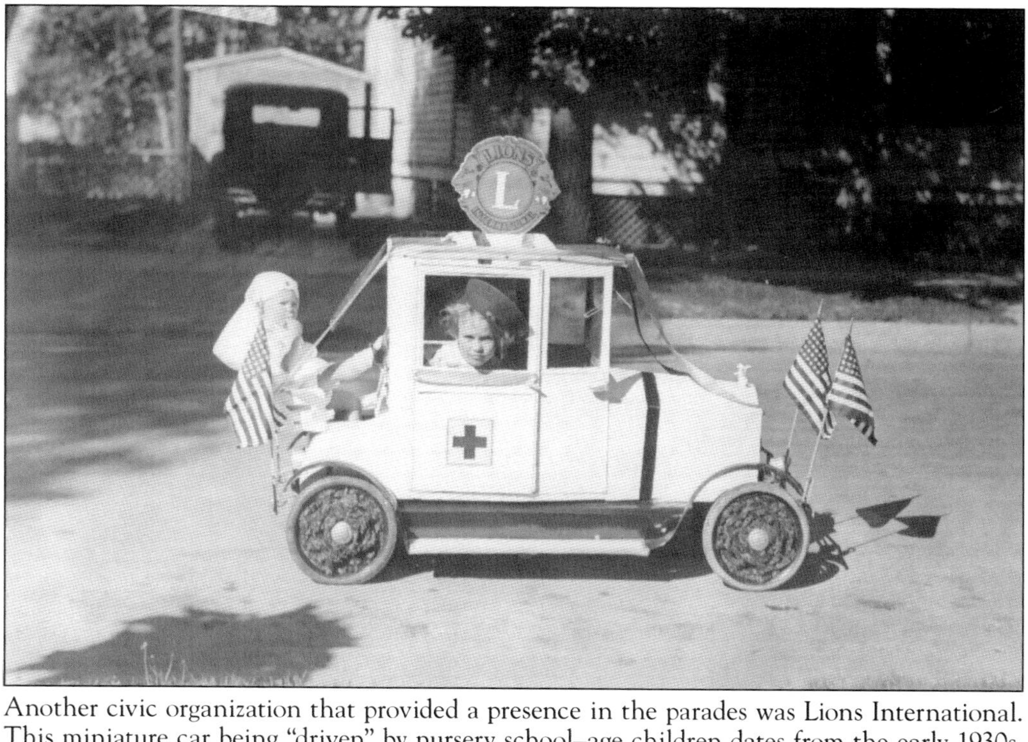

Another civic organization that provided a presence in the parades was Lions International. This miniature car being "driven" by nursery school–age children dates from the early 1930s. (BCHS.)

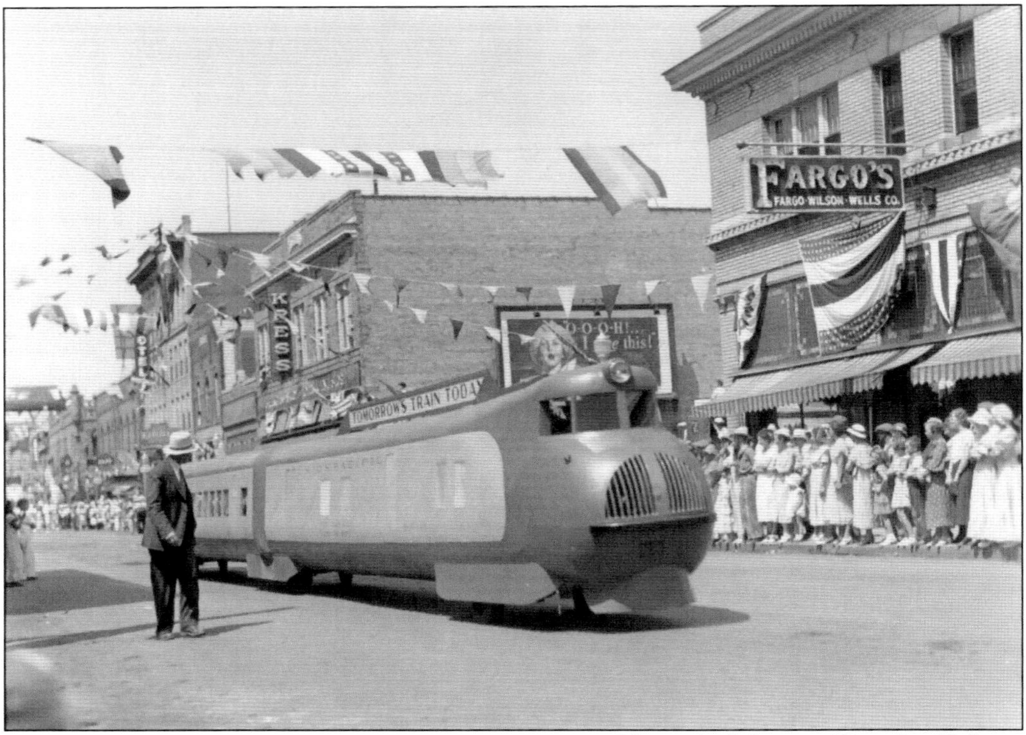

Not to be left out of Fourth of July events, the Union Pacific Railroad also contributed floats to the parades as a means of advertising. This early 1930s float advertises "Tomorrow's Train Today," presumably in reference to the streamlined trains then in development. (BCHS.)

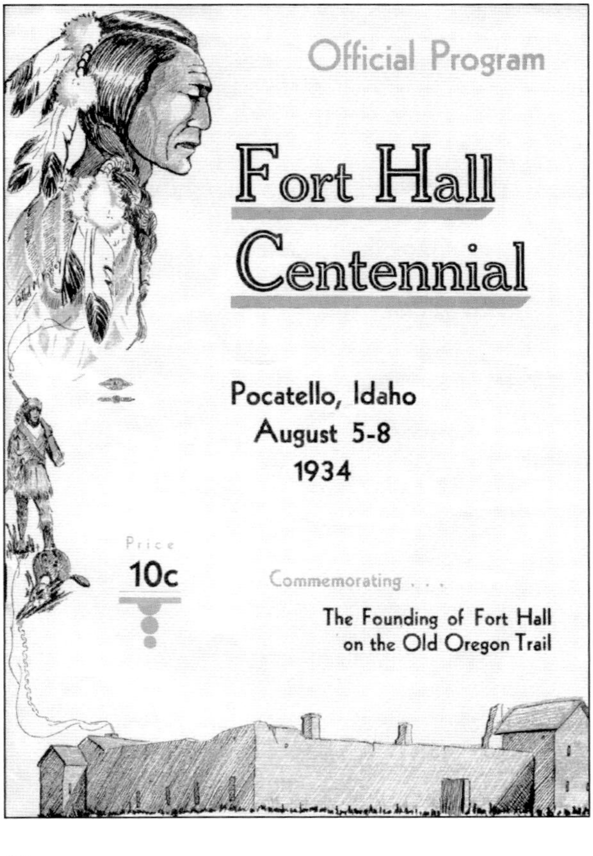

One of the major events in Pocatello in the 1930s was the centennial celebration of the founding of Fort Hall in 1834. The celebration was held from August 5 to 8, 1934, and featured a number of events, including a parade. This souvenir program was sold at the celebration and shows how the legacy of the tribes of the area was still celebrated, notwithstanding the history of relations between them and the white settlers. (BCHS.)

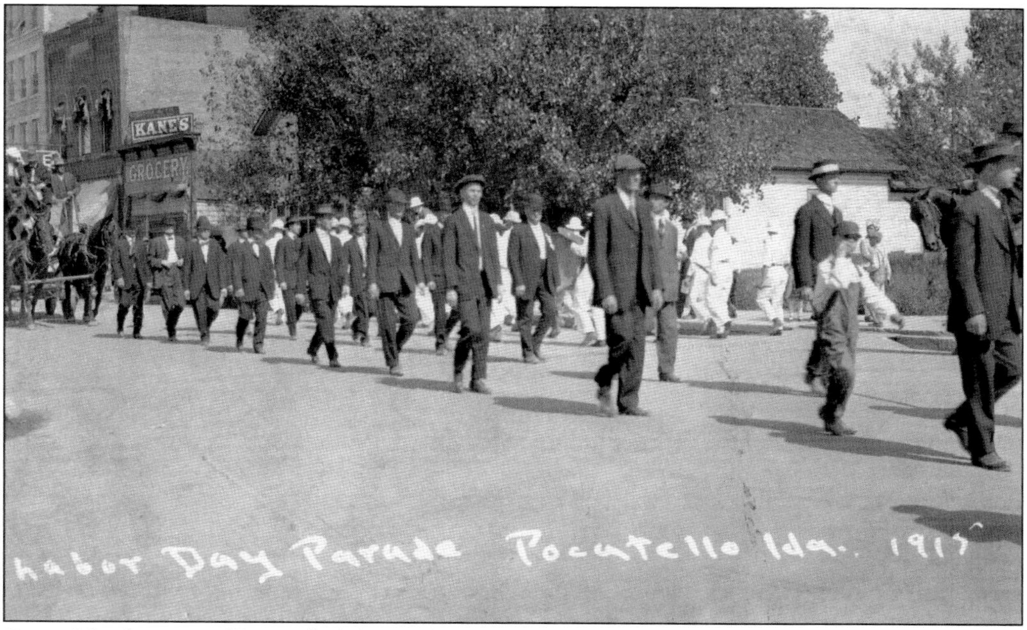

One of the features of Pocatello life was the strong identity the city had with the labor movement. The high point of the year for the labor movement was Labor Day, when the labor movement made its case for greater representation in the workplace. This 1915 photograph shows labor members marching through downtown Pocatello. (BCHS.)

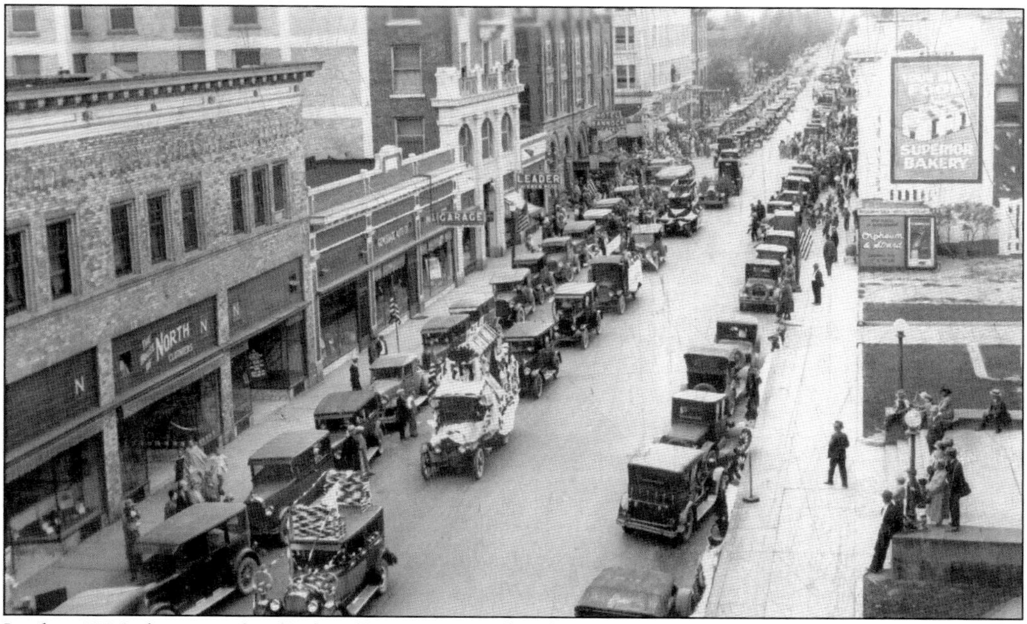

In this 1926 photograph of Labor Day in Pocatello, the movement has gained in terms of numbers and strength over the years. The participants are marching south on Arthur Street. The Bannock Hotel is visible on the left side of the street. (BCHS.)

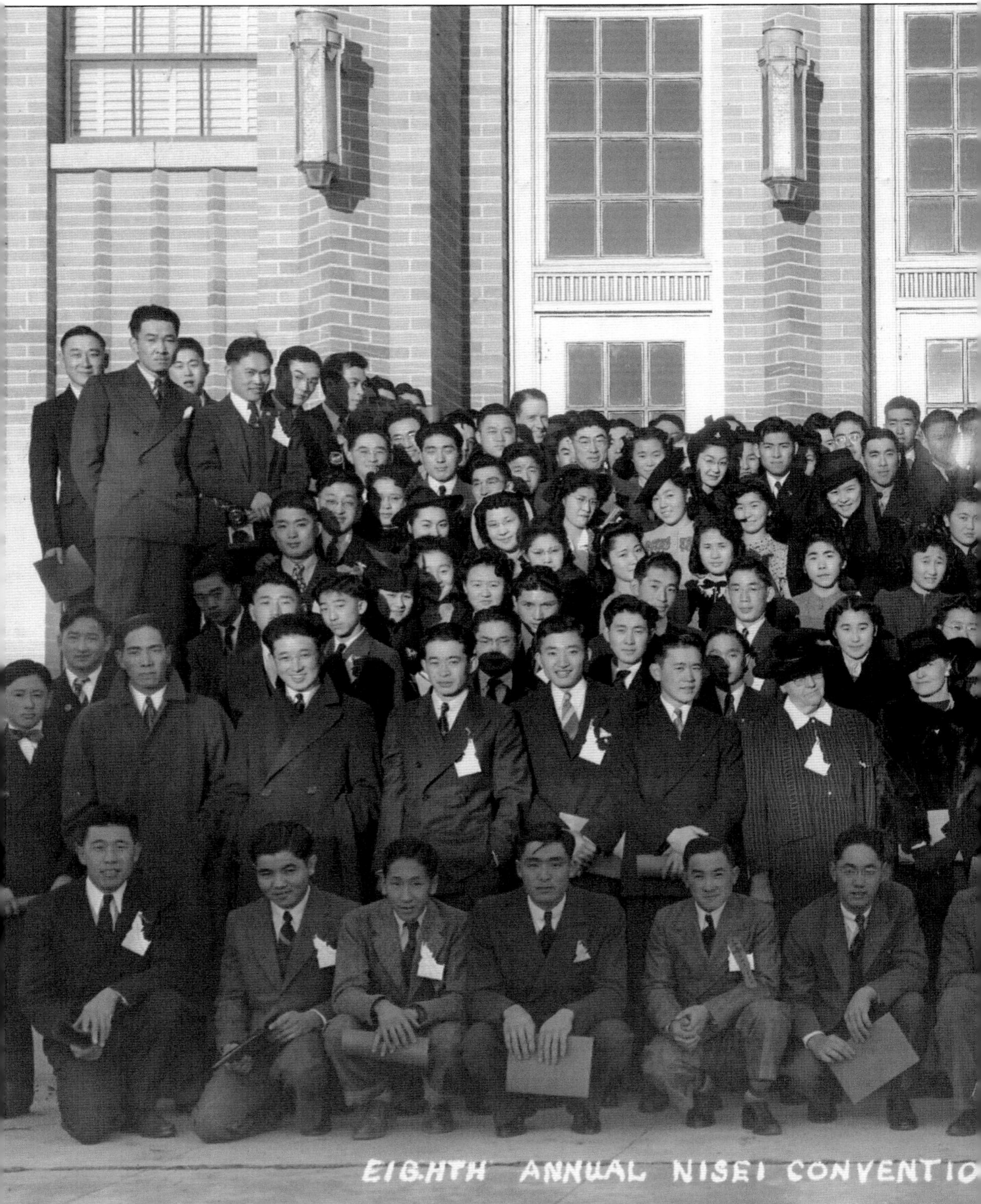

The Japanese-American community was one of the largest such communities in the Intermountain region of the western United States, and as such, was able to play host to events such as the Nisei Convention held in the city on November 22, 1940. Within a year and a half of this photograph

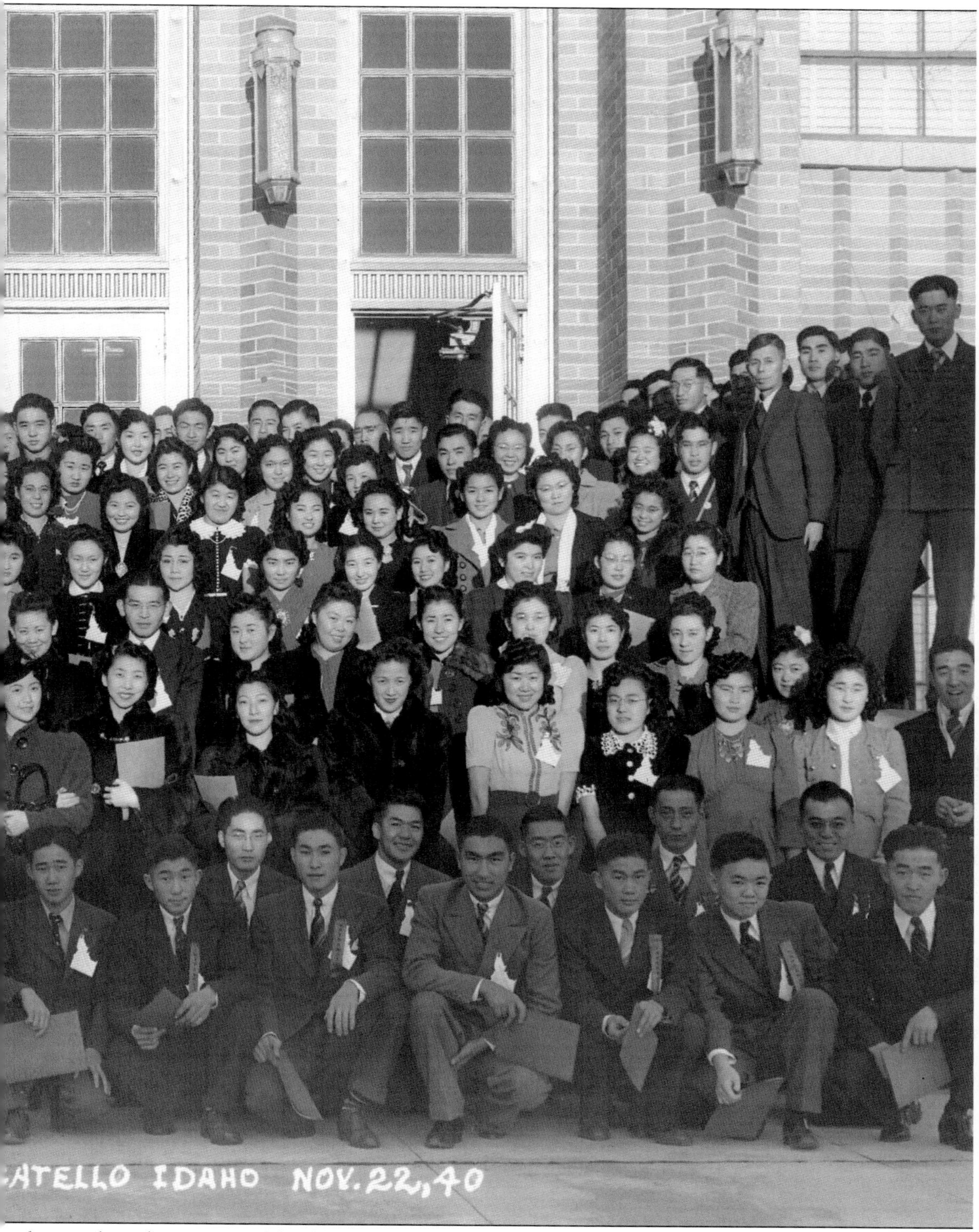

being taken, the majority of the delegates posing here would be interned by the federal government as "enemy aliens" during World War II. (BCHS.)

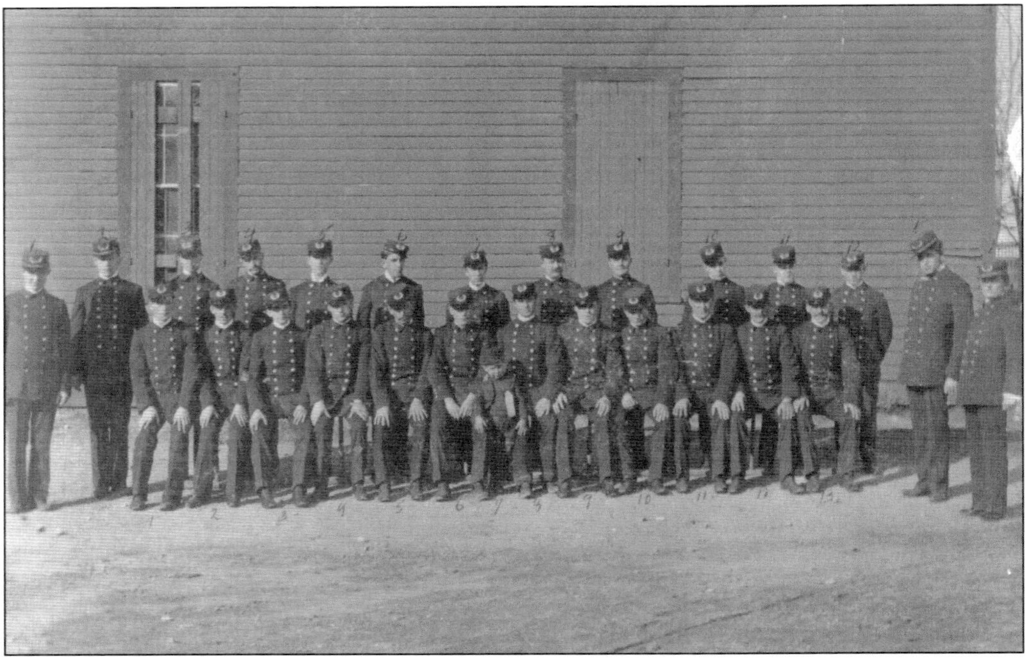

The railroad company provided the first public safety services in Pocatello. The Oregon Short Line firefighters are pictured in this 1900 photograph. (BCHS.)

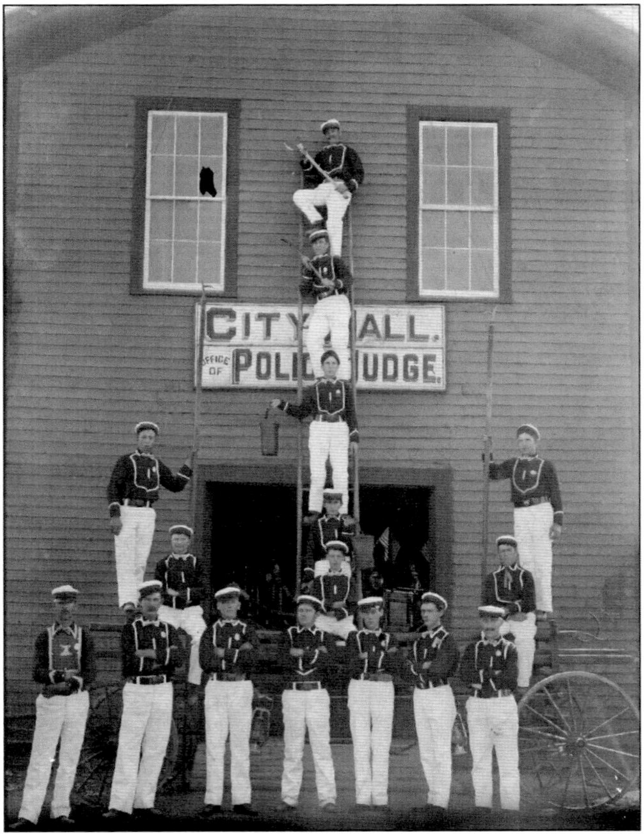

Pocatello would eventually provide its own firefighting force, set up in conjunction with the Oregon Short Line force in 1886. In the early days of the fledgling city, the force was entirely staffed with volunteers. In this 1896 Benedicte Wrensted photograph, firefighters pose in front of the then courthouse and police headquarters. Members of the fire department are, from top to bottom on the ladder, Walter Slater, Fred Cox, Fred Brown, Jimmy Regan, and George Kinport (mascot); from left to right on the fire wagon are George Brinson, John Steinman, John Tillitson, and Bob Forest; (front row) William Brinson, Bill Price, George Corbridge, Dan Jacobsen, George Firdell, Dave Kinport, and Henry Peake. Note that the window on the top left is smashed in, possibly due to a training exercise held previously. (BCHS.)

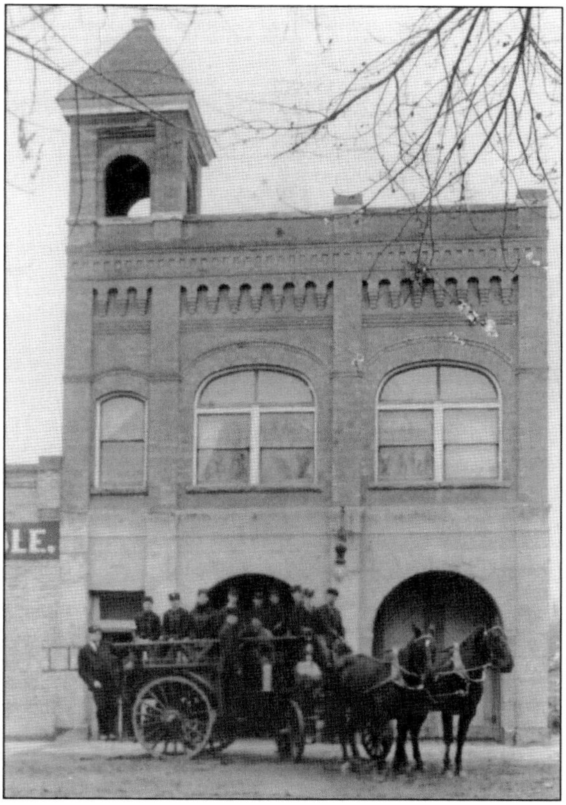

The Pocatello Fire Department, in keeping with other fire departments at the time, initially utilized horse-drawn fire engines. This 1907 photograph shows one of the first vehicles used by the department. (BCHS.)

This 1914 photograph shows both Pocatello fire engines being deployed (apparently for the benefit of the photographer), along with a wagon for use by the fire chief. (BCHS.)

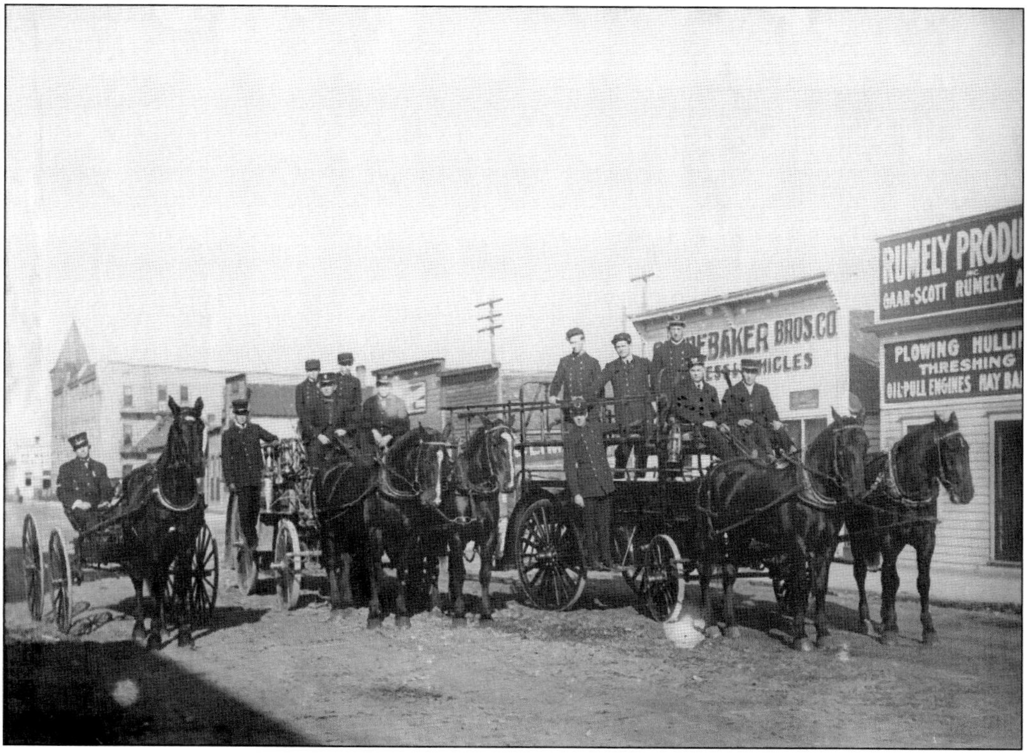

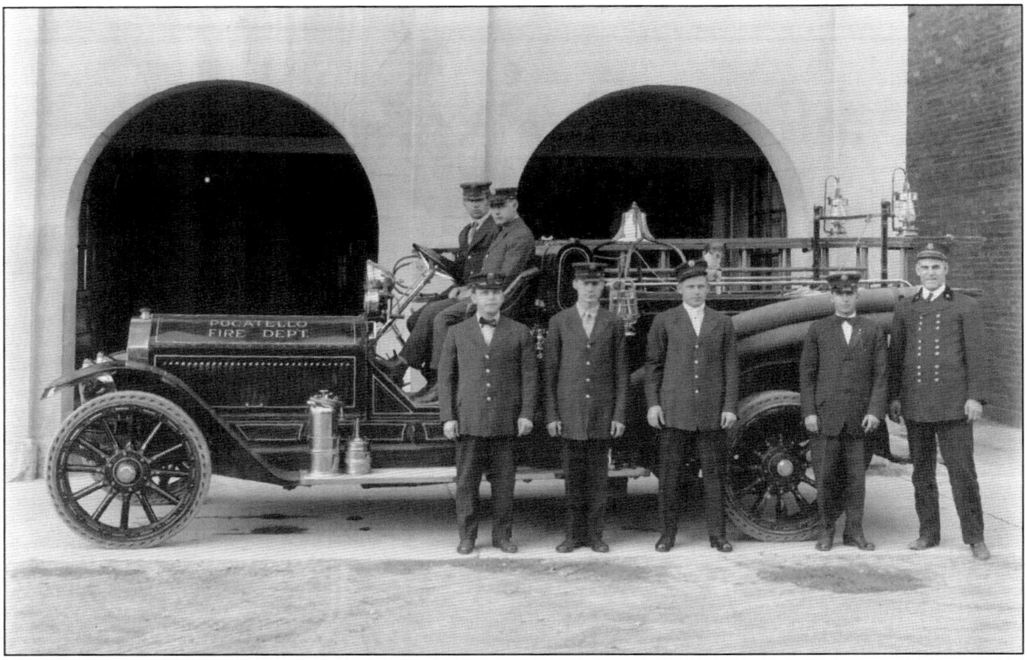

In due course, the Pocatello Fire Department acquired a gasoline-powered fire engine for use in its work. In this 1916 photograph chronicling the arrival of the new engine, the Pocatello Fire Department chief, A.B. Canfield, can be seen on the right. This fire engine has been preserved and is located in the Bannock County Historical Museum. (BCHS.)

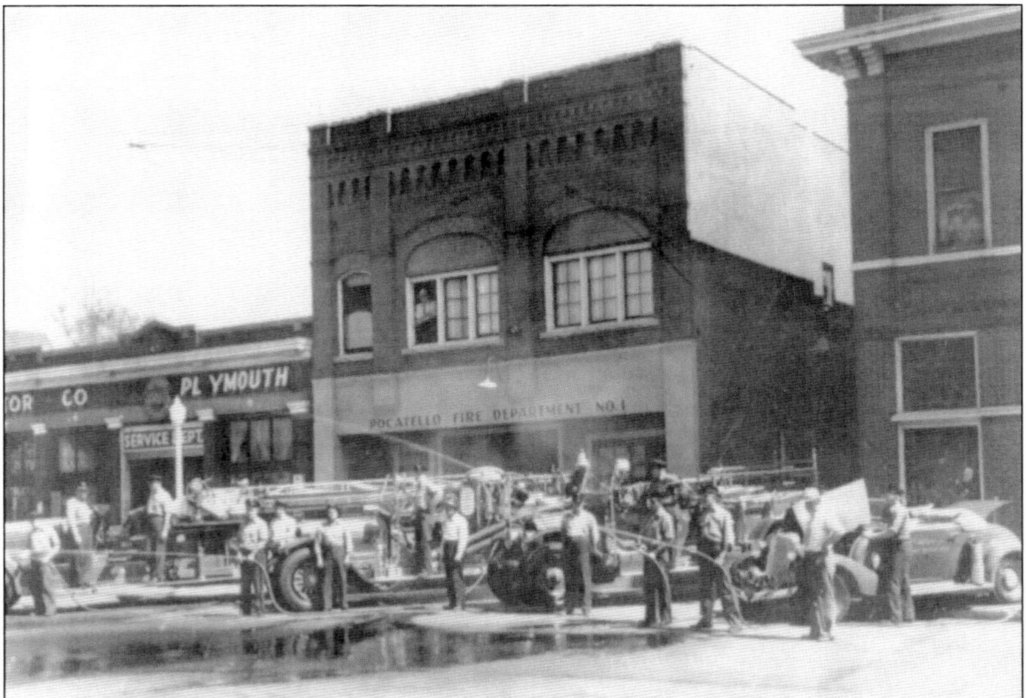

These firefighters are washing down their engines in this 1930s photograph. The original 1916 Fire Engine No. 1 is visible in the center. (BCHS.)

Along with a firefighting force, Pocatello soon acquired a police force as part of its public safety structure. This 1903 photograph of the Pocatello Police includes, from left to right, Hersey Ford, E.W. Smith, ? Bunderson, and Peter Wrensted. Peter Wrensted was Benedicte Wrensted's brother. (BCHS.)

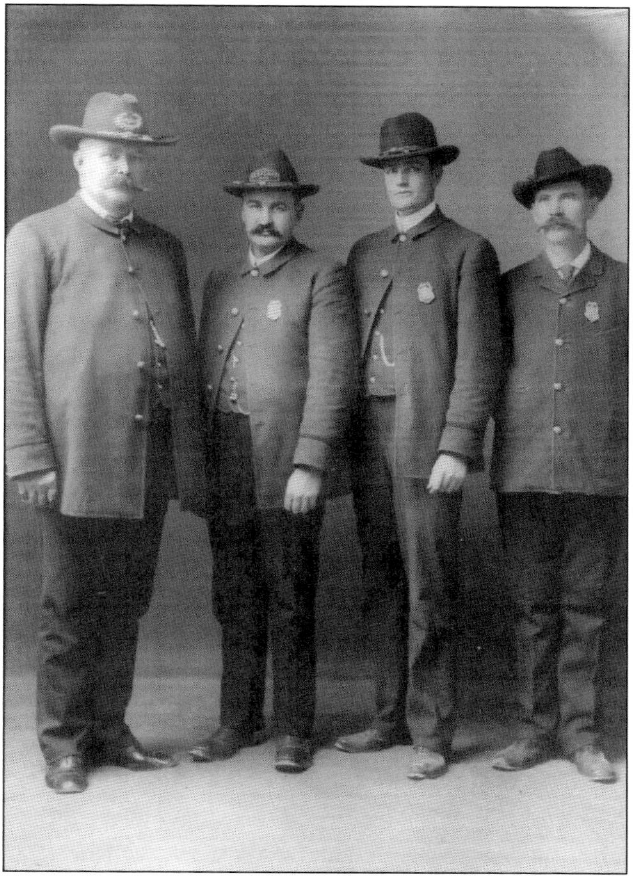

Along with the fire department, the Pocatello Police Department also went to gasoline-powered vehicles to carry out their duties. This publicity photograph shows John Ellis, the then chief of police, at the car crank handle. (BCHS.)

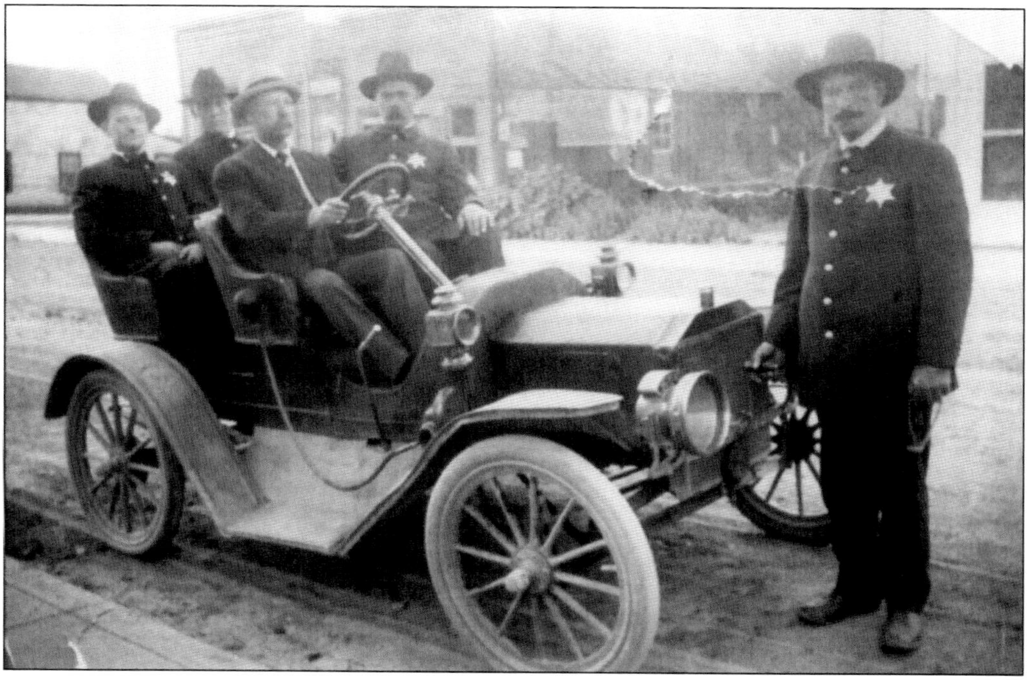

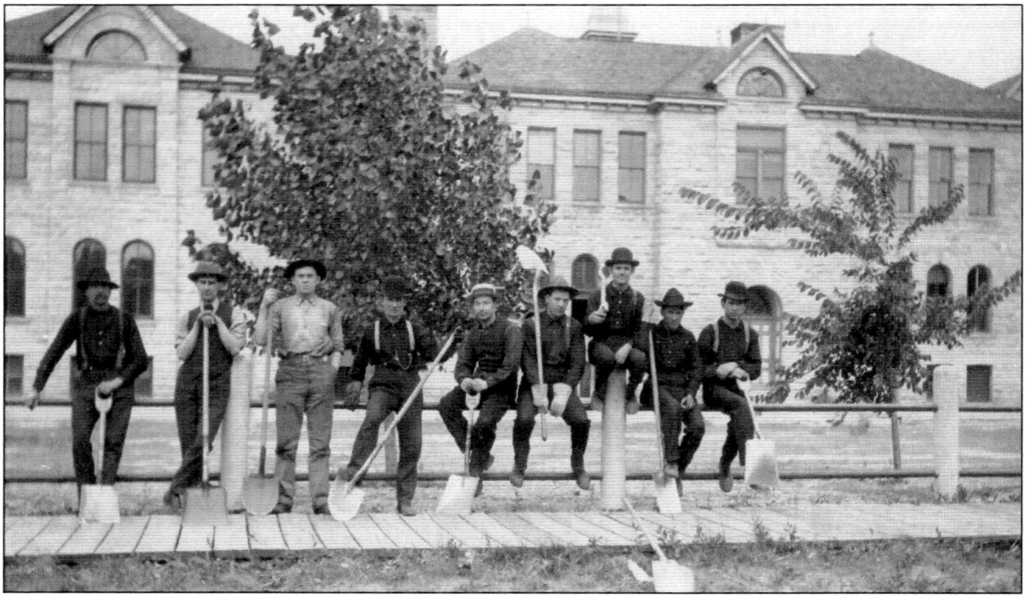

As was common throughout the United States in the early part of the 20th century, the state of Idaho imposed a poll tax so that a registered voter could be considered eligible to participate. The failure to pay this tax would lead to the miscreants being sentenced to perform work for the community. In this photograph, taken about 1905, these shop men are performing work on city property located at the back of the West Side School (Pocatello High School) on Garfield Avenue. (BCHS.)

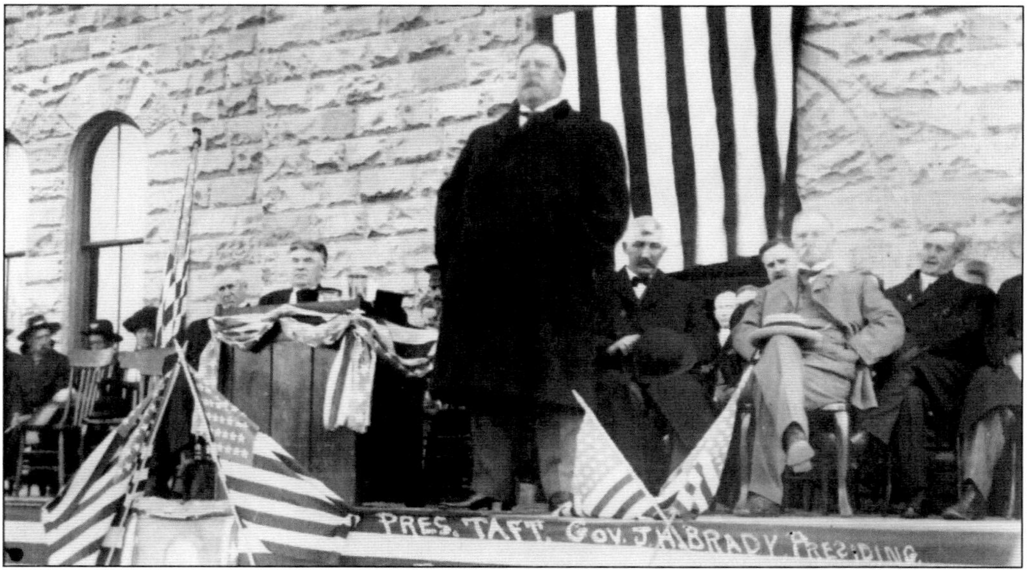

Given its importance in Idaho politics, Pocatello soon attracted politicians on all levels seeking support—and votes. One notable visitor to the Gate City was Pres. William Howard Taft, who paid a visit on October 6, 1911, to dedicate the newly built Center Street viaduct. The visit was initially at risk, due to the objections of the mayor of Pocatello, J.M. Bistline, a member of the Democratic Party (President Taft was a Republican), but these objections were eventually overcome. In this photograph, Taft is speaking at Pocatello High School, with Idaho governor J.H. Brady on the stage behind him. (BCHS.)

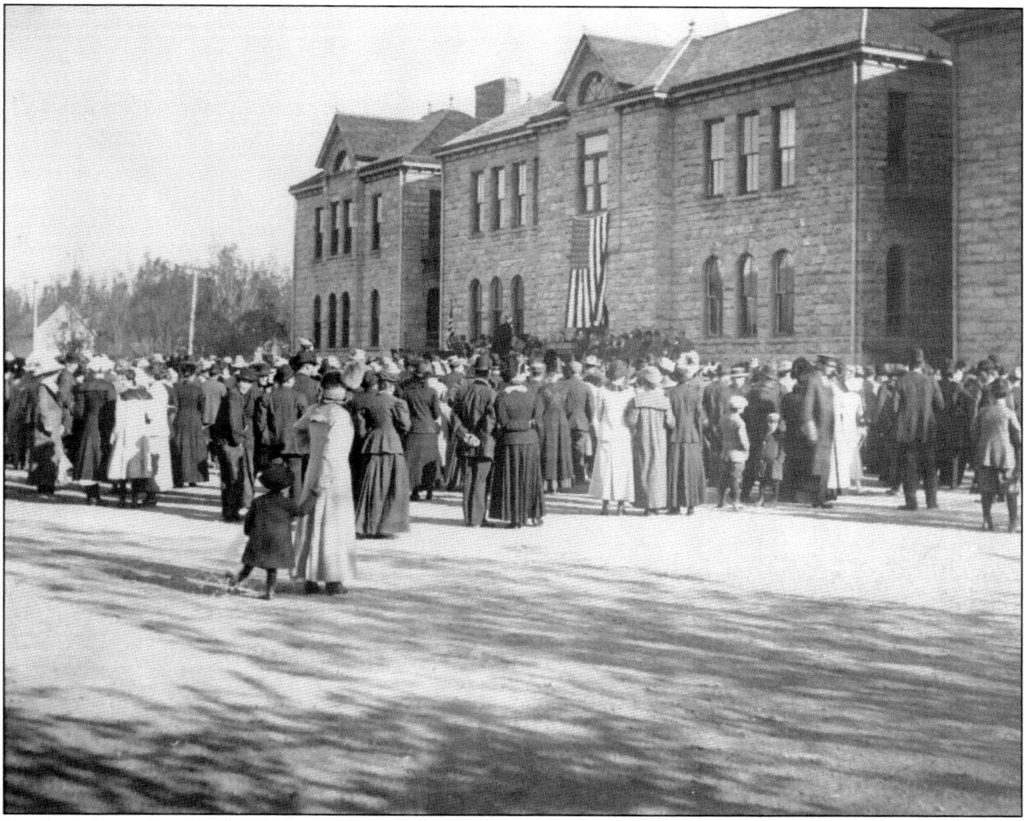

In this photograph, Pocatello residents have come to witness President Taft's speech. (BCHS.)

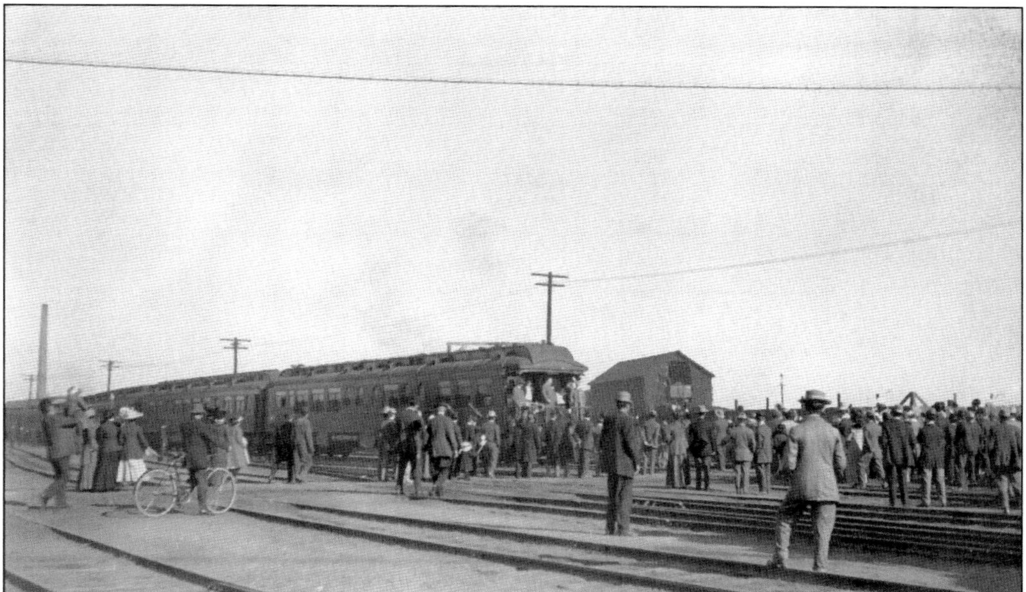

Another noteworthy politician who visited Pocatello during this period was William Jennings Bryan, who paid a visit to the city in 1915. In this photograph, Bryan is seen speaking before a gathering of Pocatello residents and members of the press from his railroad car. (BCHS.)

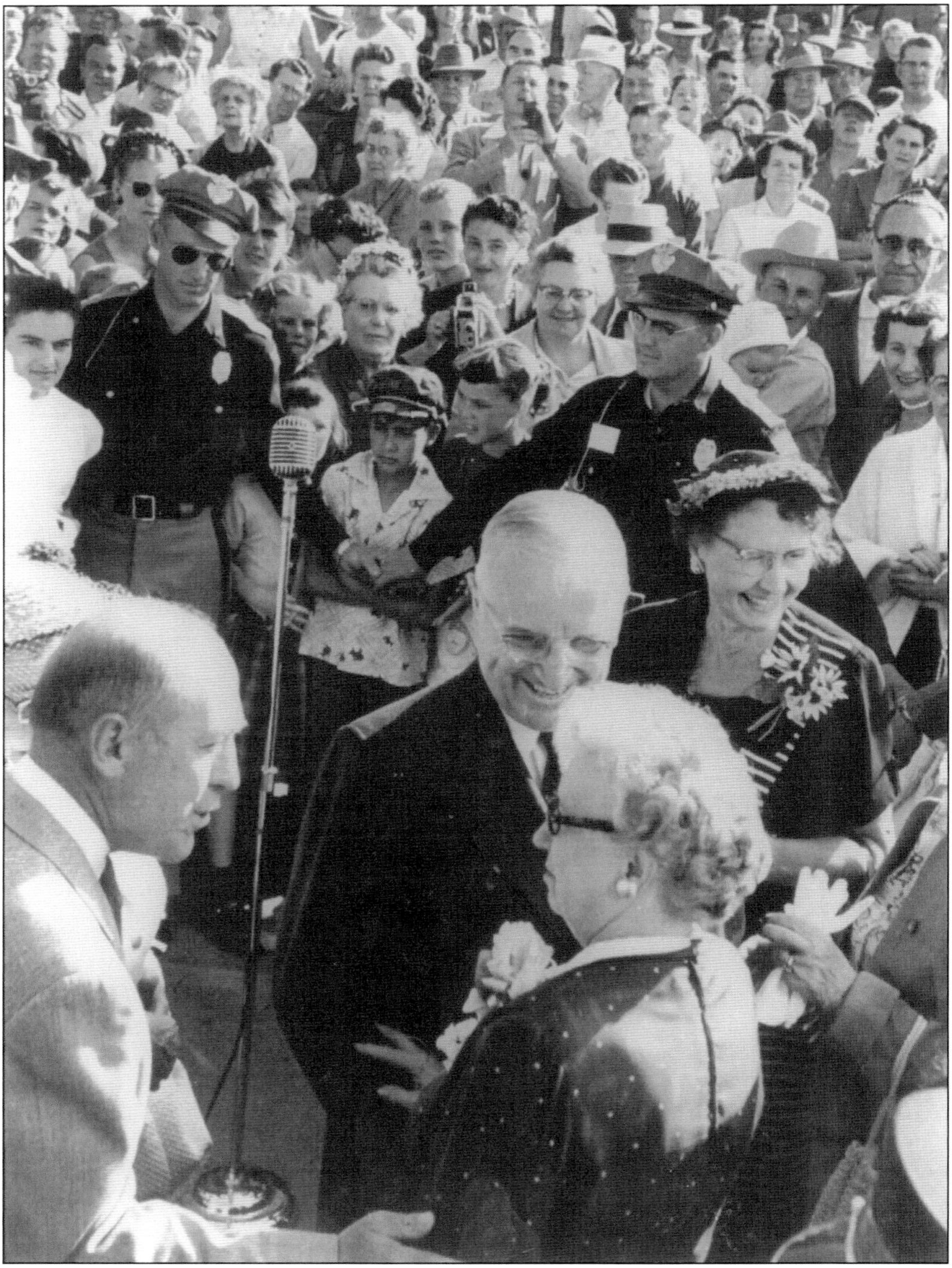

Yet another noteworthy visitor to Pocatello was former president Harry Truman in 1955. The president's visit to the city was part of a national tour that was undertaken at the time, following the "whistle-stop" campaign tour he undertook during the 1948 presidential race. (BCHS.)

Four

Commerce

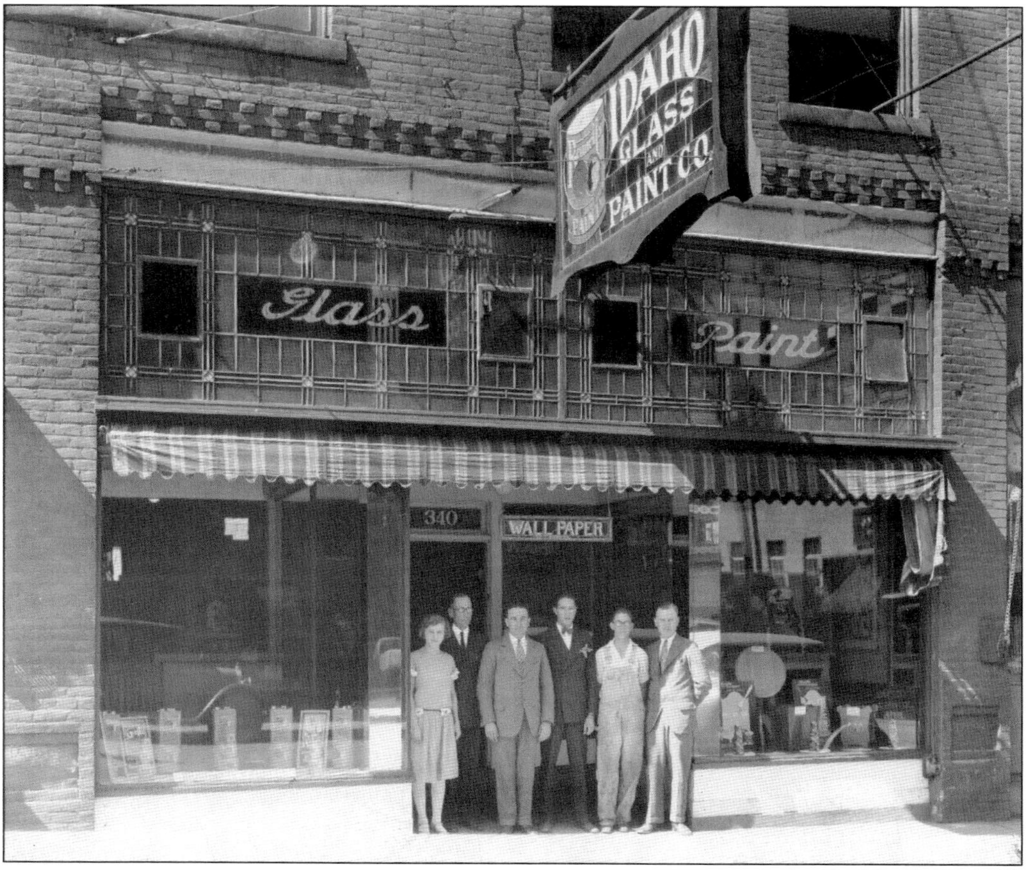

This photograph of the Idaho Glass and Paint store at 340 West Center Street, taken at some time in the 1930s, is emblematic of most of the businesses in Pocatello's history—family-owned operations, generally of small scale, and tasked with serving the community at large. (BCHS.)

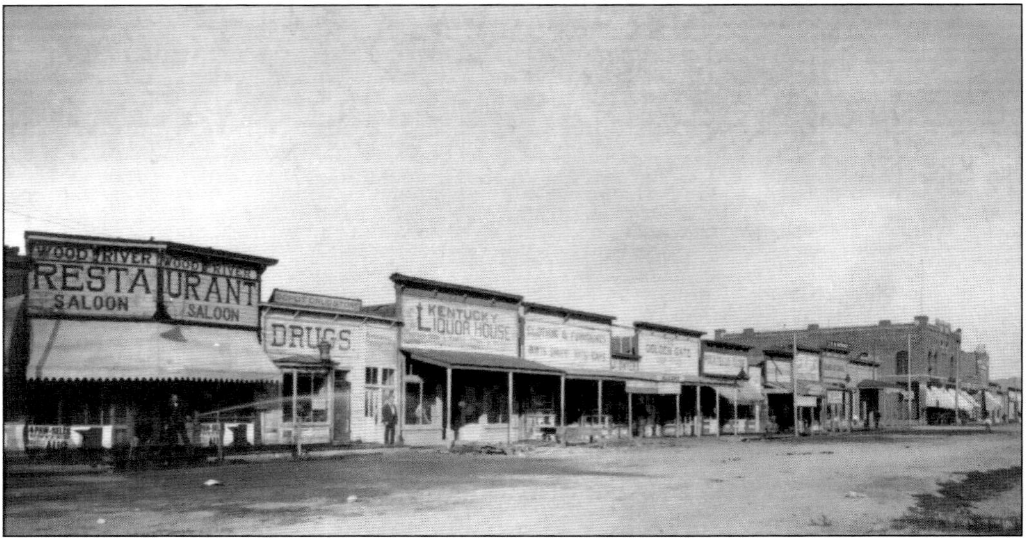

This c. 1895 photograph of Front Street (later First Avenue) shows early commerce in Pocatello. There are a number of restaurants and drinking establishments, along with a clothier and a drugstore. In keeping with the early nature of Pocatello, most of the structures here are made of wood, with false fronts featured prominently. (BCHS.)

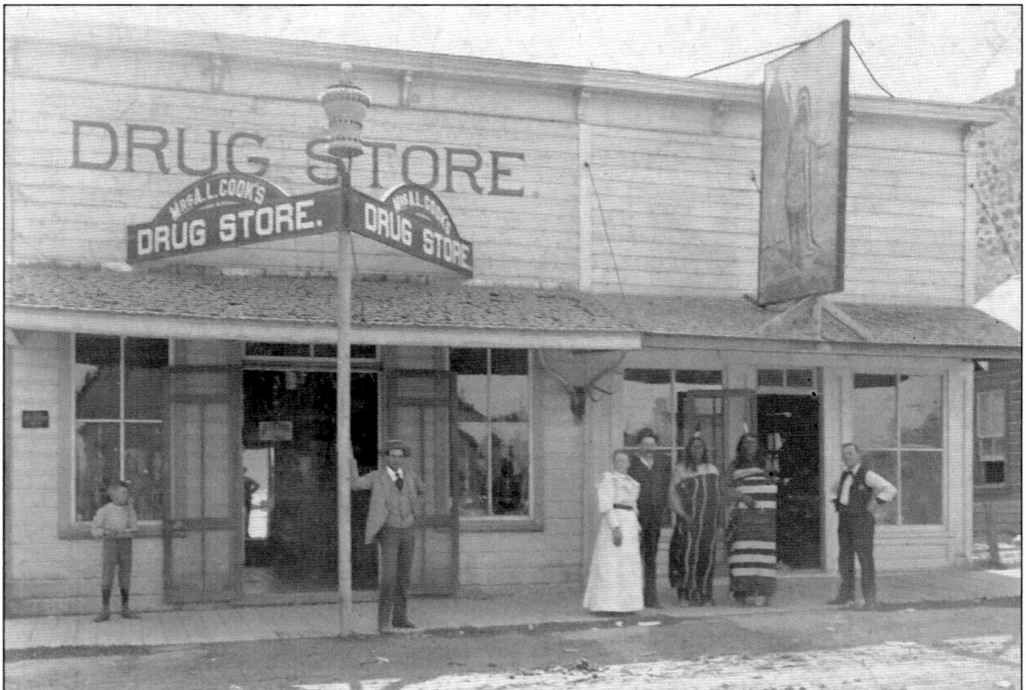

One of the earliest retailers in Pocatello that was able to survive the turbulent frontier days was Mrs. A.L. Cook's drugstore on 333 West Center Street. This wooden building was constructed in 1887 and served as the location for the drugstore until a more permanent structure was built in 1900. Mrs. Cook first opened the Indian Curio Shop, pictured in the right side of the building shown, which sold moccasins, beaded clothing, gloves, and more, all of which were made by the local Native Americans. (NAA.)

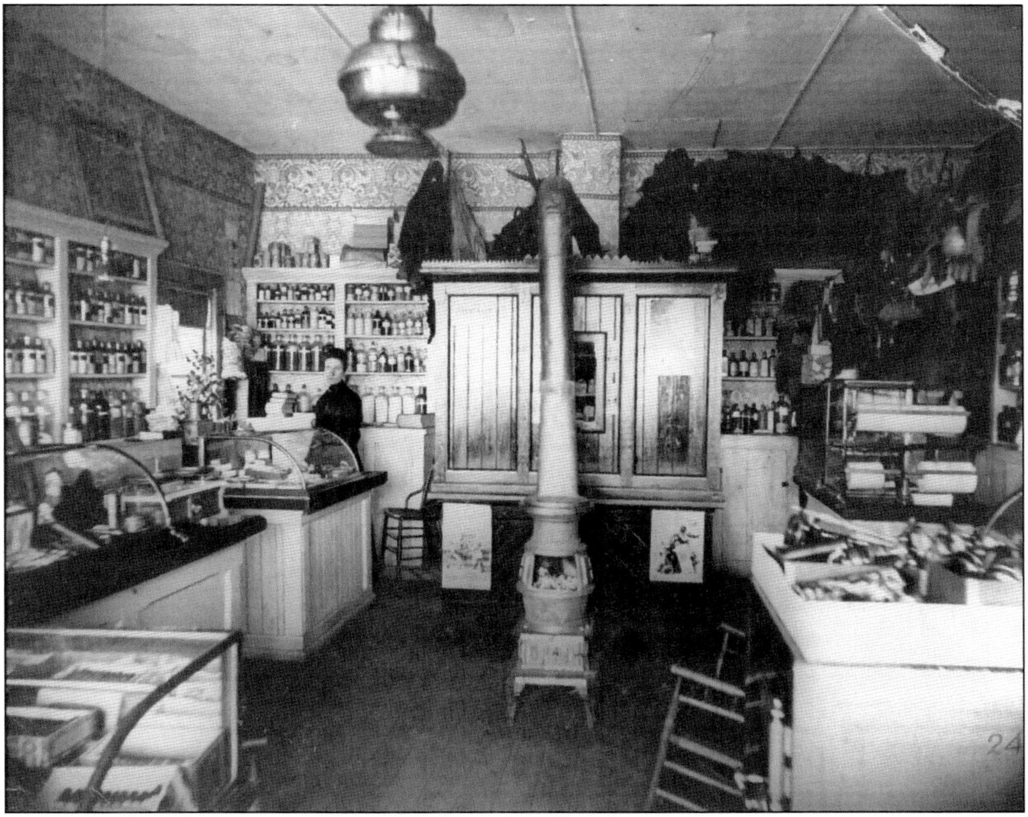

This c. 1888 photograph of the interior of Mrs. A.L. Cook's drugstore shows Mrs. Cook just behind the counter on the left. (ISU.)

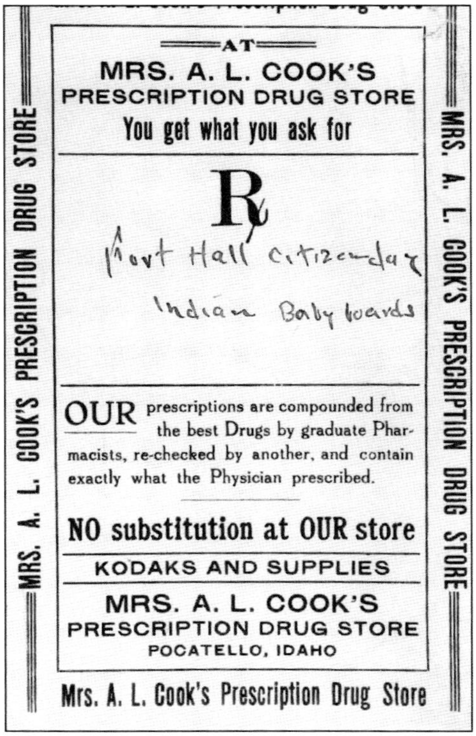

This flyer from Mrs. A.L. Cook's drugstore most probably dates from the 1890s. The main slogan in the flyer—"You get what you ask for"—would indicate the main appeal to prospective customers. (BCHS.)

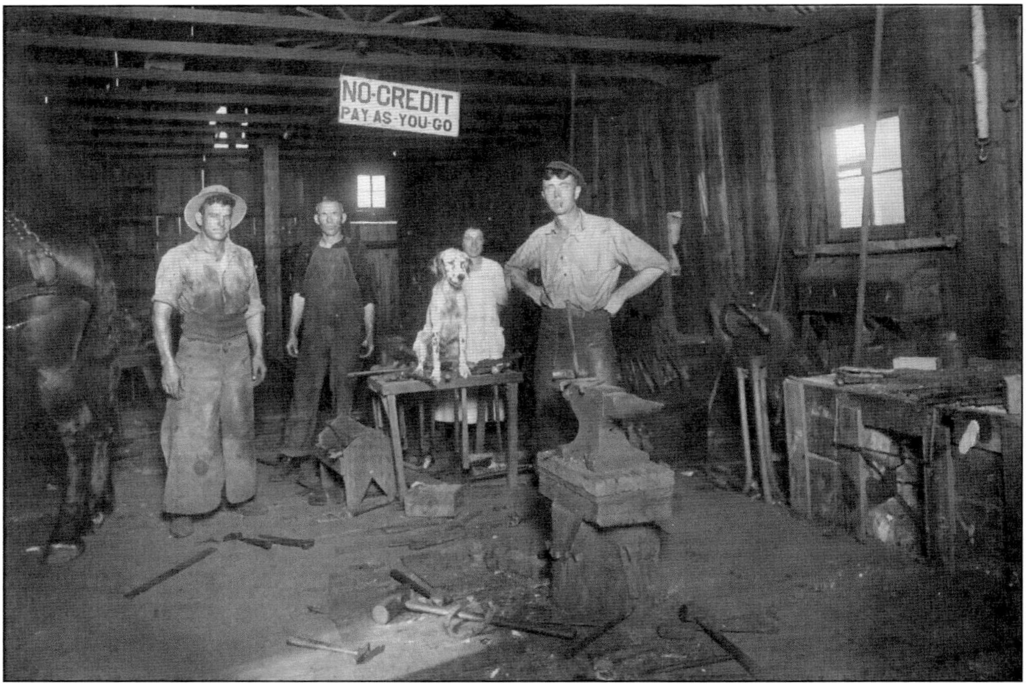

In an era when the horse was still a necessity for transportation and work, horse farriers were a necessary component of everyday life. This farrier shop provides a glimpse of how the business worked. Of particular interest is the sign advising that the business was "pay-as-you-go," indicating that some customers were delinquent in paying for services rendered. (BCHS.)

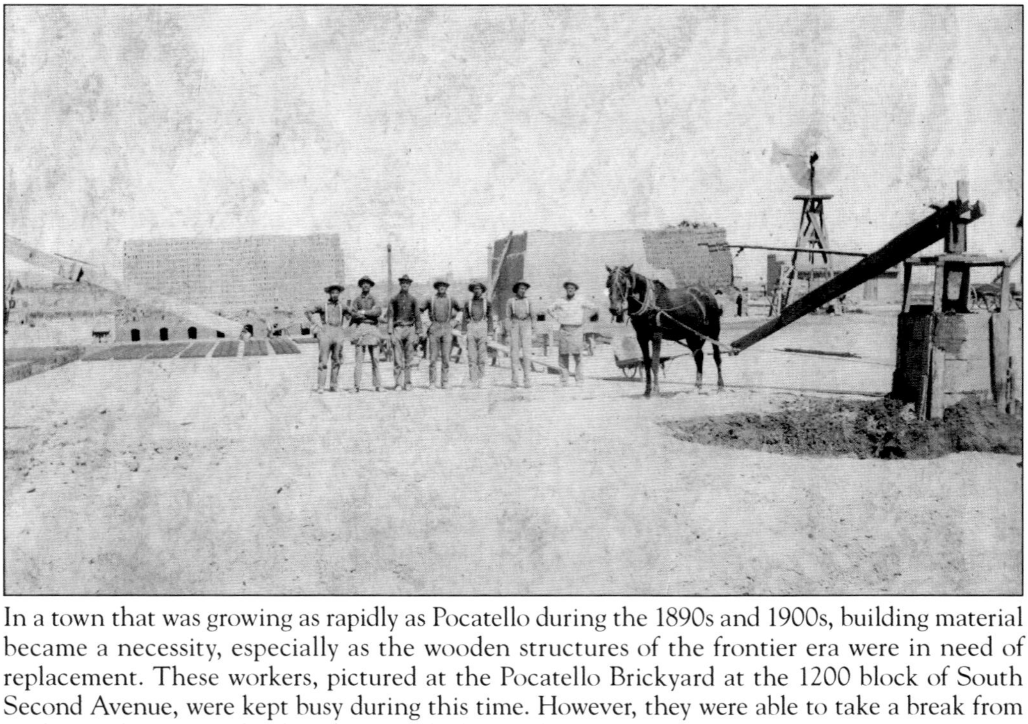

In a town that was growing as rapidly as Pocatello during the 1890s and 1900s, building material became a necessity, especially as the wooden structures of the frontier era were in need of replacement. These workers, pictured at the Pocatello Brickyard at the 1200 block of South Second Avenue, were kept busy during this time. However, they were able to take a break from work in order to pose for this photograph. (BCHS.)

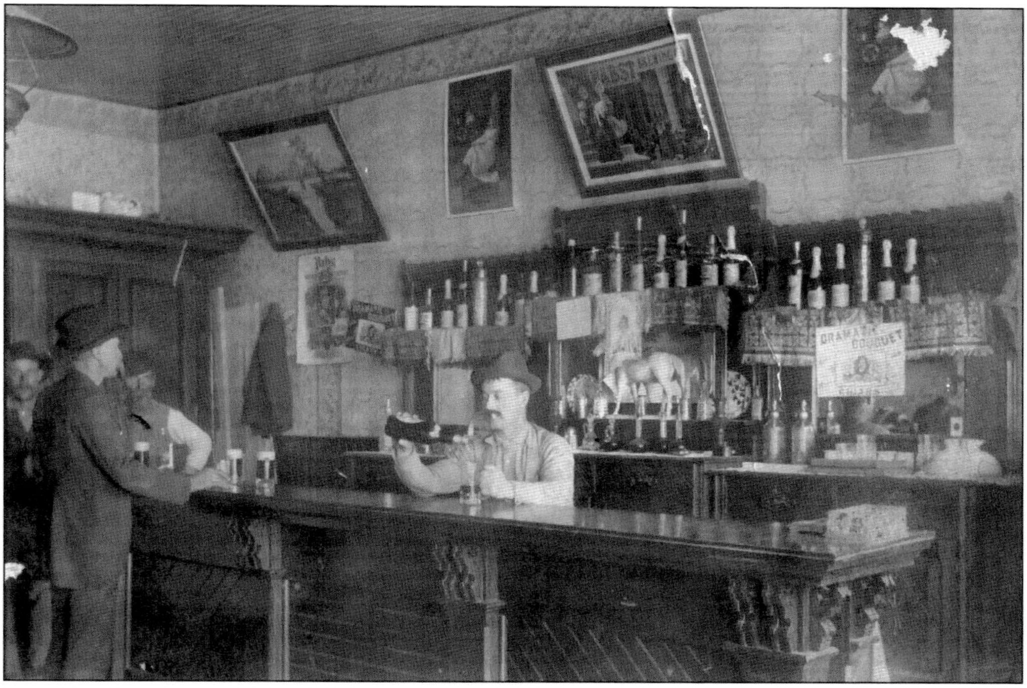

One of the most popular establishments that survived the frontier era in Pocatello was the drinking saloon. Initially, saloons appealed to railroad workers and ranch hands working in the area as they passed through the town. The A.L. Roulet saloon, located on the 500 block of North Main Street, is pictured at the turn of the century. (BCHS.)

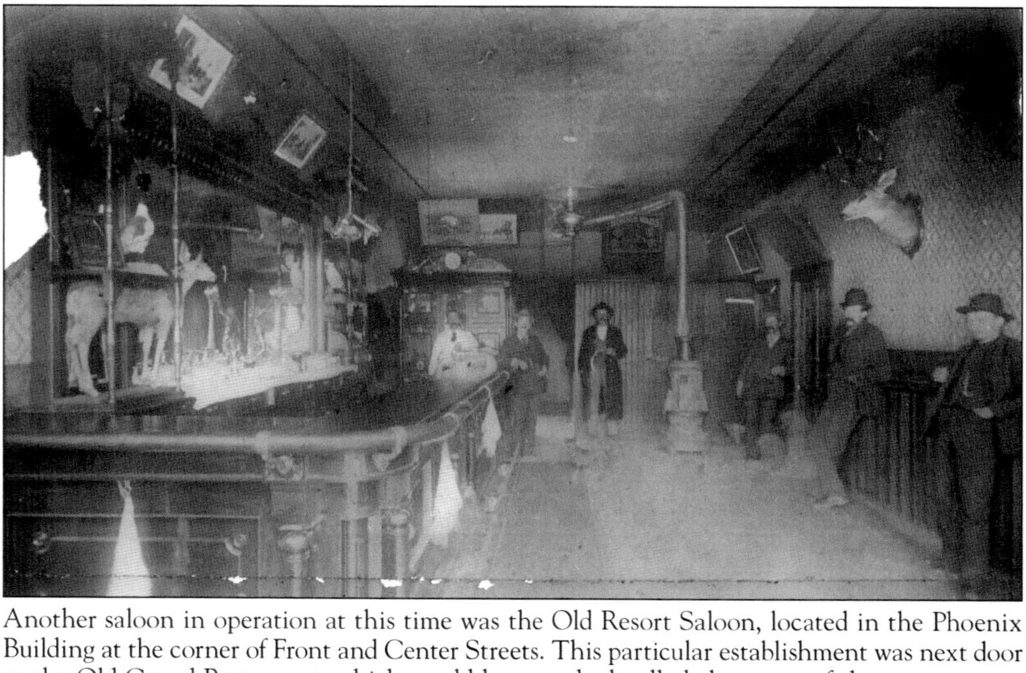

Another saloon in operation at this time was the Old Resort Saloon, located in the Phoenix Building at the corner of Front and Center Streets. This particular establishment was next door to the Old Grand Restaurant, which would have undoubtedly led patrons of the restaurant to have an after-dinner refreshment. The popularity of the saloon can be ascertained by the claim that it was "the swellest joint in town." (BCHS.)

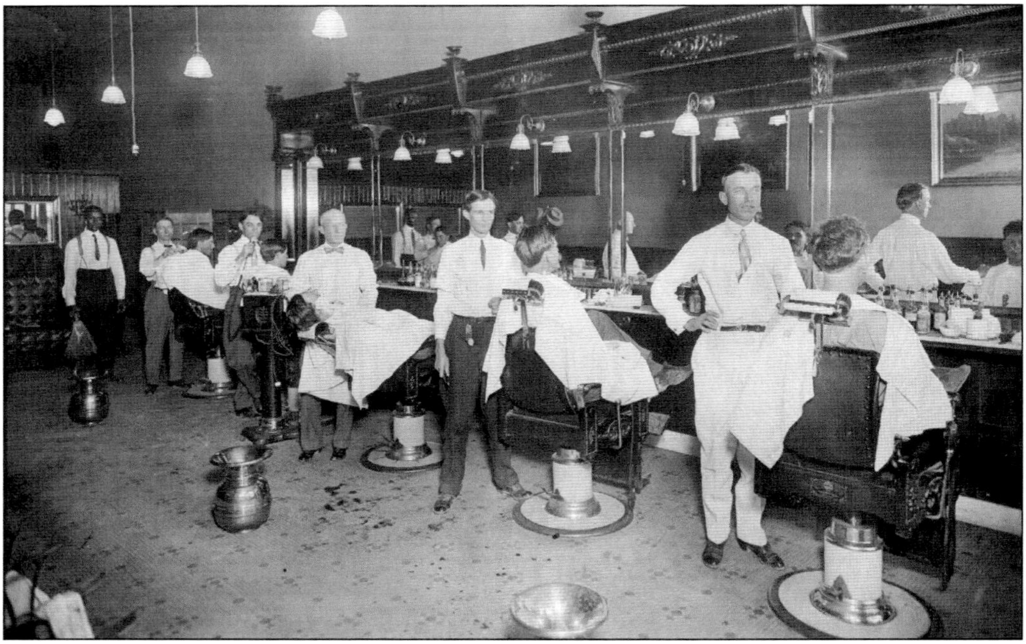

As Pocatello grew larger and more prosperous, establishments began to come into being that appealed to a more prosperous class. One such establishment was the Earley Day barbershop, which provided haircuts and shaves (using a straight razor) to its clients. The brass spittoons were a typical accessory for barbershops of the time. (BCHS.)

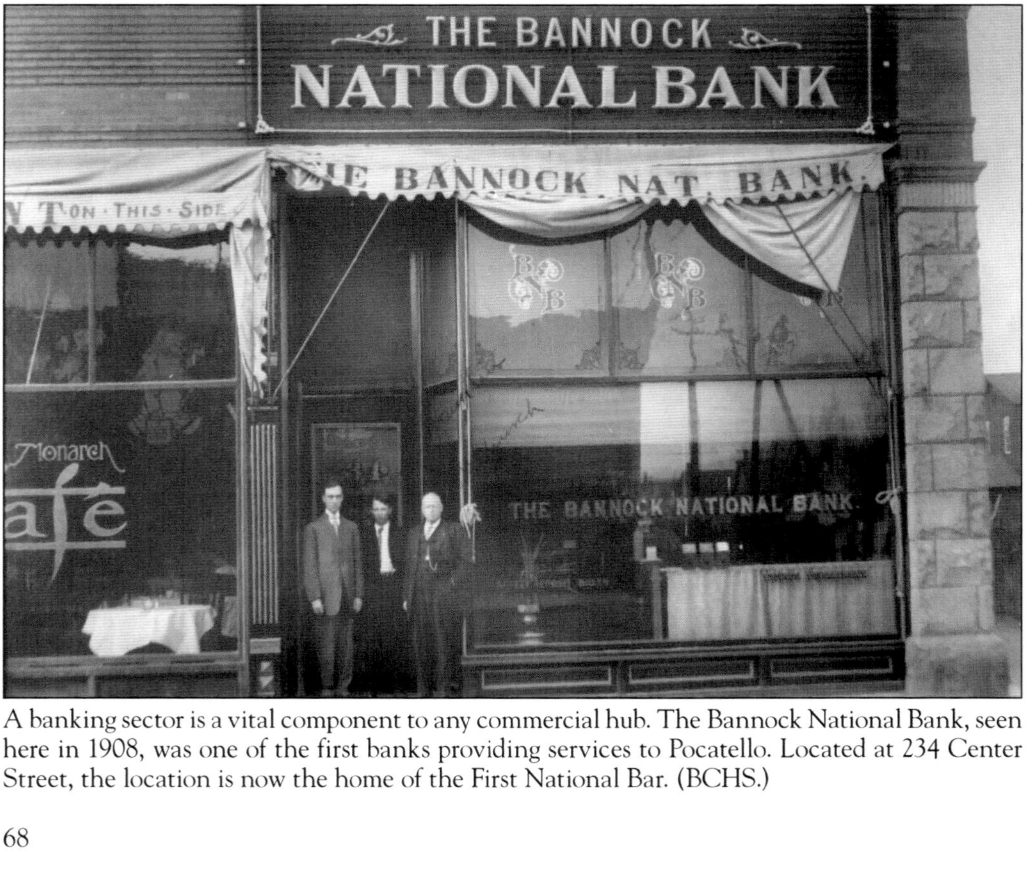

A banking sector is a vital component to any commercial hub. The Bannock National Bank, seen here in 1908, was one of the first banks providing services to Pocatello. Located at 234 Center Street, the location is now the home of the First National Bar. (BCHS.)

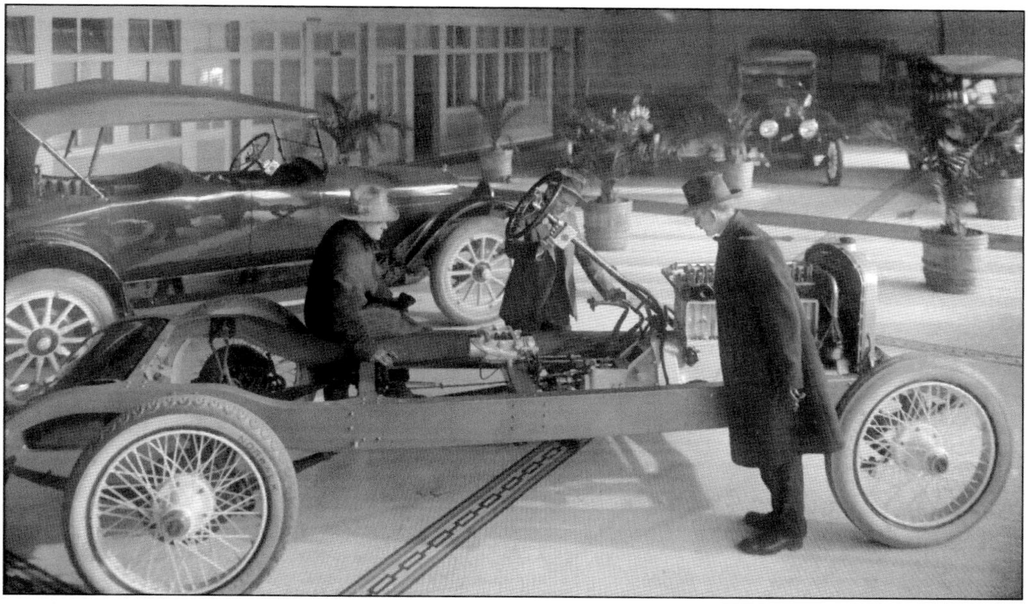

As the United States moved from horses to automobiles, car sales and servicing soon became a staple of American life. In Pocatello, one of the first auto dealers was the Trist Automobile Company, which was initially located on the 600 block of West Center Street and was the Ford dealer for the Pocatello region. In this 1917 photograph, the showroom floor of Trist Automobile is visible. The stripped-down chassis is apparently meant to show how the new motorized cars are constructed "under the hood." (BCHS.)

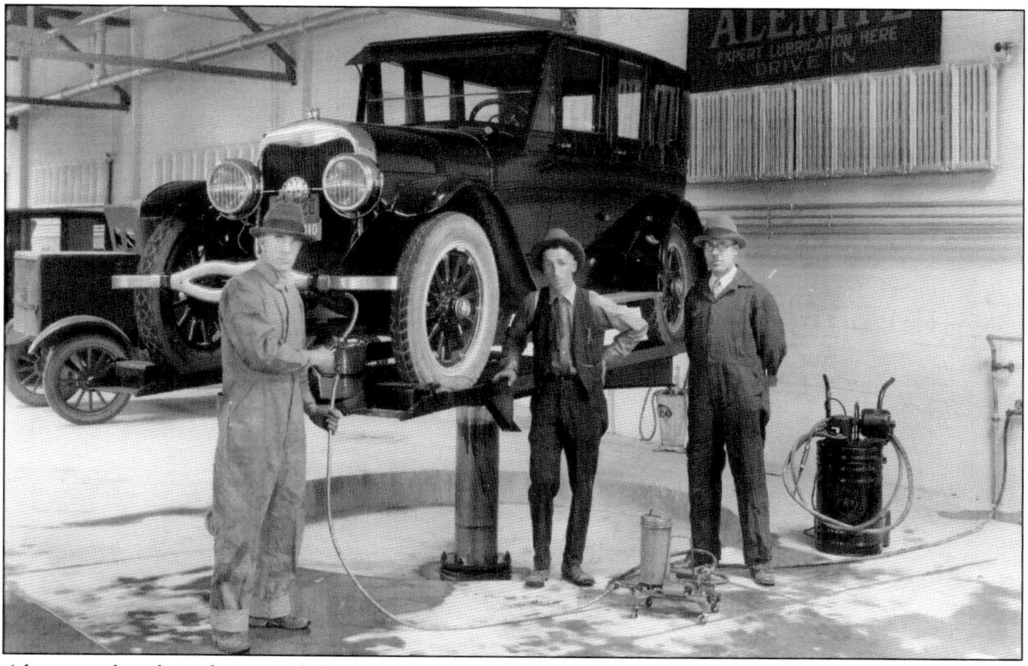

Along with sales of automobiles, Trist Automobile also provided service for the cars that were sold by the dealership. In this 1928 publicity photograph, the repair shop is in operation. Trist Automobile became Amphlett Chevrolet Company in 1930, later to become Intermountain Chevrolet in 1936. In 1960, Intermountain Chevrolet moved to Garrett Way. (BCHS.)

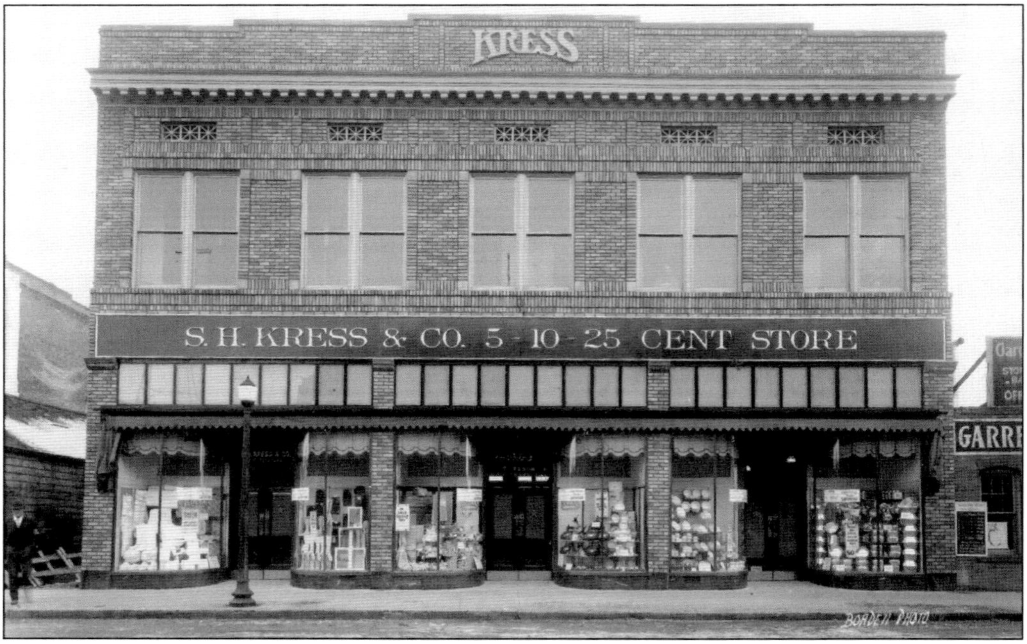

One of the major retailers of consumer goods was the S.H. Kress store, which offered a range of consumer goods. Seen here just prior to its opening, S.H. Kress was a familiar shopping venue for generations of Pocatello residents. Located on South Main Street, it was one of the major retailers in the area. (ISU.)

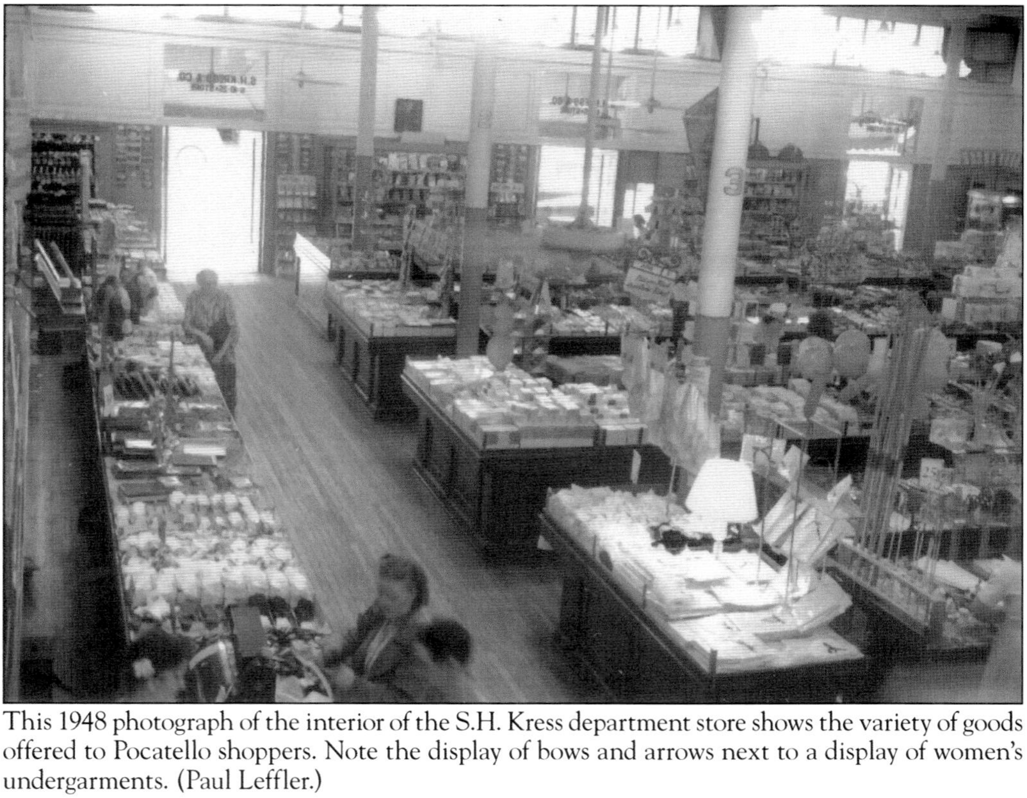

This 1948 photograph of the interior of the S.H. Kress department store shows the variety of goods offered to Pocatello shoppers. Note the display of bows and arrows next to a display of women's undergarments. (Paul Leffler.)

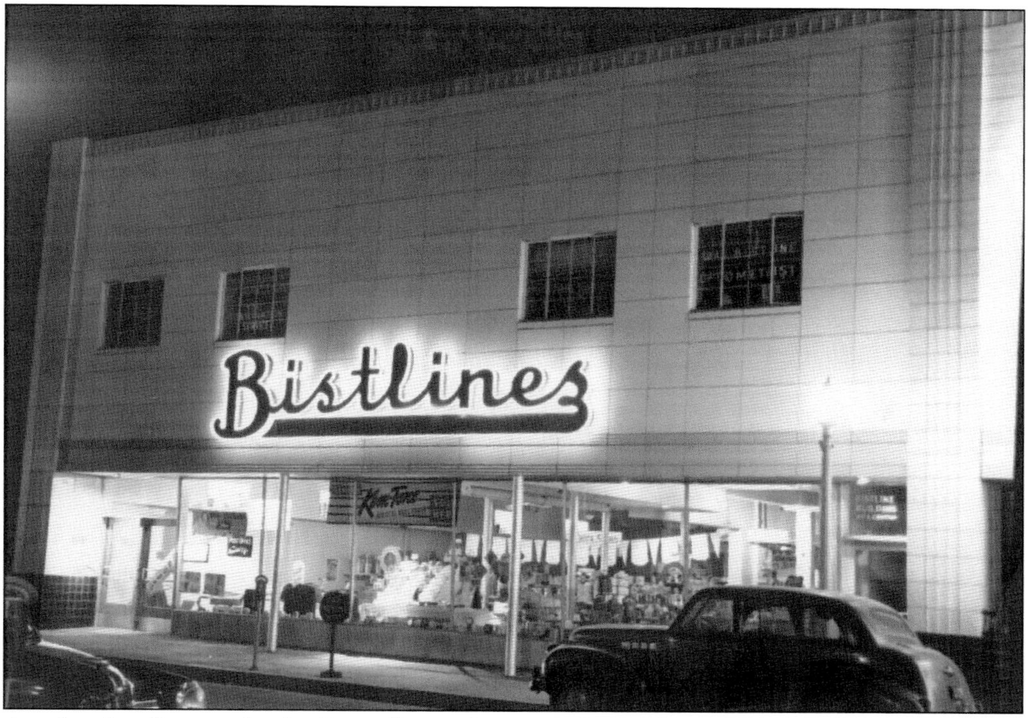

Another familiar retailer for Pocatello residents was the Bistline Lumber Company, located at 427 East Center Street. Bistline Lumber, in addition to selling lumber, also sold hardware and farm implements, including horse harnesses. (BCHS.)

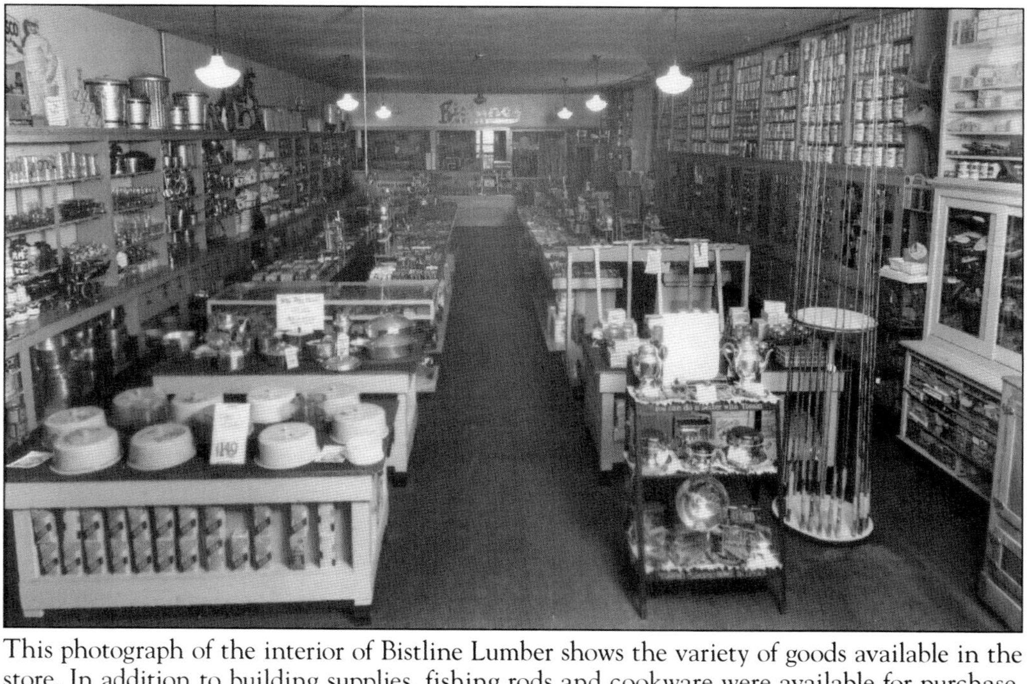

This photograph of the interior of Bistline Lumber shows the variety of goods available in the store. In addition to building supplies, fishing rods and cookware were available for purchase. The Bistline Lumber building was eventually torn down, and the site now serves as a parking lot for a Bio-Mat USA location. (BCHS.)

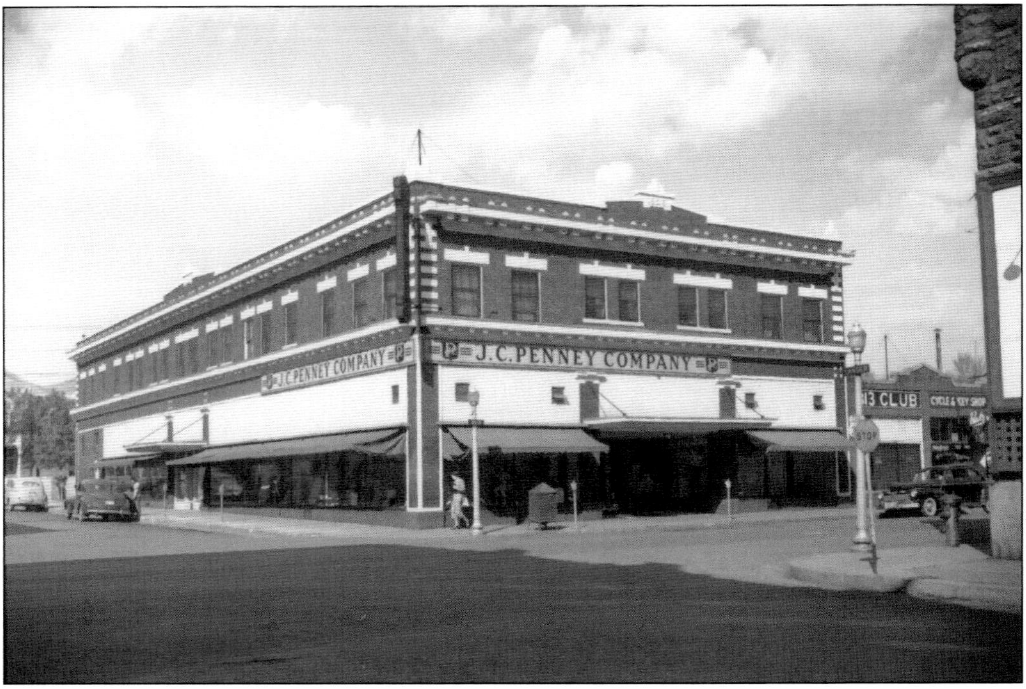

Major national retail chains have always had a presence in Pocatello. One such retailer was J.C. Penney, located on the 300 block of North Main Street. This location served as the Pocatello outlet for the national chain until 1982, when it relocated its Pocatello store to the Pine Ridge Mall on the outskirts of the city. (Paul Leffler.)

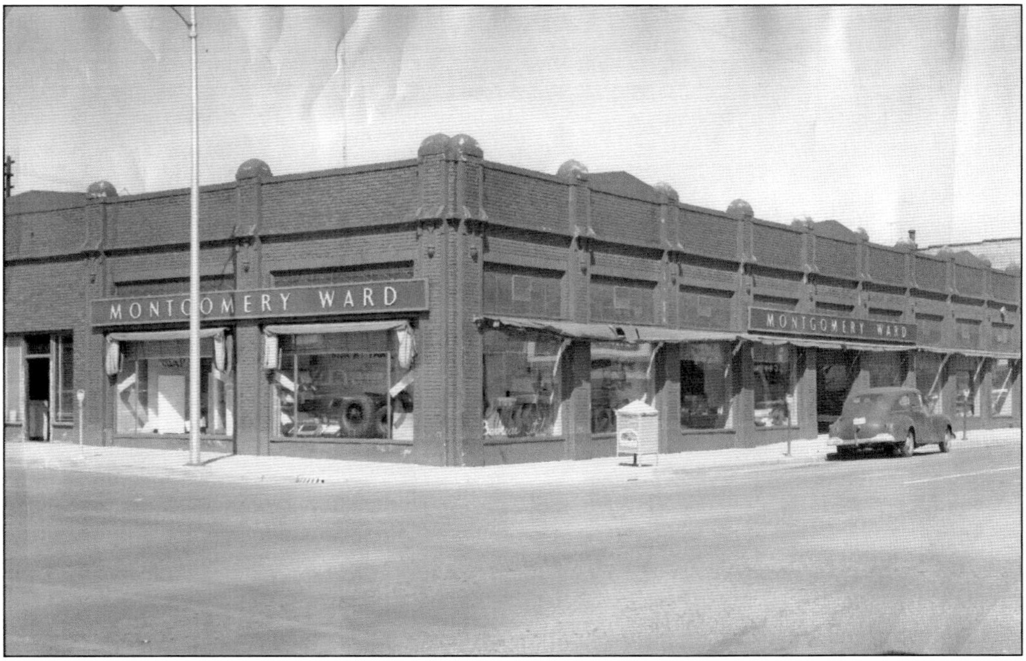

Another major national retailer with a Pocatello presence was Montgomery Ward. Located on South Main Street for many years, it was eventually torn down after the company moved its outlet to the new Pocatello Mall. (BCHS.)

Five

Education

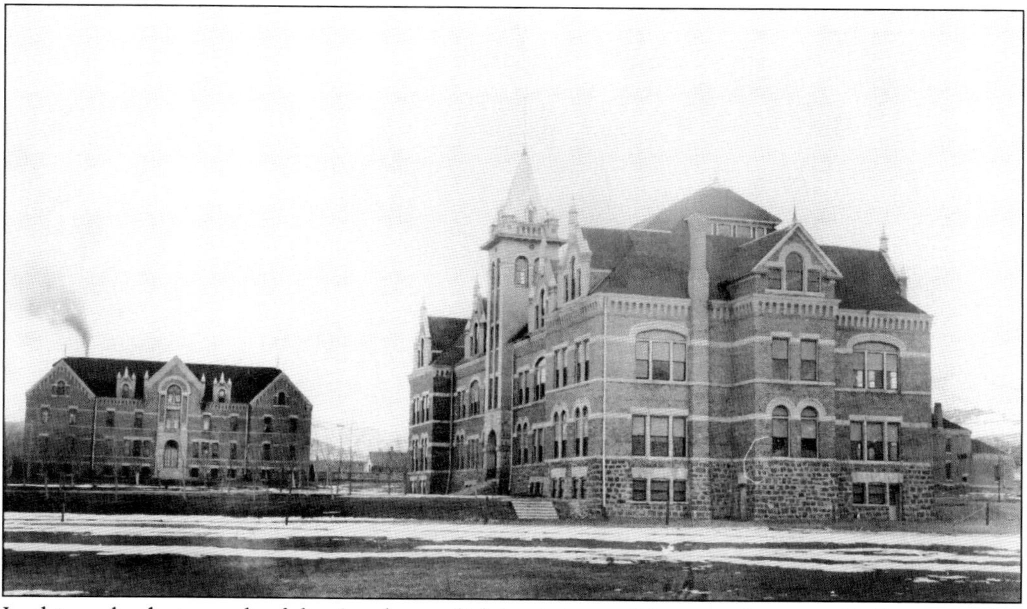

In this early photograph of the Academy of Idaho, it is possible to see Swanson Hall to the right, and Faris Hall to the left. Both were part of the original Academy of Idaho campus when it opened in 1901. Faris Hall was demolished in 1959; Swanson Hall was demolished in 1973. (Bistline.)

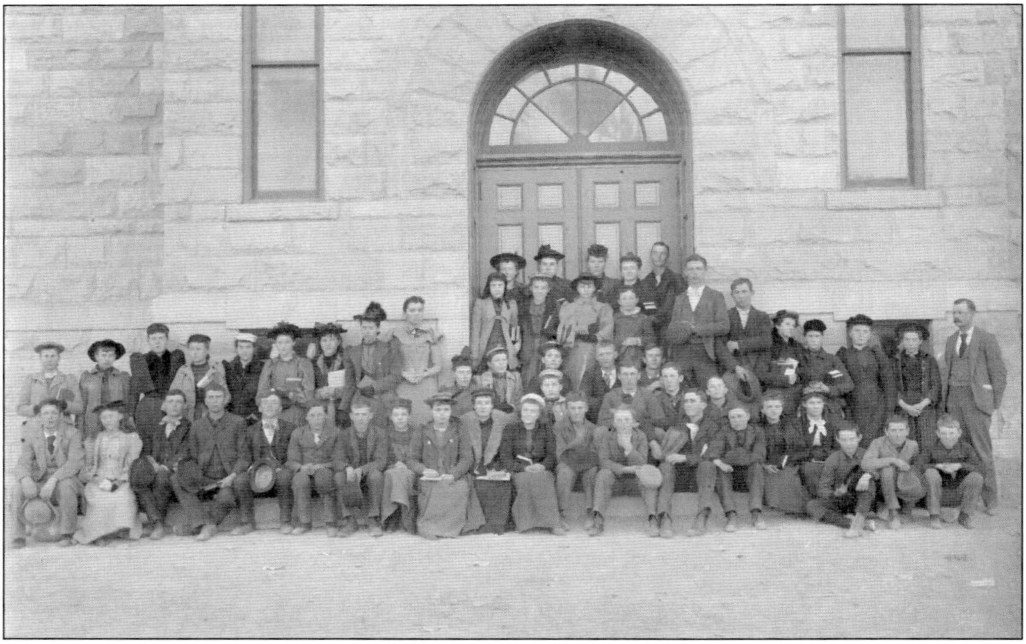

Pocatello erected permanent buildings for educational purposes at an early point in its history. The West Side School, later renamed Pocatello High School, provided an educational facility to those schoolchildren living on the West Side of Pocatello at all grade levels. This 1893 photograph shows the eighth, ninth, and tenth grade classes attending West Side School. (BCHS.)

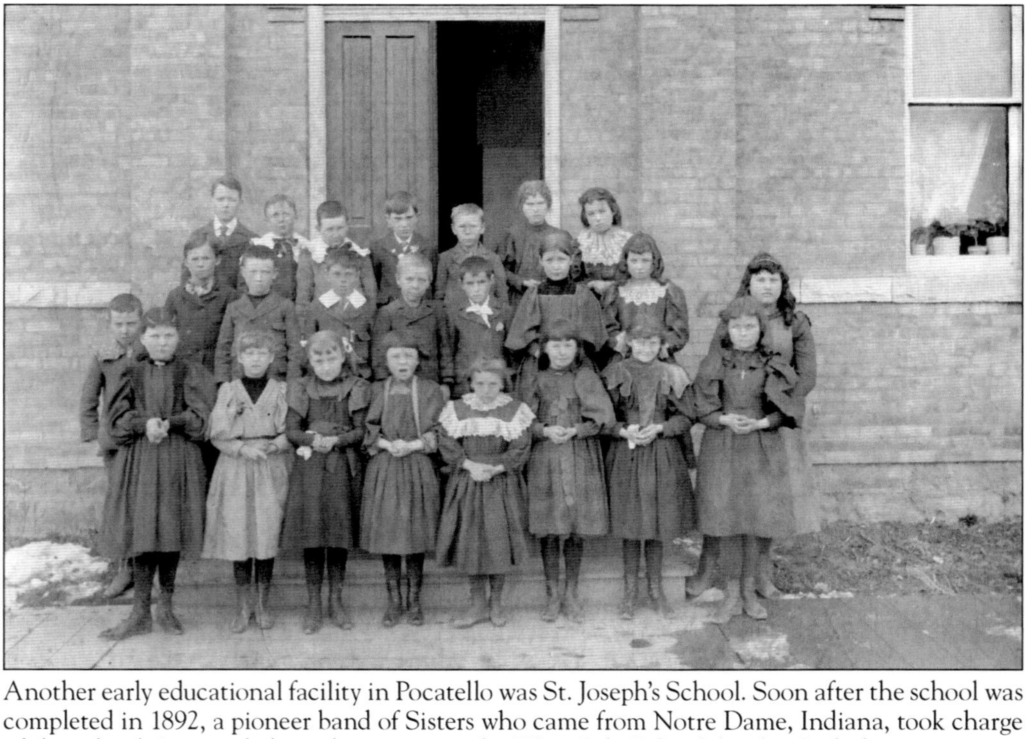

Another early educational facility in Pocatello was St. Joseph's School. Soon after the school was completed in 1892, a pioneer band of Sisters who came from Notre Dame, Indiana, took charge of the school. It provided an alternative to the West Side School for the Catholic community. This 1896 photograph shows the student body. (BCHS.)

St. Joseph's School, seen here sometime in the 1920s, continued to serve those who sought a Catholic education for their elementary and middle school children. St. Joseph's closed its doors in 1968 when the Holy Cross Sisters were no longer able to supply Sisters as faculty. (ISU.)

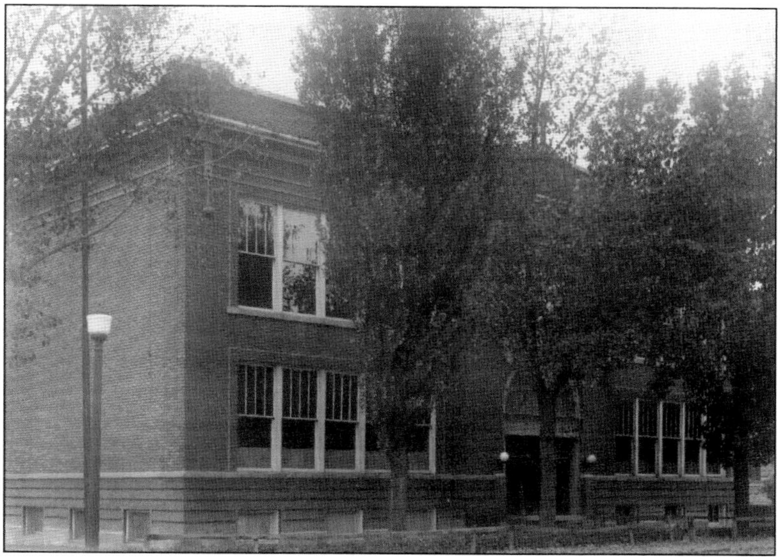

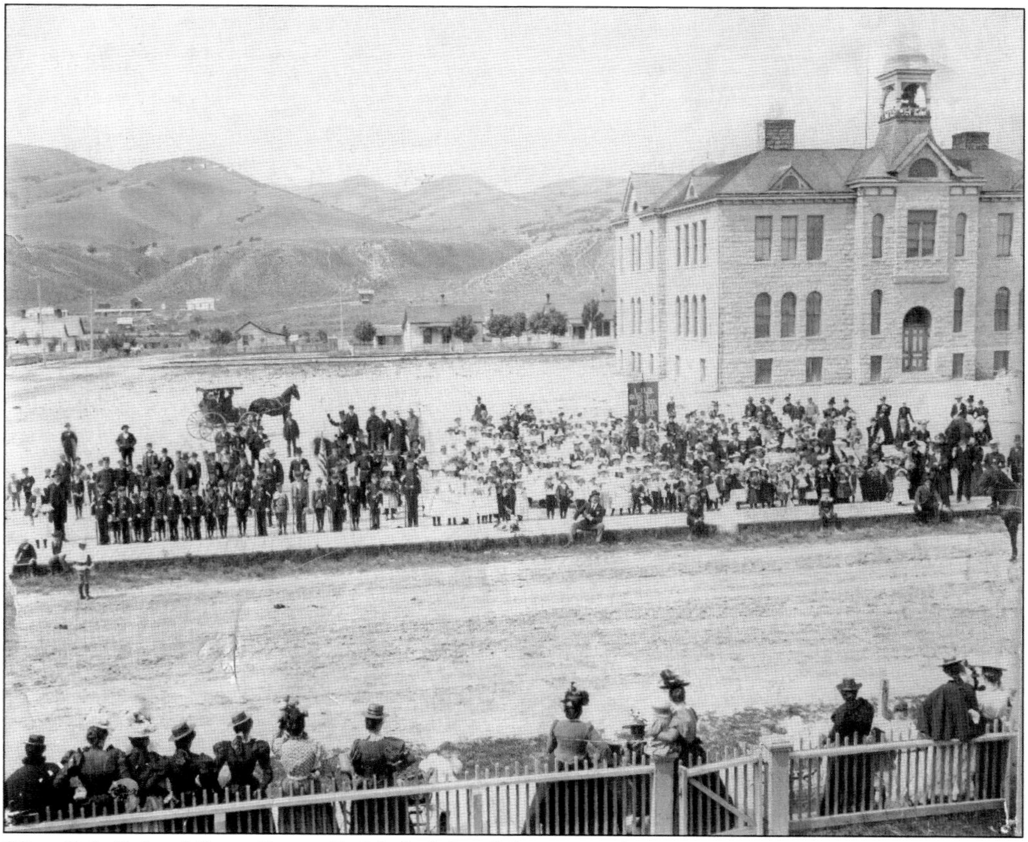

West Side School (later Pocatello High School) became a feature of Pocatello life, and numerous functions passed by its facade during the early history of Pocatello. This 1902 photograph seems to show a civic parade. Note the corps of cadets in the left background. (BCHS.)

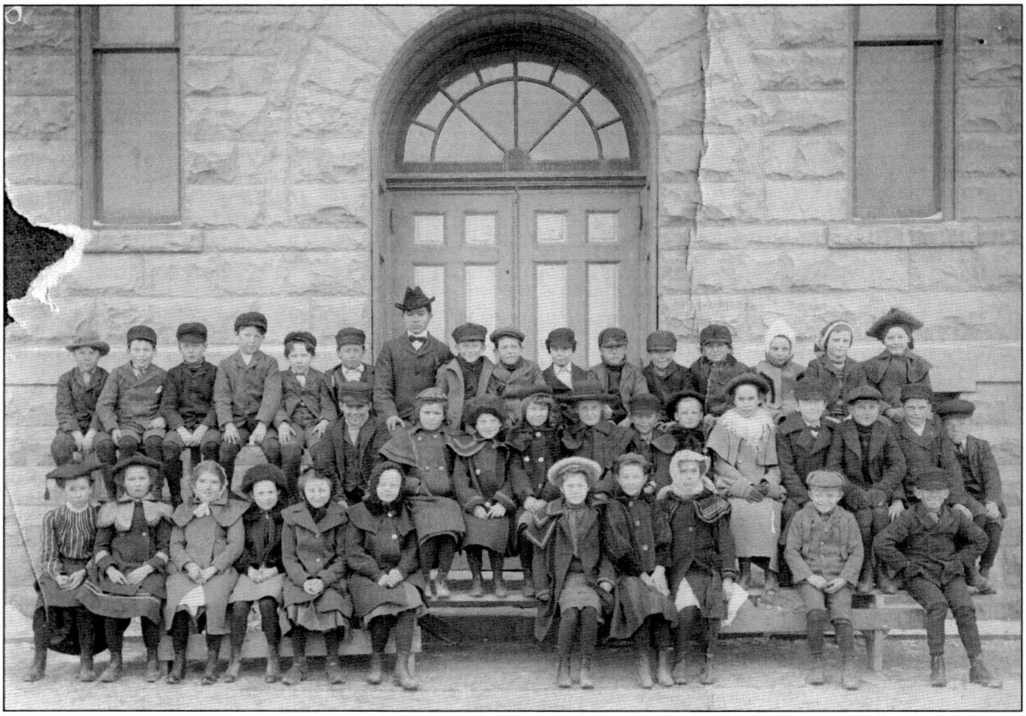

In the early days of Pocatello's history, the West Side School functioned as the main educational facility for the growing town. As such, it accommodated all grade levels, as shown in this 1908 photograph of an elementary class. Note the teacher in the center background; minority educators were generally uncommon at this time. (BCHS.)

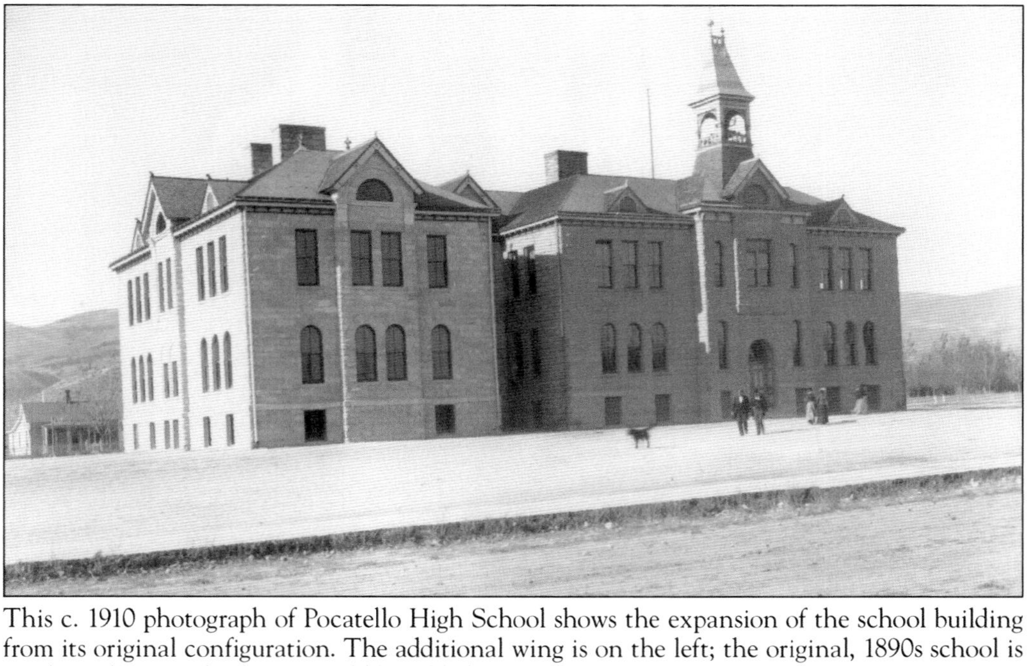

This c. 1910 photograph of Pocatello High School shows the expansion of the school building from its original configuration. The additional wing is on the left; the original, 1890s school is on the right. Another wing would be added to the right of the original structure in due course. (BCHS.)

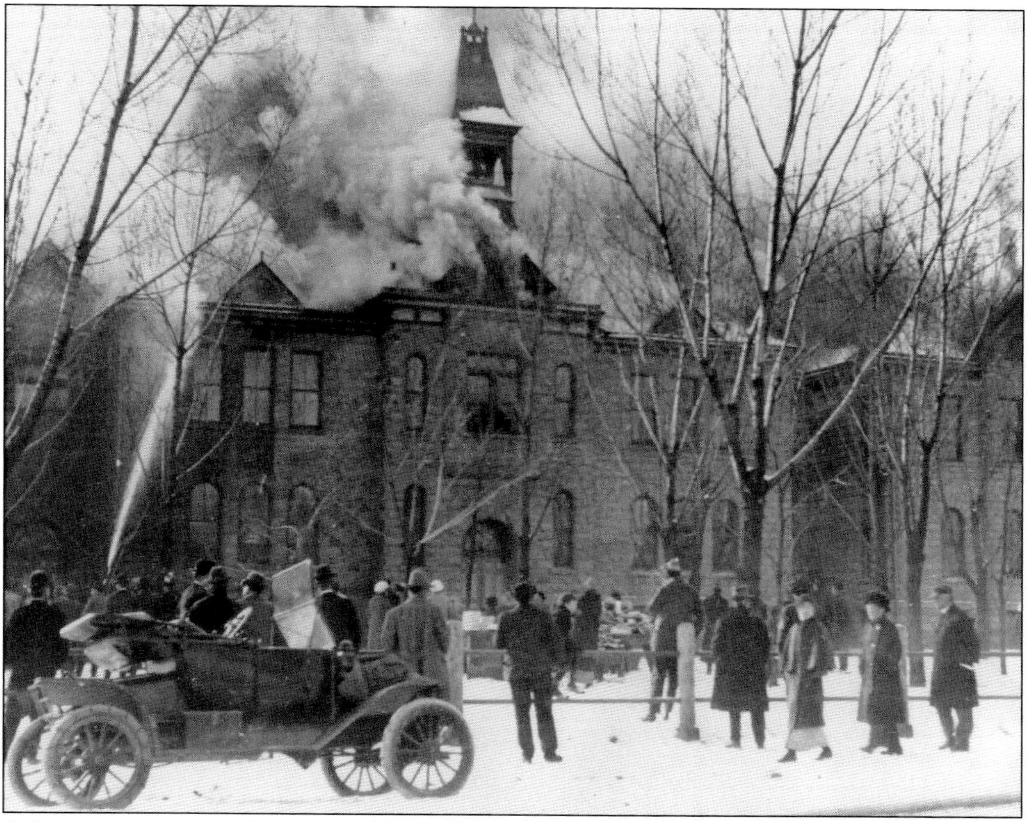

A devastating event in the history of Pocatello High School was the fire that broke out on December 16, 1914. The fire consumed a substantial amount of the building, and required considerable rebuilding before it once again could be fully utilized as an educational facility. (BCHS.)

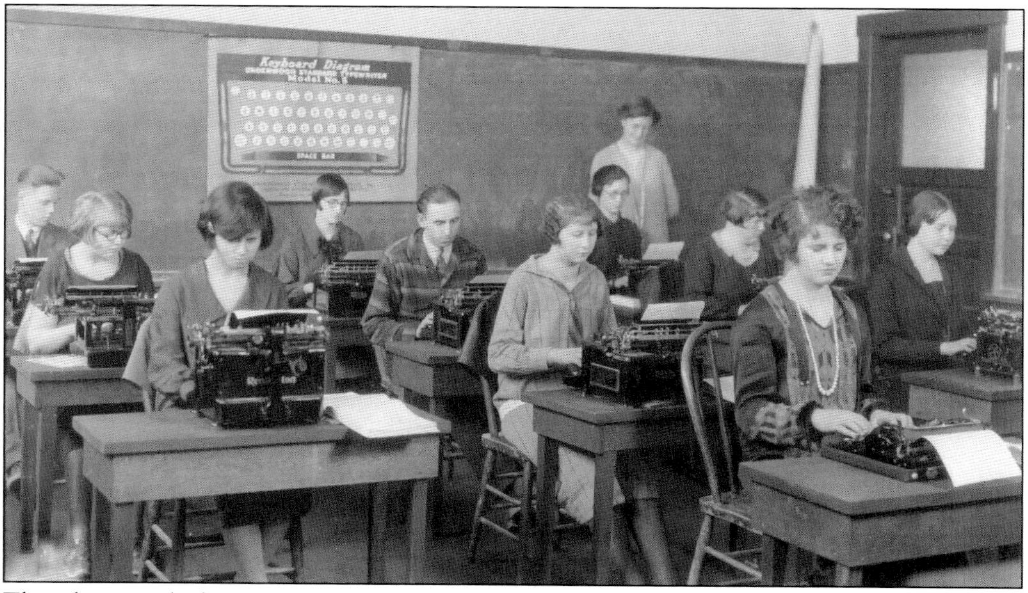

This photograph shows a typewriting class at Pocatello High sometime in the late 1920s. Note the keyboard diagram posted on the chalkboard at the back of the classroom. (BCHS.)

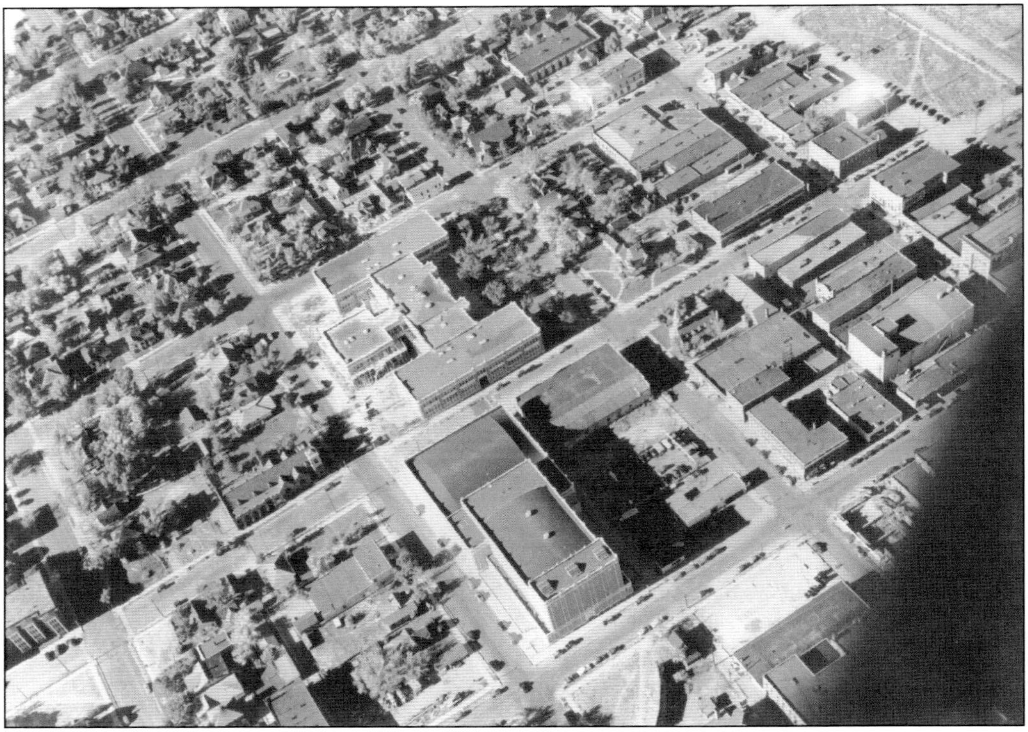

This 1940 aerial photograph of Pocatello High School shows the expansion of the campus from its early days as West Side School. The main campus can be seen in the center, with the gymnasium directly south of the main structure. (Paul Leffler.)

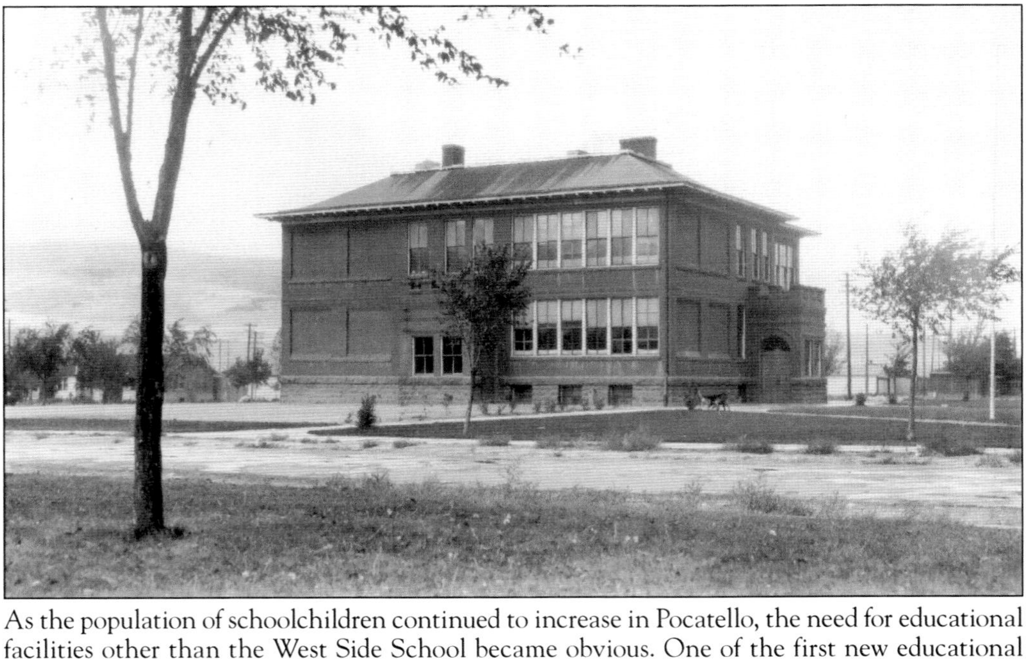

As the population of schoolchildren continued to increase in Pocatello, the need for educational facilities other than the West Side School became obvious. One of the first new educational structures was the North Ward School (later Lincoln School), completed in 1910 and pictured here sometime in the 1920s. Lincoln School was demolished in 1961. (ISU.)

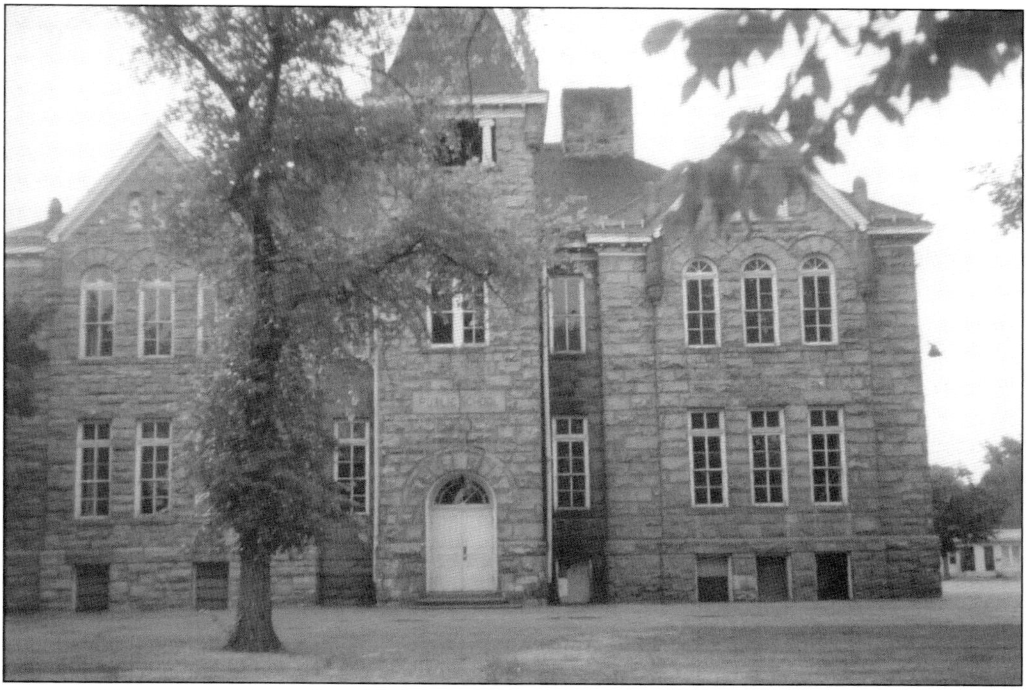

A vital addition to the Pocatello school system was the East Side School (later Bonneville School). Built in close proximity to the Bannock County Courthouse, the East Side School was a familiar sight to generations of East Side schoolchildren. (BCHS.)

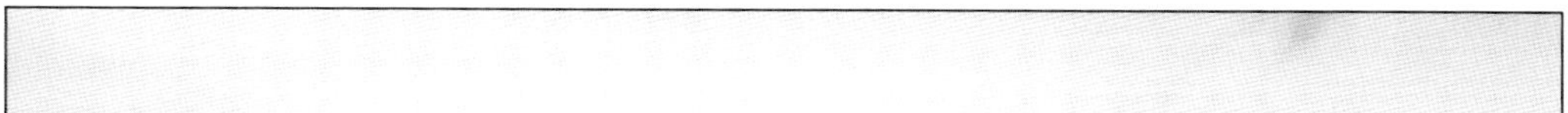

Whittier School, located on South 4th Avenue, was constructed in 1914. It was considered to be as modern as the science of school building allowed at that time. As a testament to the rapid growth of Pocatello during this period, Whittier School was fully enrolled a year after its opening. Whittier School closed at the beginning of the 1982 school year and was later razed. The location is now a parking lot for Idaho State University. (ISHS.)

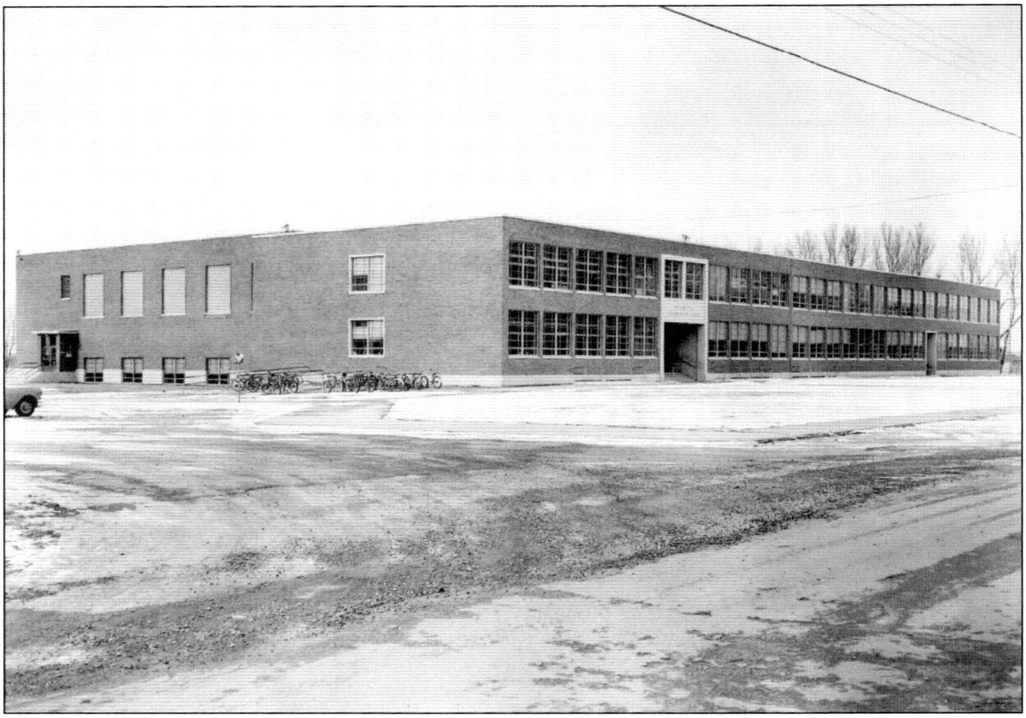

One of the last junior high schools constructed, Alameda Junior High was opened in 1952. Located on McKinley Avenue at Alameda Road, this facility served as a junior high until a drop in enrollment in the Pocatello school district forced its closure in 2000. Used as a continuation school for the district, it is scheduled to reopen as a middle school in 2013. (ISU.)

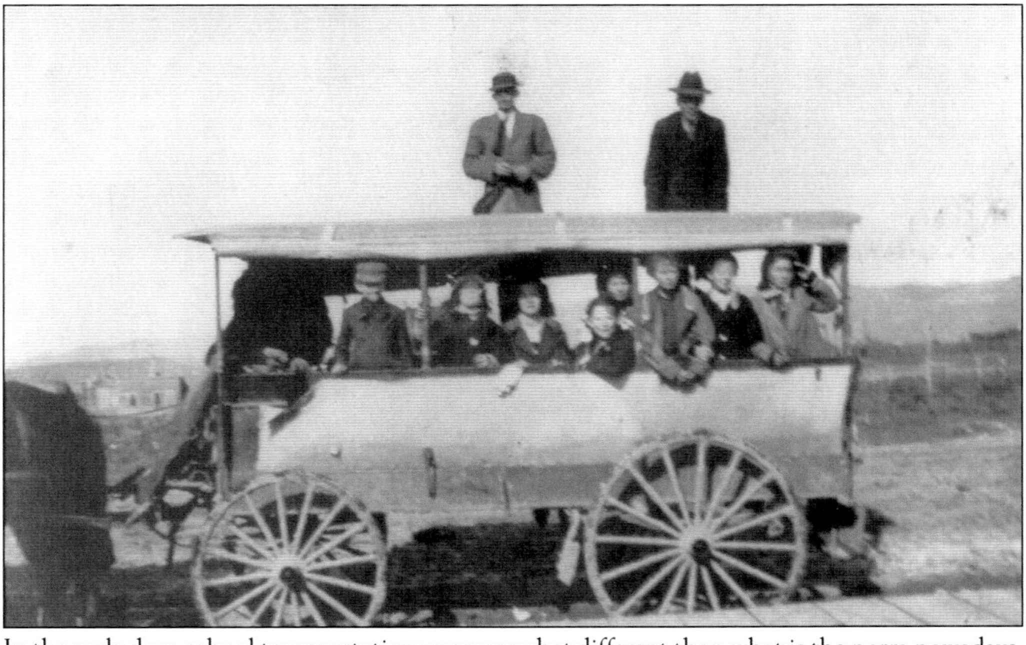

In the early days, school transportation was somewhat different than what is the norm nowadays. This photograph, taken in 1905, purports to show the first school bus in Pocatello. Note that this "bus" is very similar to the wagons used by farmers and businesses at the time. (BCHS.)

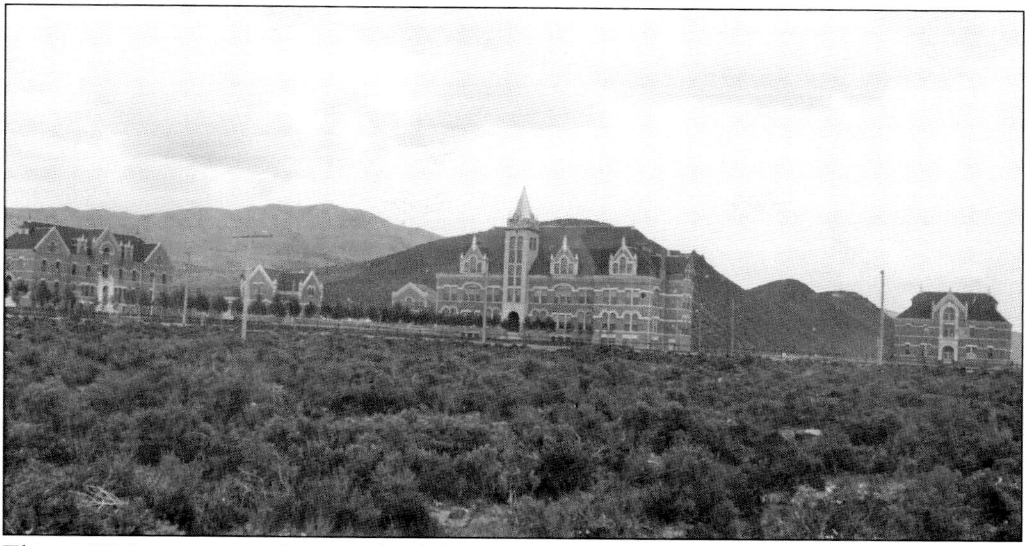

This c. 1908 panoramic photograph of the Academy of Idaho shows the center of the campus at the time. In the center is Swanson Hall, Faris Hall is to the left, and the women's dorm (later renamed Turner Hall) is to the right. The generally isolated aspect of the campus relative to Pocatello proper is apparent here. (BCHS.)

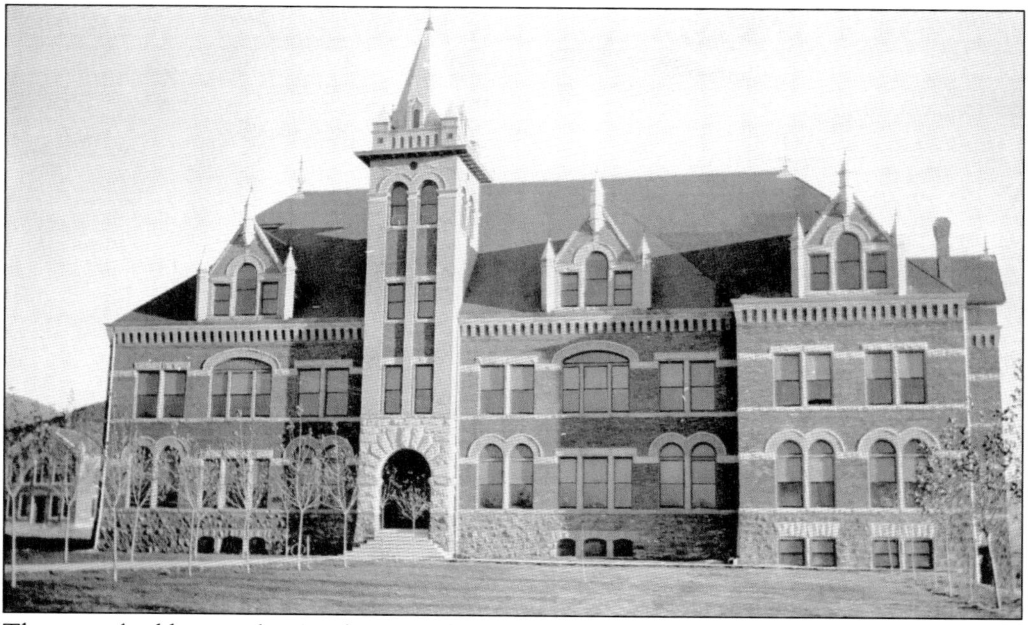

The main building at the Academy of Idaho—and the signature structure right up until the Idaho State College phase of the institution—was Swanson Hall. A combination of lecture and recital halls as well as administrative departments, Swanson Hall was the featured center of the campus for decades. (ISU.)

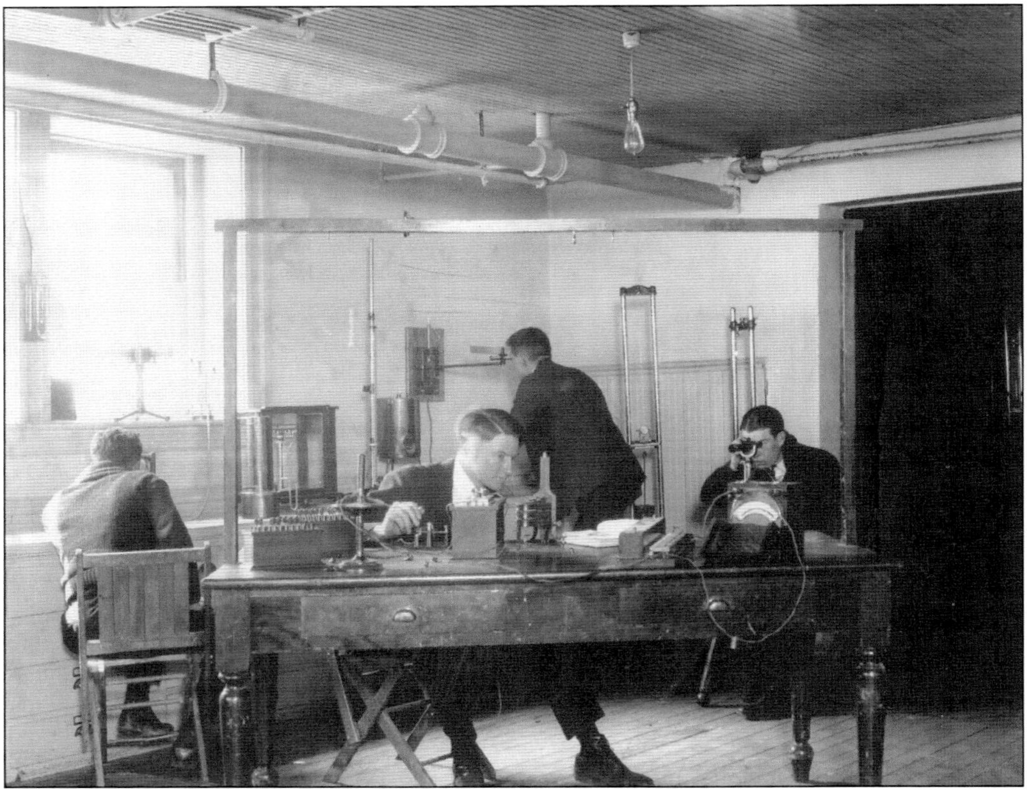

Swanson Hall held many departments of the university. The physics lab was located in the basement. This 1922 photograph shows students conducting an experiment under the direction of Ralph H. Waters. (ISU.)

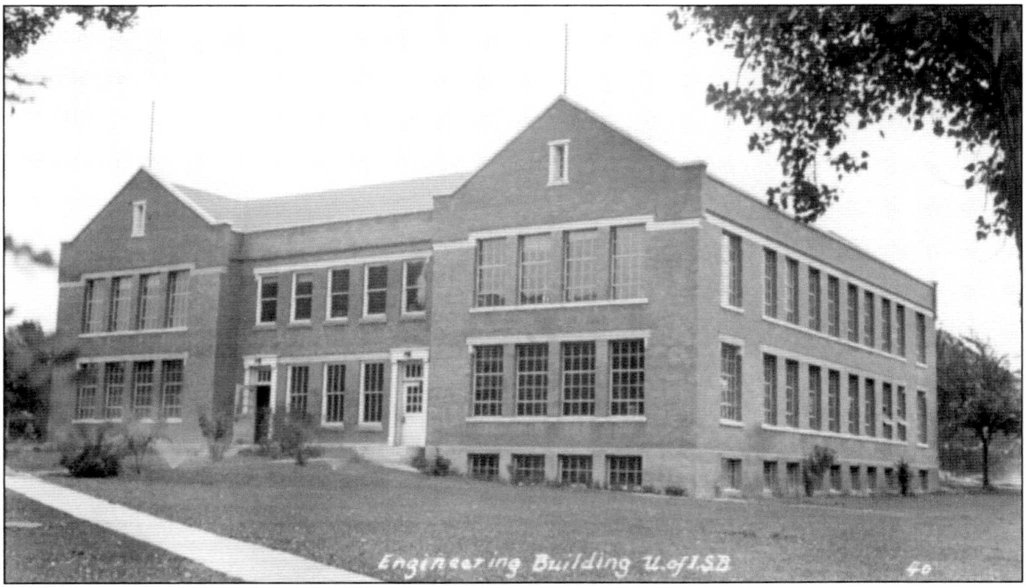

One of the original structures of the Academy of Idaho was the Engineering Building. Originally built in 1903, it was expanded in 1909 and 1925. The home of the Engineering Department for decades, the building was demolished in 1971. (ISU.)

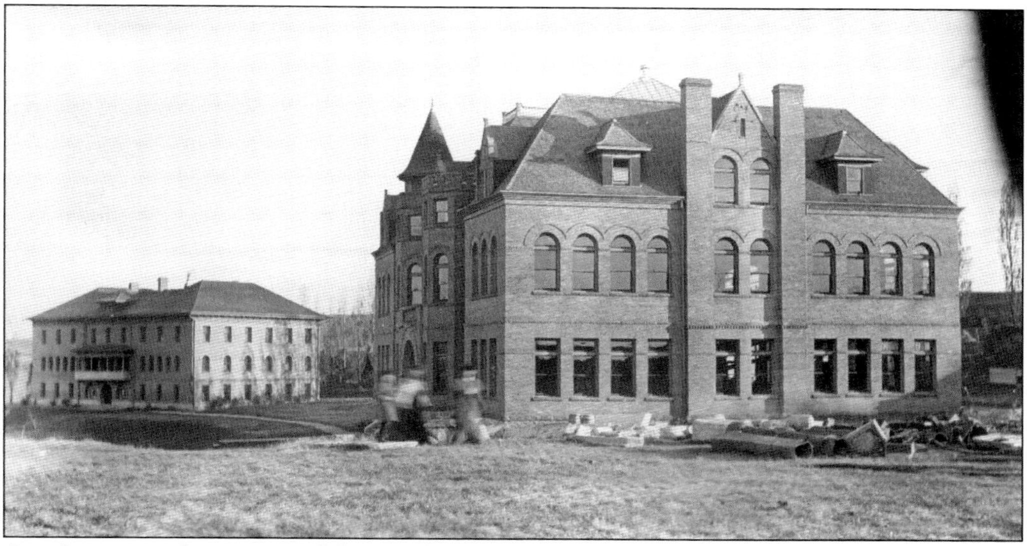

Another original structure of the Academy of Idaho was the boy's dormitory, seen here under construction in 1909. (Bistline.)

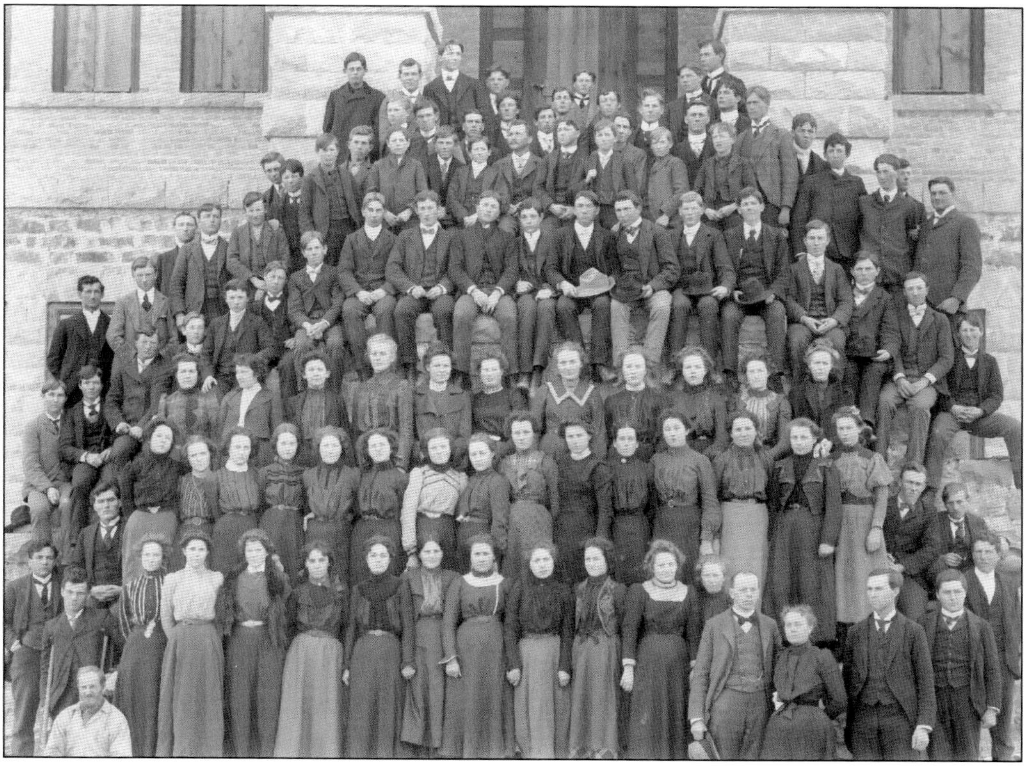

The student body of the Academy of Idaho consisted of what would otherwise be considered high-school students and traditional college students. Note the number of women in the 1905 student body. (BCHS.)

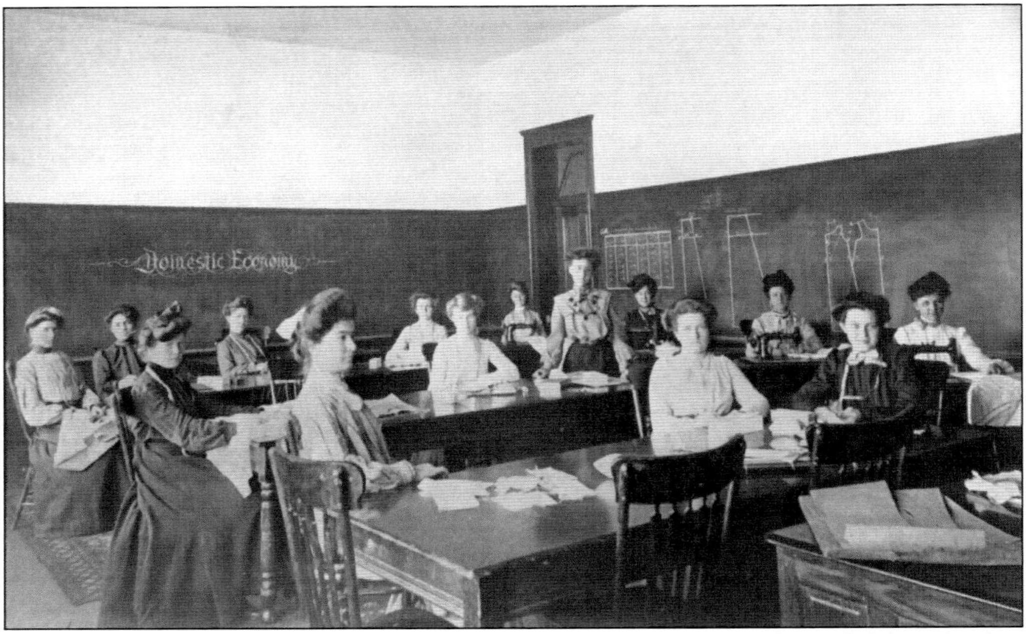

This 1904 photograph shows a course in domestic engineering at the Academy of Idaho. The class consists entirely of women, indicating the role of gender in higher education. (BCHS.)

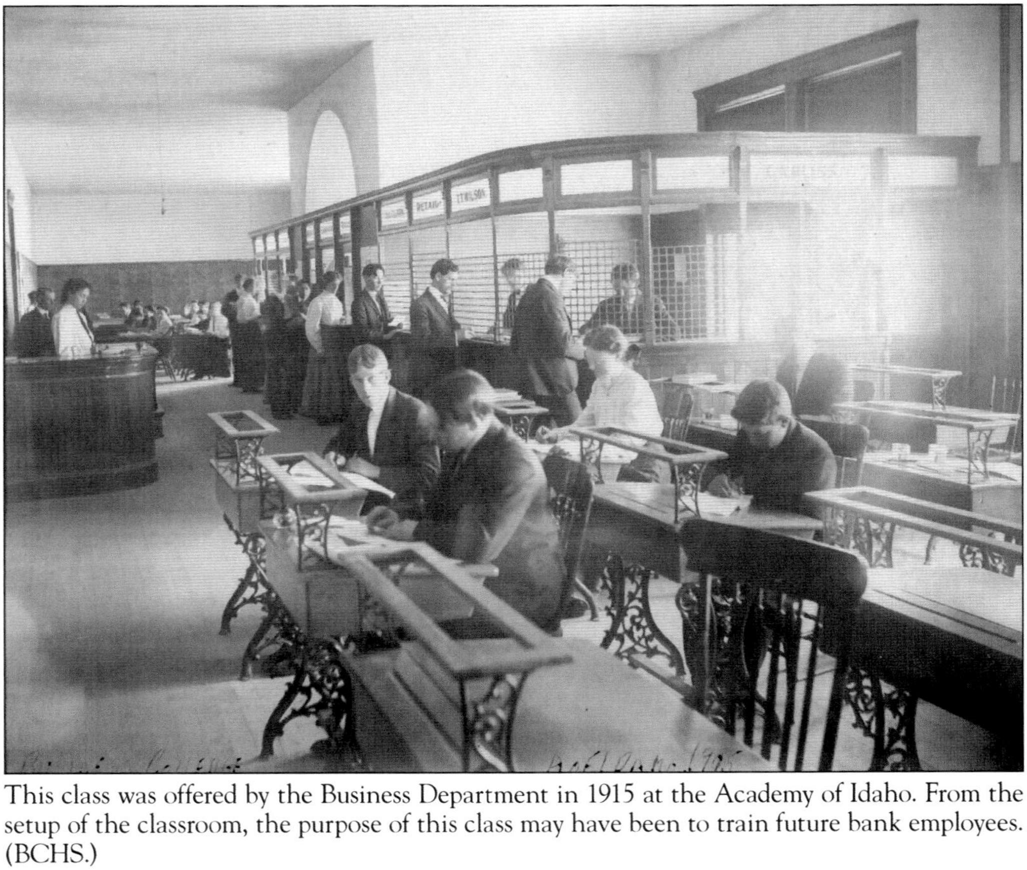

This class was offered by the Business Department in 1915 at the Academy of Idaho. From the setup of the classroom, the purpose of this class may have been to train future bank employees. (BCHS.)

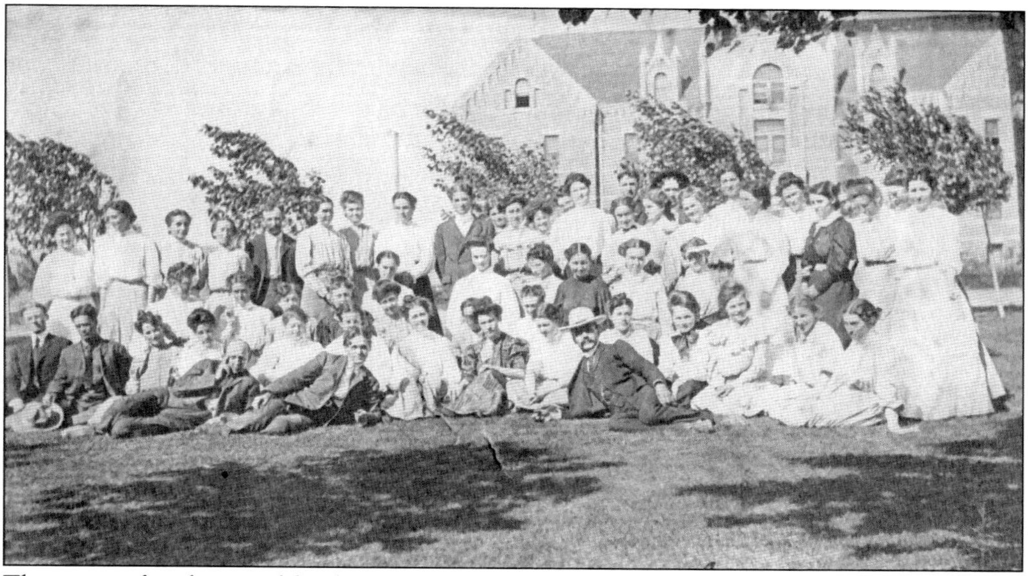

This group of students and faculty partaking in summer courses at the Academy of Idaho in 1906 posed in front of Swanson Hall. Again, note the ratio of women students to men. (BCHS.)

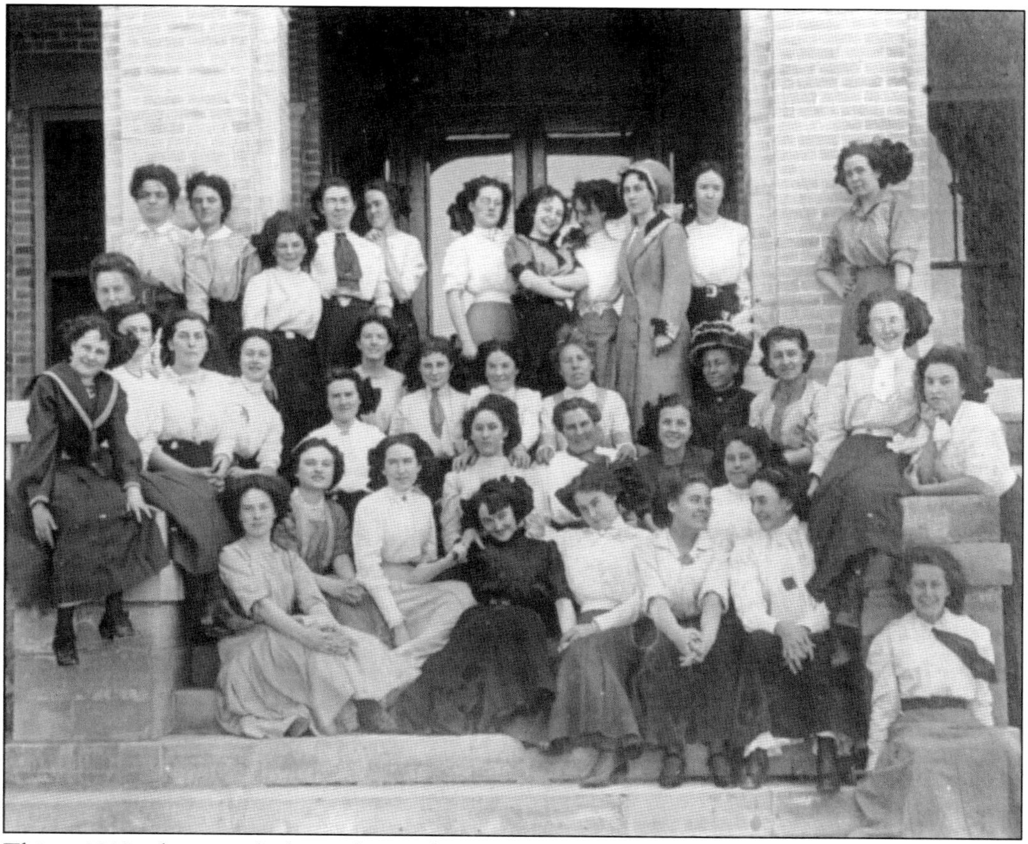

This c. 1910s photograph shows the residents of the women's dorm at the Academy of Idaho just as a wind gust blew in, a hazard of Pocatello life. (BCHS.)

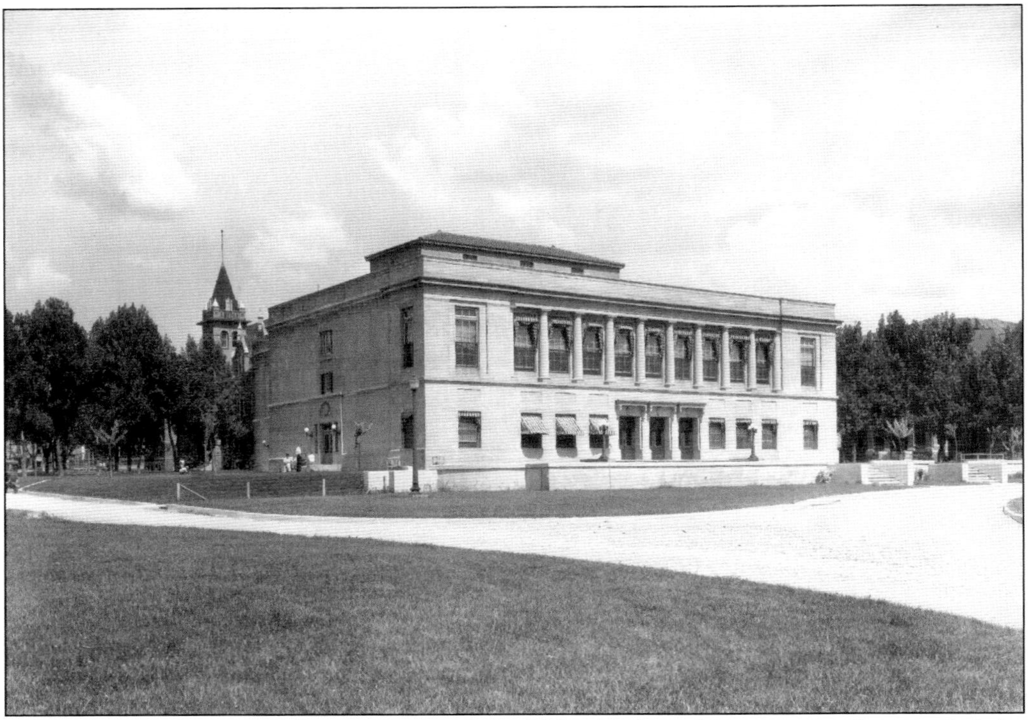

When the Academy of Idaho was renamed the Idaho Technical Institute, it also signaled the growth of the campus itself. One noteworthy structure is Frazier Hall, which was built in 1924. Frazier Hall is still in use at Idaho State University today. (ISU.)

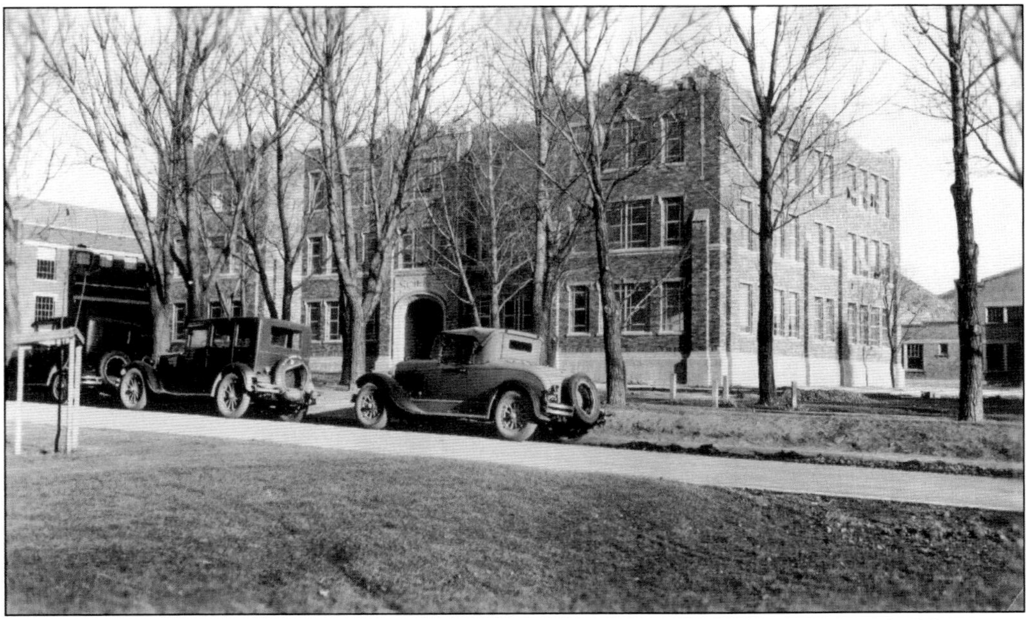

Another notable addition to the Idaho Technical Institute prior to its rechristening as the University of Idaho, Southern Branch, was the Science Building. Later renamed Baldwin Hall, this building was the home of science programs at the university before being razed in 1992. (ISU.)

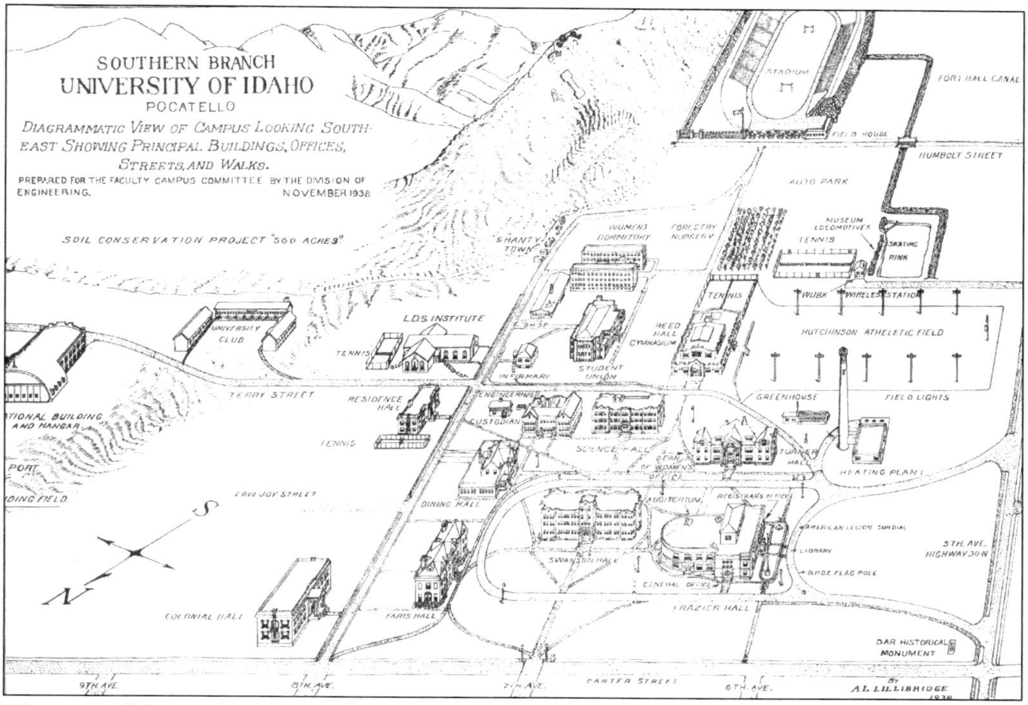

This map of the campus of the University of Idaho, Southern Branch, drawn by A.E. Lillibridge, shows how the campus would have looked in 1938. Many of the original Academy of Idaho buildings are visible, along with additions from the expansion period after World War I. However, the Student Union building, shown here, was not actually completed until 1939. (ISU.)

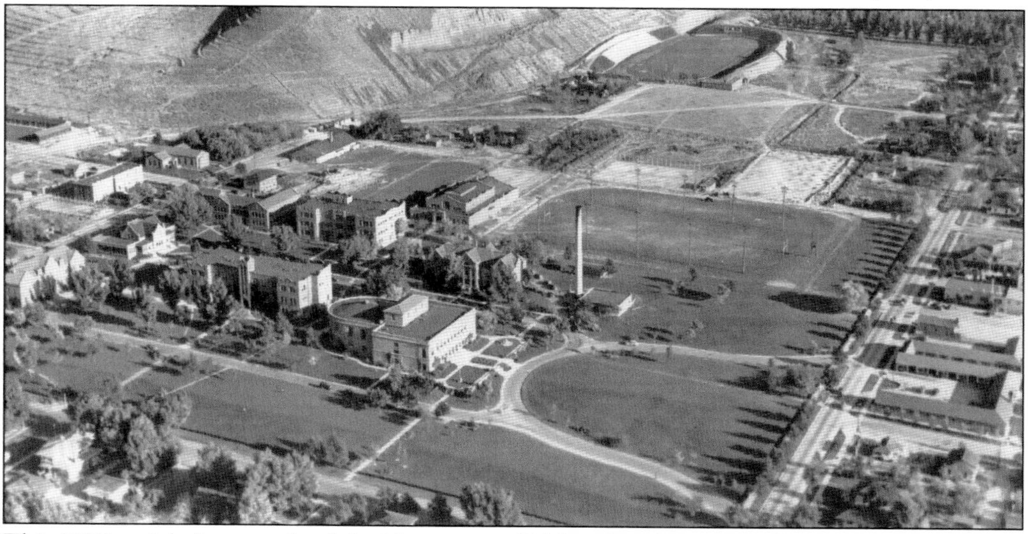

This 1938 aerial photograph of the University of Idaho, Southern Branch, shows the expansion of the campus. The Spud Bowl can be seen at the top of the photograph, with the main campus directly to the north of the stadium. Swanson Hall and Frazier Hall are visible in this photograph, with the Science Hall and Turner Hall directly east of these structures. Reed Hall, the site of the gymnasium for the university, is alongside Turner Hall. The new Student Union Building, which would become the Administration Building, is still at the foundation stage. Also noticeable is the terracing work done on Red Hill by the Civilian Conservation Corps. (Paul Leffler.)

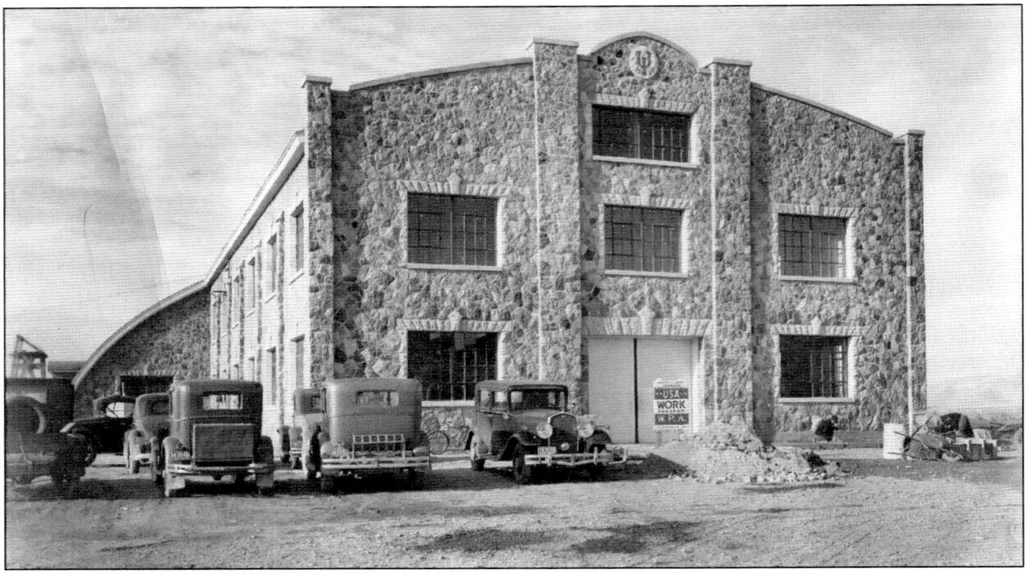

One of the programs offered at the University of Idaho, Southern Branch was an aviation program. This involved both the maintenance and flying of aircraft. To maintain the aircraft used in the program, a combined hangar and maintenance shop was built by the WPA in 1938. This photograph shows the facility just before completion. The building is still in use as the location of the College of Technology for Idaho State University. (BCHS.)

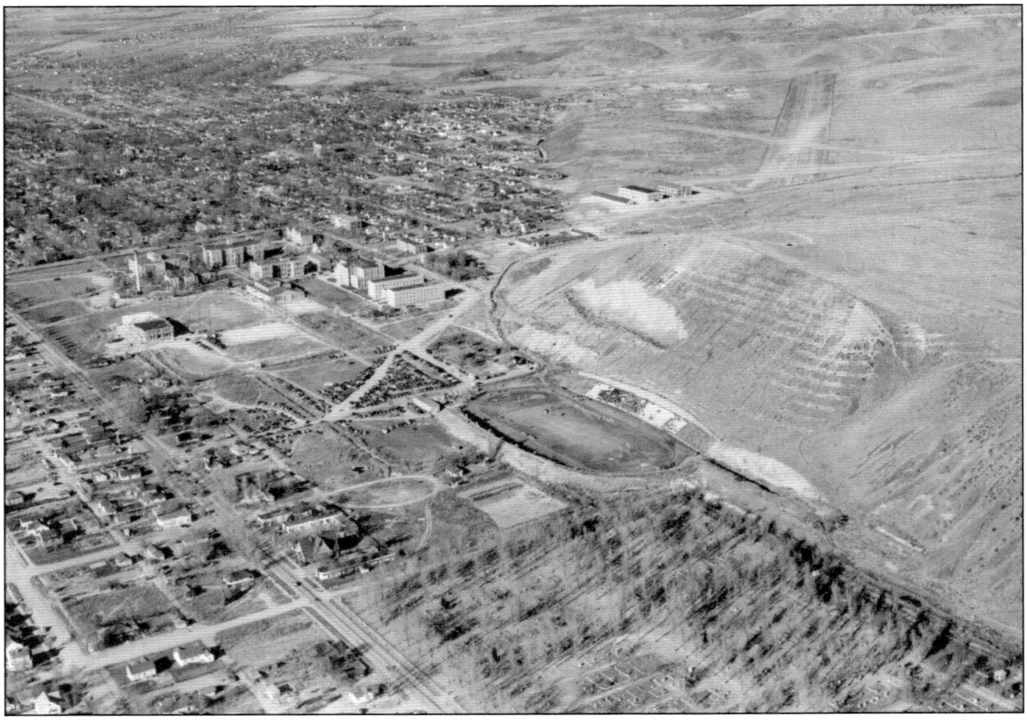

In this c. 1939 aerial photograph of the University of Idaho, Southern Branch, landing strips associated with Hamm Field are at the top right of the photograph. Hamm Field was used as a training facility for both prospective pilots as well as aircraft technicians; a pilot-training program was set up by the federal government in 1939. (ISU.)

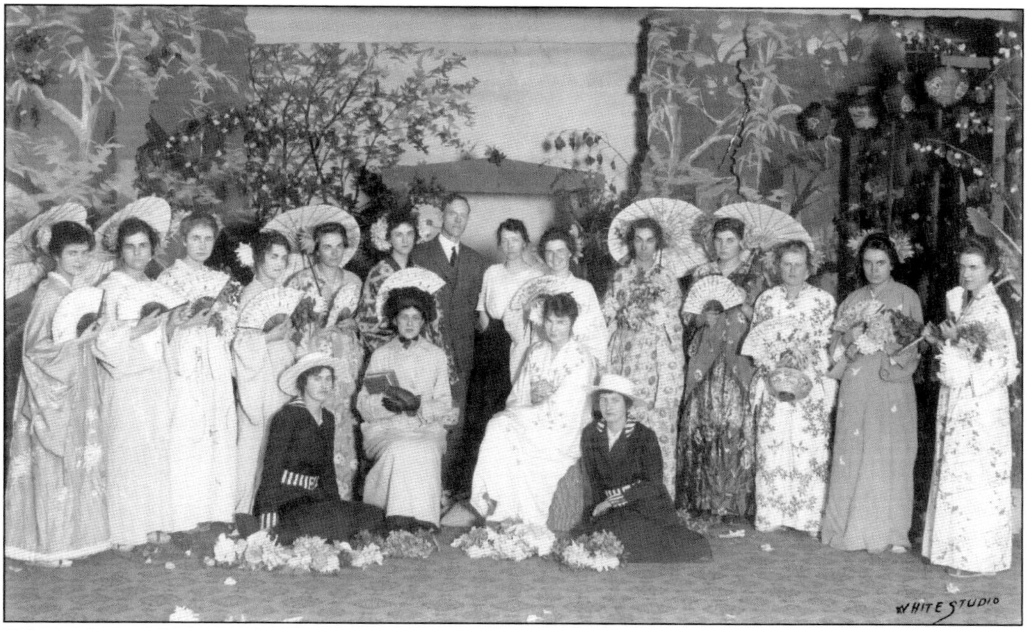

While the students at the university campus were engaged in academic studies, there were also opportunities to engage in social activities. This photograph, apparently from the Academy of Idaho period, shows women students involved in what seems to be a Japanese evening. This sort of event was popular in the early part of the 20th century. (ISU.)

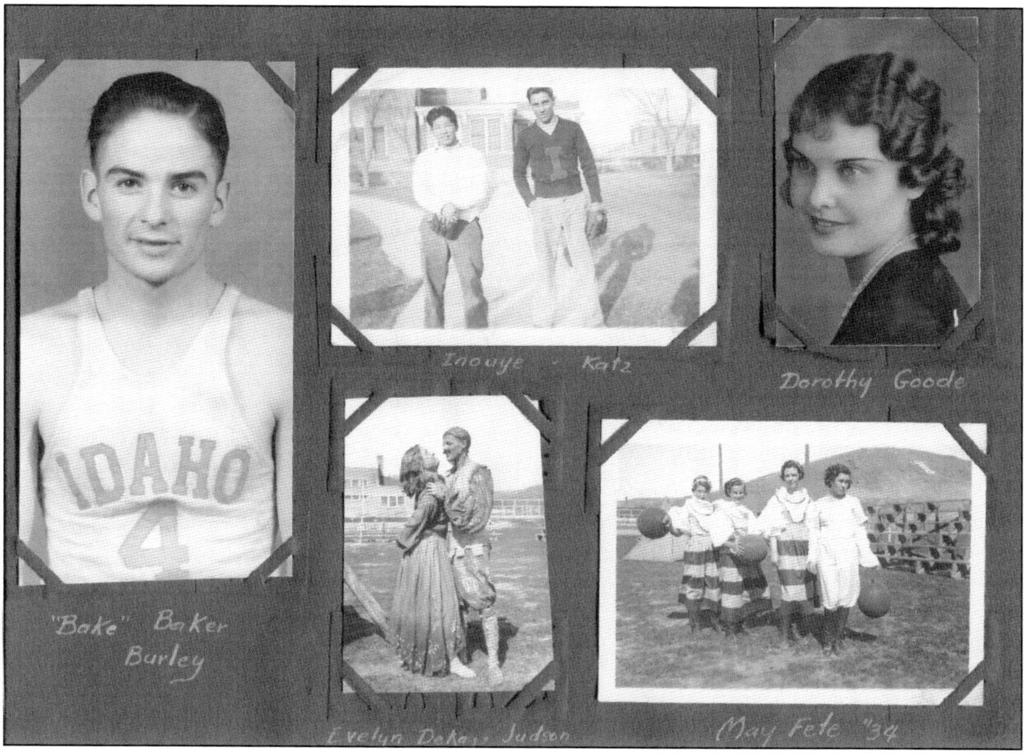

This is a page from a student's scrapbook from the 1930s. Note the combination of athletic and theatrical photographs featured here. (ISU.)

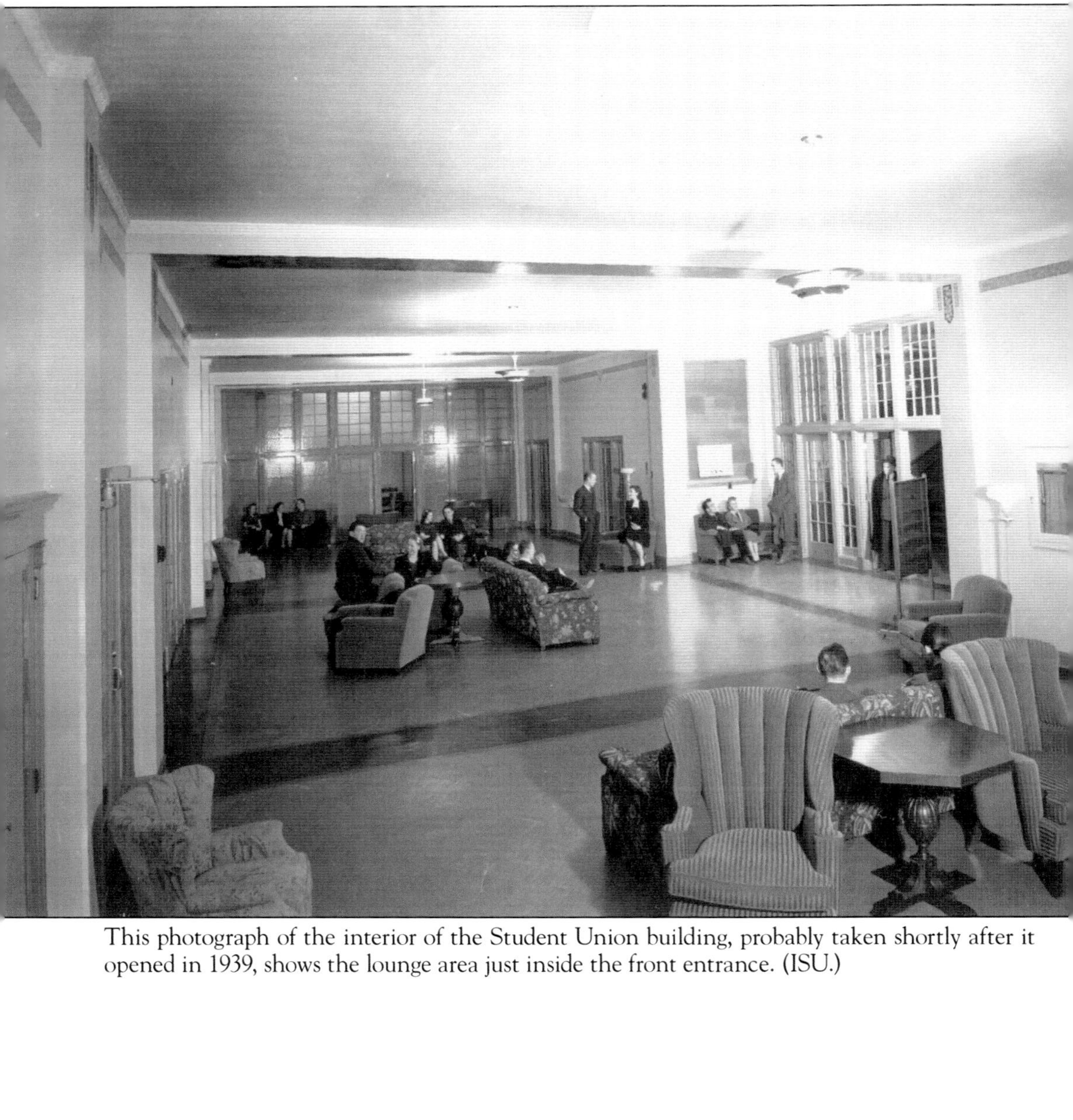

This photograph of the interior of the Student Union building, probably taken shortly after it opened in 1939, shows the lounge area just inside the front entrance. (ISU.)

Six

Sports and Recreation

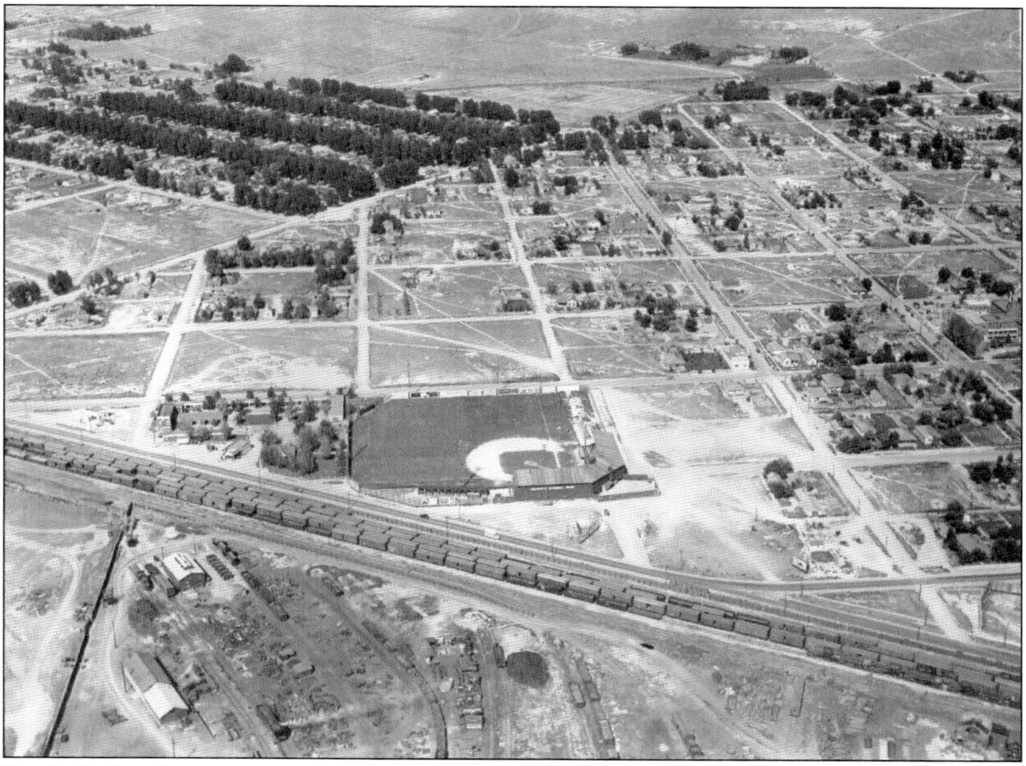

Baseball played an important role in the history of the development of Pocatello. From its earliest days as a frontier town, baseball leagues were a feature of Pocatello life. An important milestone in the history of baseball in Pocatello was the construction of Pocatello Baseball Park (later renamed Halliwell Park) in 1938–1939, located northeast of what is now Pocatello Avenue. One of the significant features of this ballpark was the installation of lights for night baseball. This was a notable feature at a time when only five major league ballparks were equipped with lights. This site is now the parking lot for the Pocatello City Hall. (Paul Leffler.)

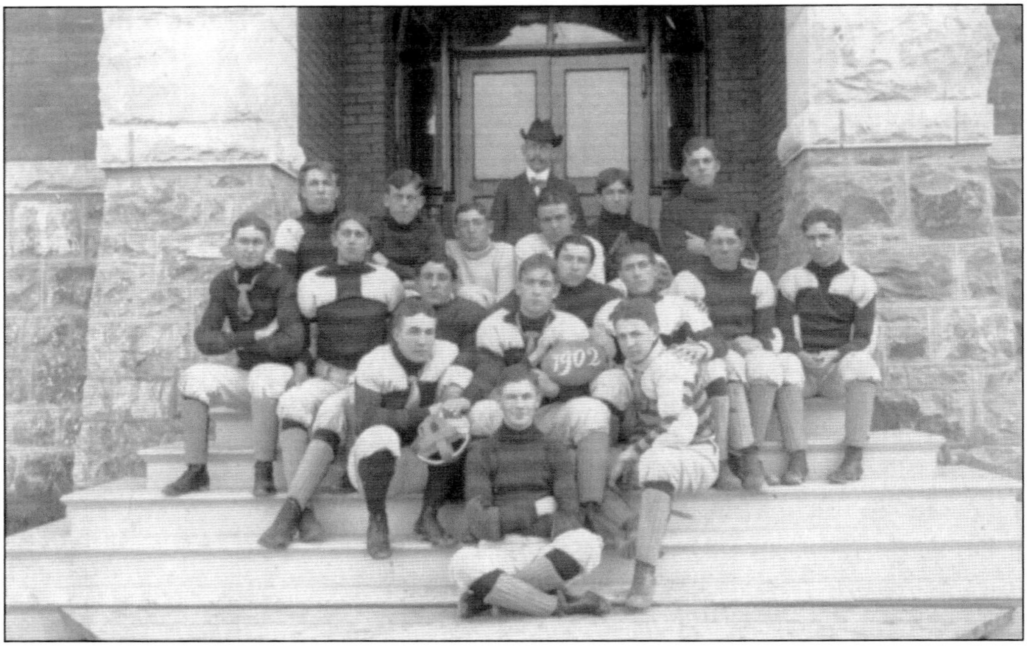

Football was played at the Academy of Idaho from its opening in 1901. This photograph of the 1902 team features, from left to right, (first row) Fred Ball, Leo Lewis, Clarence Dietrich, and J.D. Gillilan Jr. (captain); (second row) George Matthews, Quicy Hoag, unidentified, Morton Baum, Les Castle, ? Rice, Charles Matthews, and L.A. West Jr.; (third row) Emmett Kadlitz, Harry ?, H.D. Cheney (coach), Grover McGee, Lars Nielson, and Edward Bremm. The position of football coach was a voluntary one at this time. (ISU.)

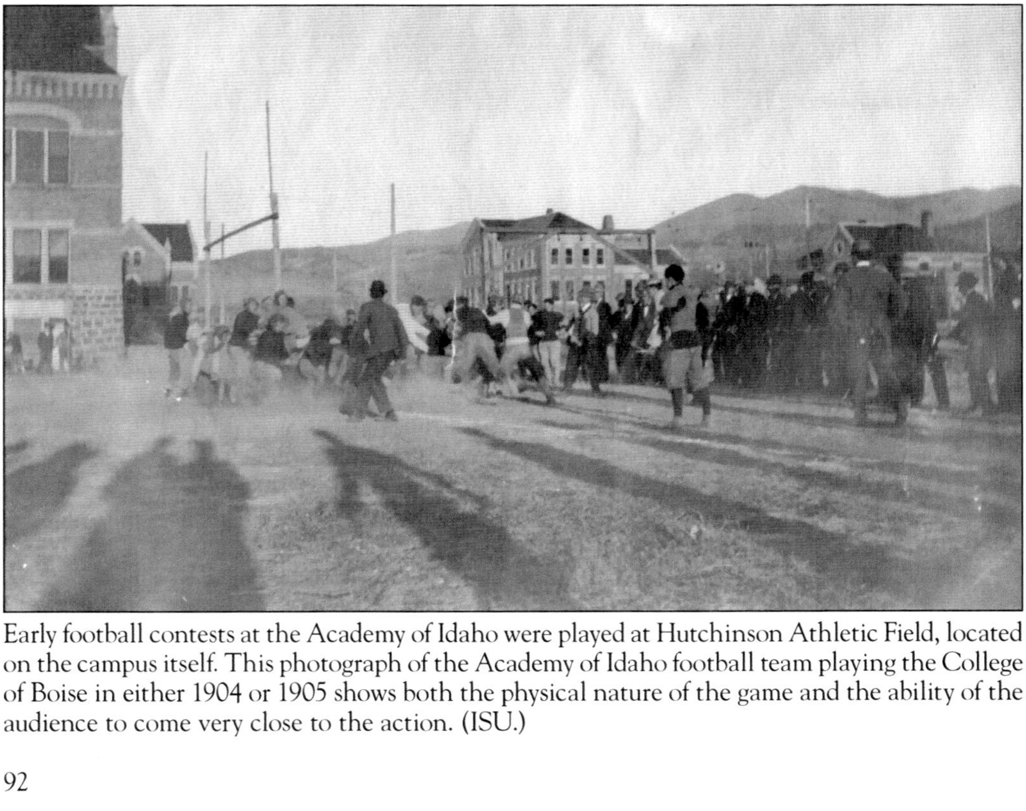

Early football contests at the Academy of Idaho were played at Hutchinson Athletic Field, located on the campus itself. This photograph of the Academy of Idaho football team playing the College of Boise in either 1904 or 1905 shows both the physical nature of the game and the ability of the audience to come very close to the action. (ISU.)

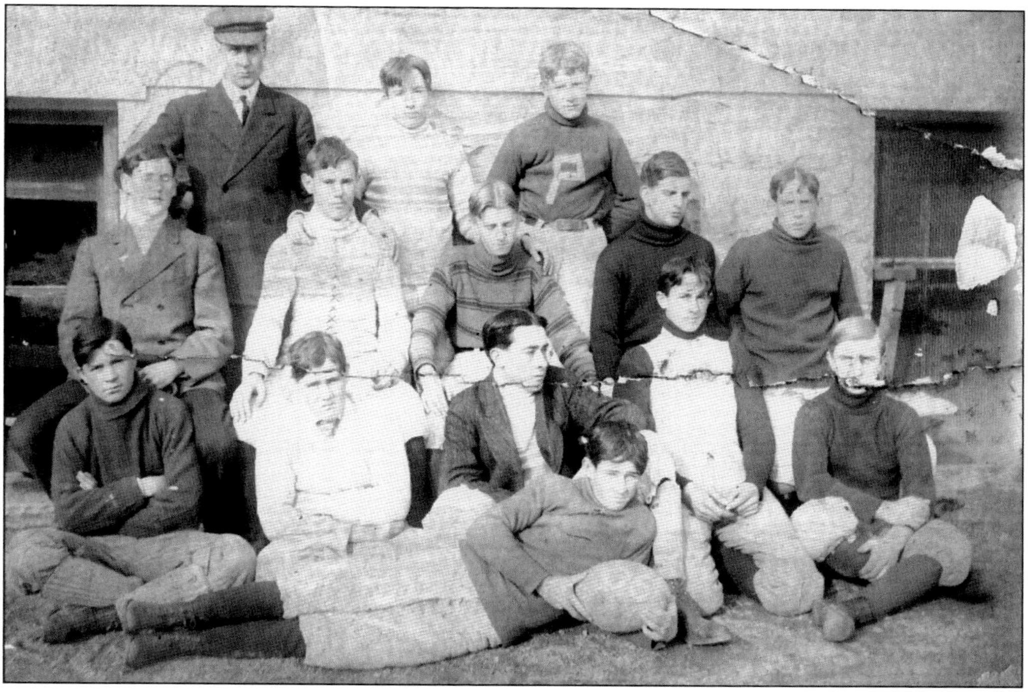

Not to be outdone by their more senior brethren, the Pocatello High School football team also competed for championship glory. This portrait of the 1906 team features, from left to right, (first row) Guy Hansen, Jim Smith, Carl Loux, Ernest Loux, and Roland Gasser; (second row) Ed. Freeman, Harold H. Huggard, Louis Whitman, Thomas Dolman, and Howard Baker; (third row) E.N. Ferris (coach and principal), Beany (or Harry) Wade, and Dayton Peck. This photograph was taken on the south side of Pocatello High School. (BCHS)

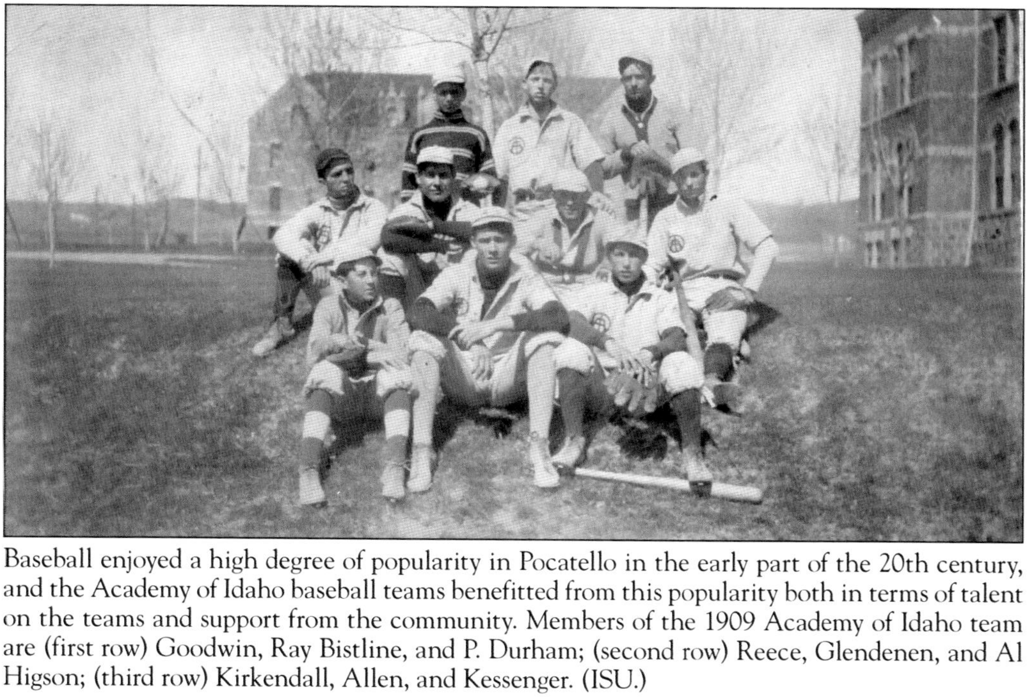

Baseball enjoyed a high degree of popularity in Pocatello in the early part of the 20th century, and the Academy of Idaho baseball teams benefitted from this popularity both in terms of talent on the teams and support from the community. Members of the 1909 Academy of Idaho team are (first row) Goodwin, Ray Bistline, and P. Durham; (second row) Reece, Glendenen, and Al Higson; (third row) Kirkendall, Allen, and Kessenger. (ISU.)

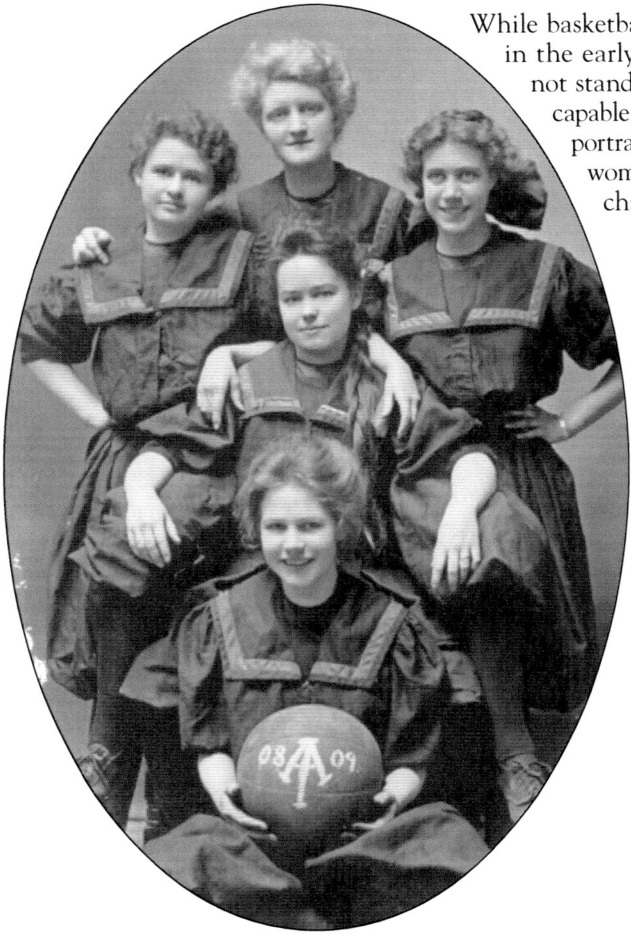

While basketball was categorized as a "girl's sport" in the early part of the 20th century, this did not stand in the way of women's teams being capable of competing at a very high level. This portrait of the 1908–1909 Academy of Idaho women's basketball team shows a group of championship-level athletes. (ISU.)

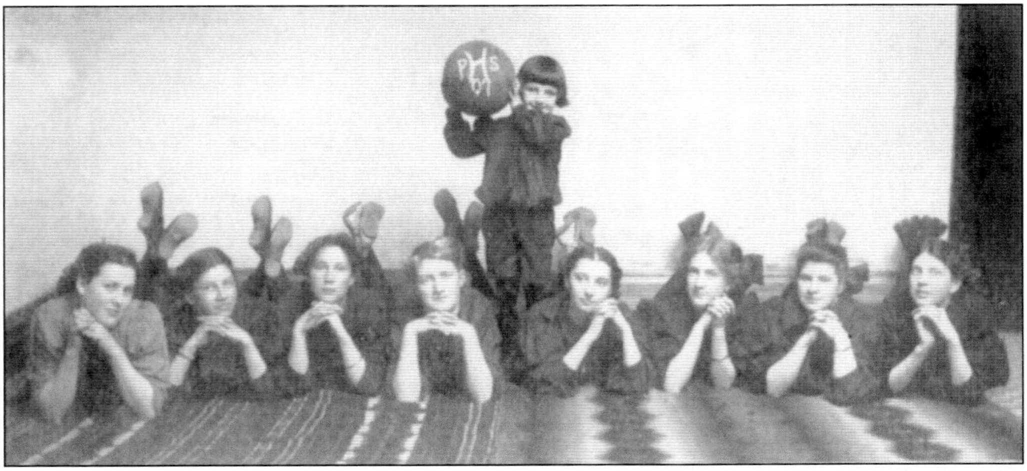

As with their male compatriots, the women's basketball team at Pocatello High School in the early part of the century performed at a level higher than would have been expected from society. This photograph, taken by the Benedicte Wrensted studio, is noteworthy for the Native American blanket being used by the players in their team photograph. This was an unusual prop for non–Native American photographs at the time. (BCHS.)

Basketball was played by both men and women at the Academy of Idaho at a highly competitive level. The members of the 1907–1908 men's championship squad include, from left to right, (first row) Howard Parsons and Roland Davidson; (second row) Ross Jones, Guy Clinderin, and Ole Olson; (third row) Leo Kessinger, Professor Morris (coach), and Raymond Peterson. (ISU.)

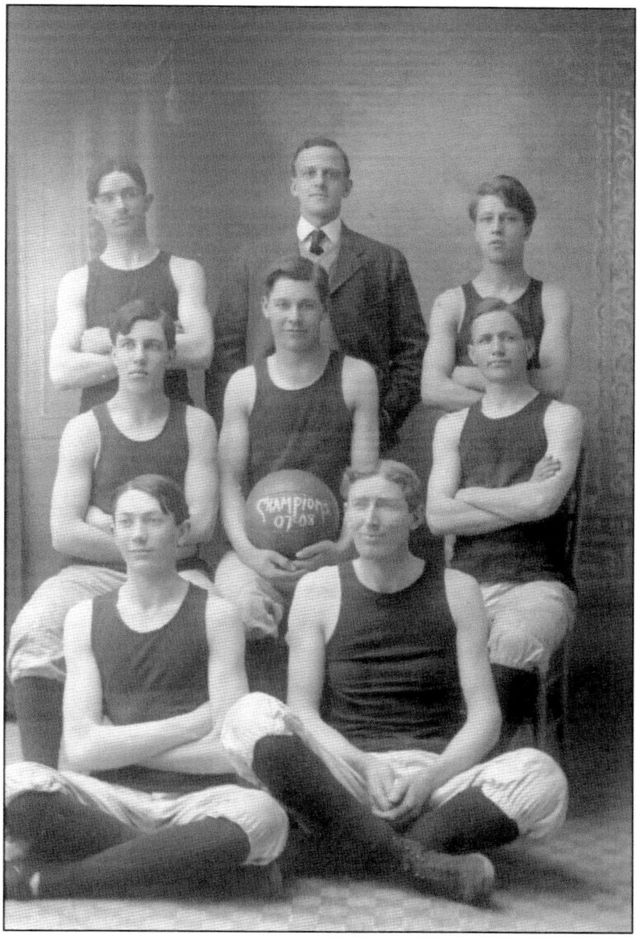

In the post–World War I period, the Idaho Tech football program continued to perform at a high level. This team photograph shows the 1921 conference and Intermountain junior college championship squad. (ISU.)

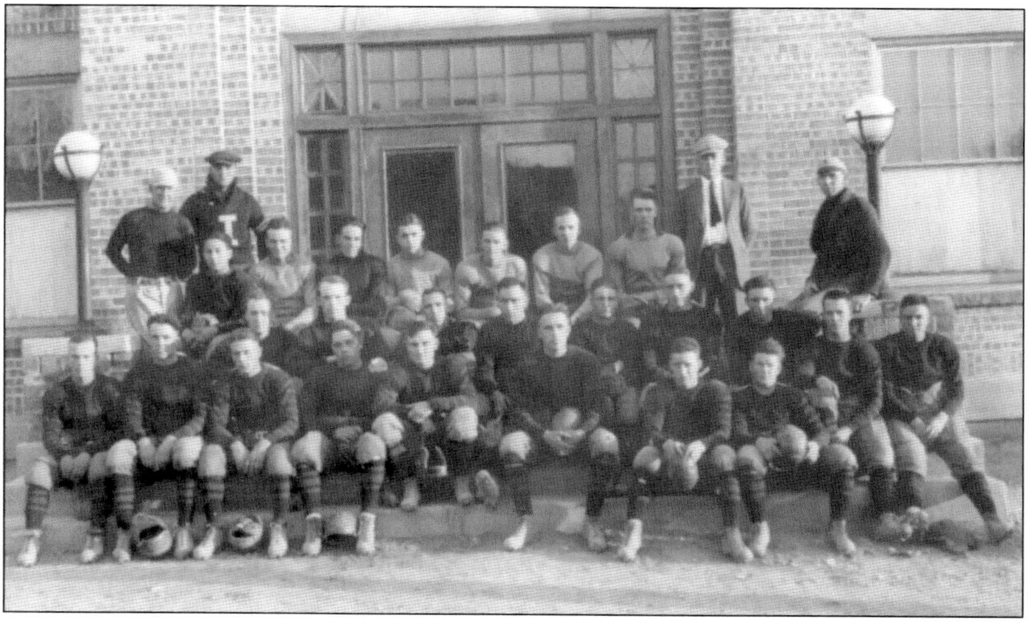

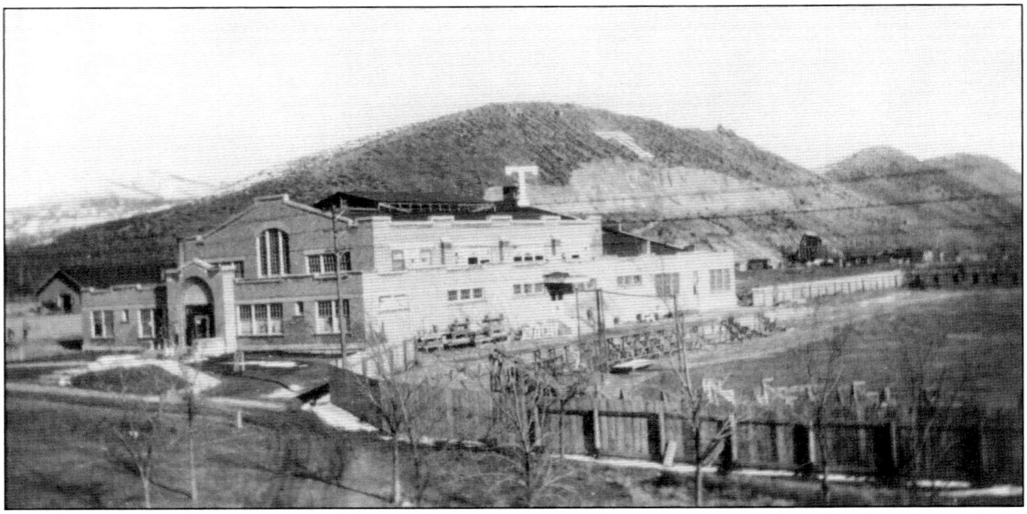

One of the noteworthy landmarks in Pocatello athletic history was Reed Hall, the home of the sports programs at the Idaho Technical Institute; the University of Idaho, Southern Branch; and for a short period, Idaho State College. Built between 1917 and 1919, the facility was torn down in 1951 in favor of a new building. (ISU.)

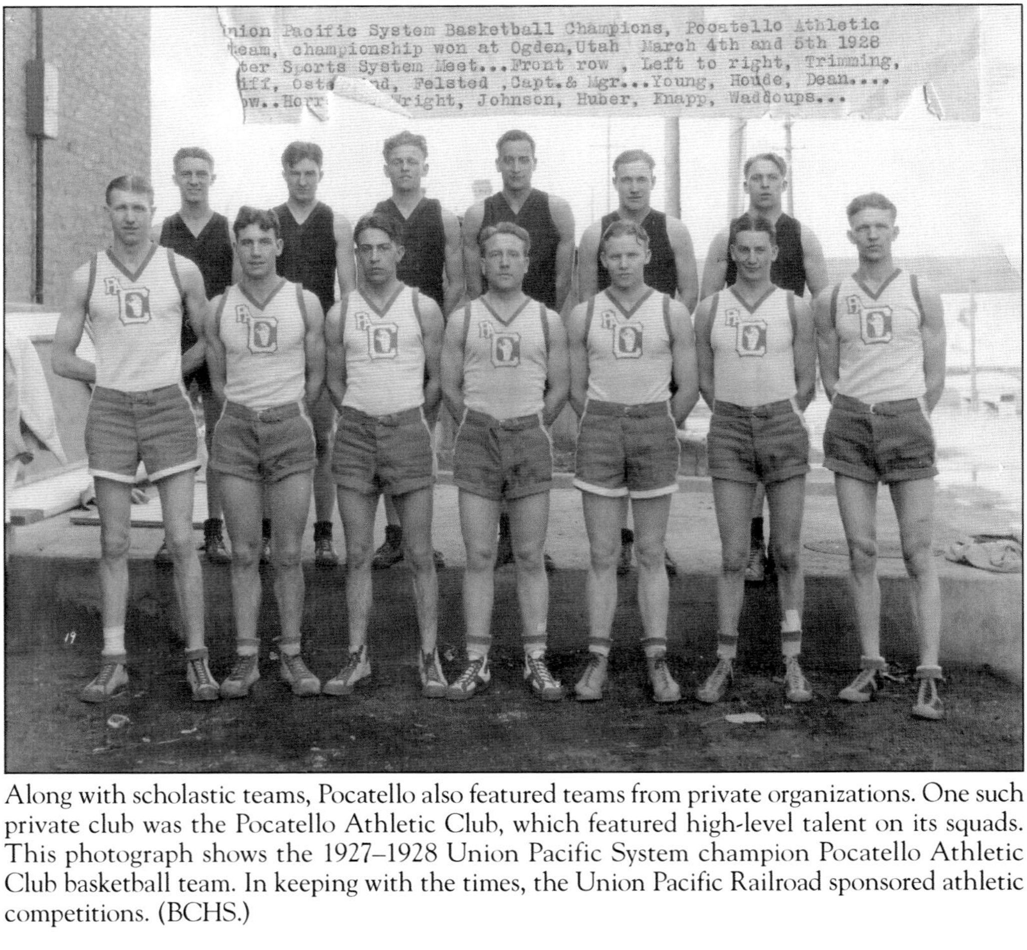

Along with scholastic teams, Pocatello also featured teams from private organizations. One such private club was the Pocatello Athletic Club, which featured high-level talent on its squads. This photograph shows the 1927–1928 Union Pacific System champion Pocatello Athletic Club basketball team. In keeping with the times, the Union Pacific Railroad sponsored athletic competitions. (BCHS.)

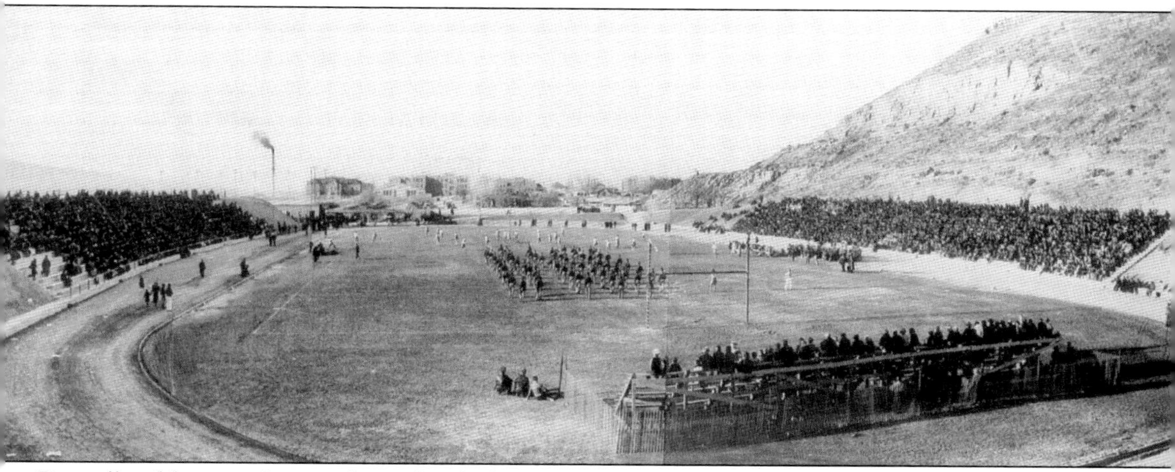

Pocatello athletics took a step forward with the opening of the Spud Bowl in 1937. This multipurpose facility was built by the WPA during the Great Depression and was used to host athletic competitions for decades until the opening of the Minidome in 1971. Today, the stadium, now known as Davis Field, is used for soccer and track and field competitions. (BCHS.)

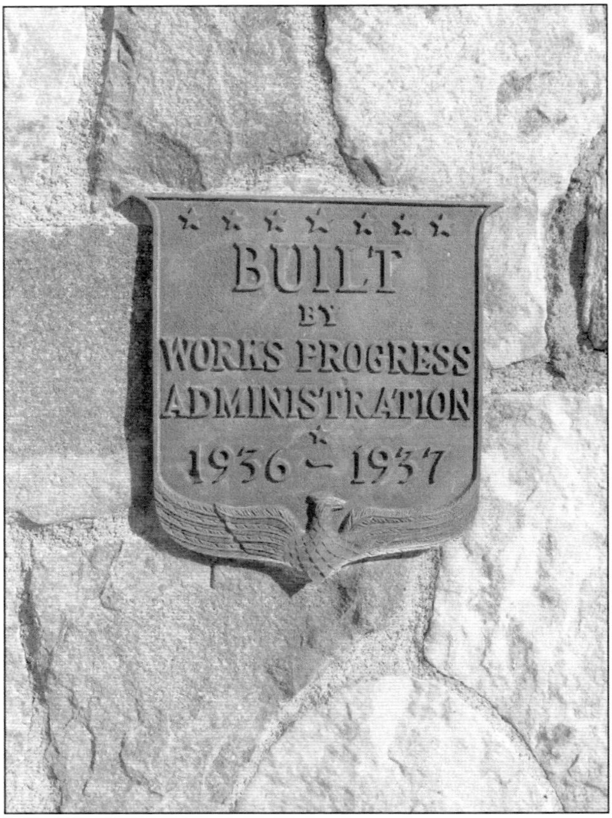

To this day, signs of the work done by the WPA are still visible at Davis Field. This plaque can be seen at the entrance to the field. (Walter Mallette.)

This photograph of the 1939–1940 Pocatello High School basketball team shows Lionel Bowser in the first row, wearing number 40. After his playing days, Bowser became the athletic director at Pocatello High School, before moving on to be the vice principal and then principal of Highland High School. (BCHS.)

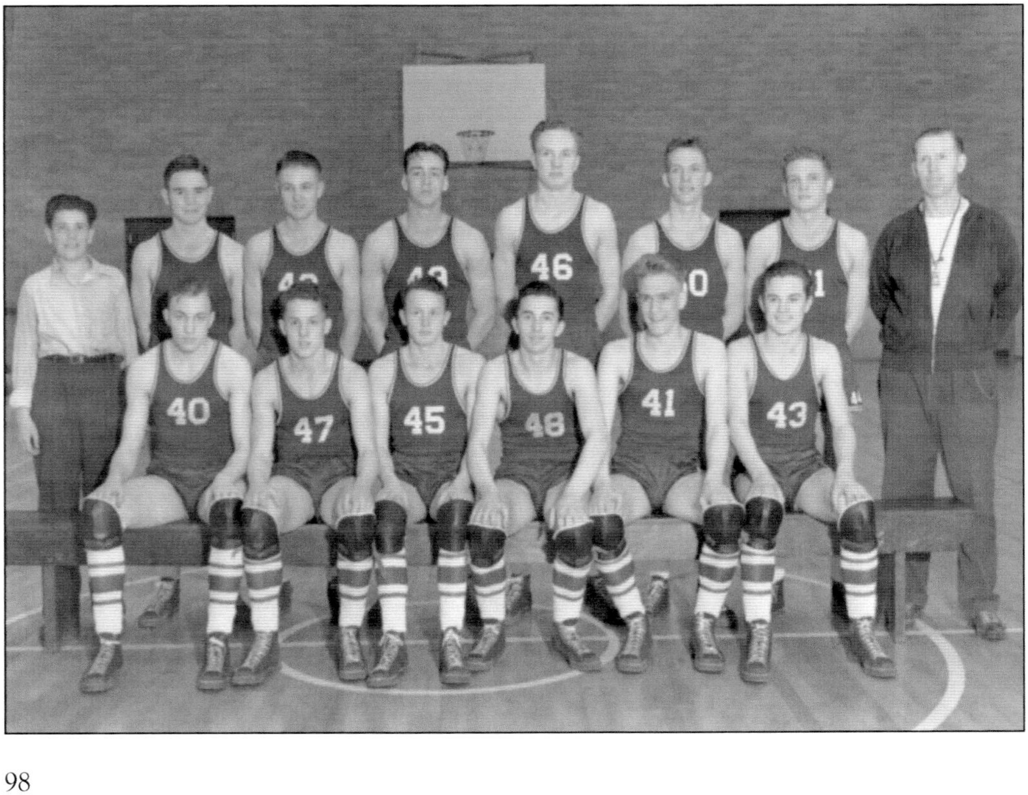

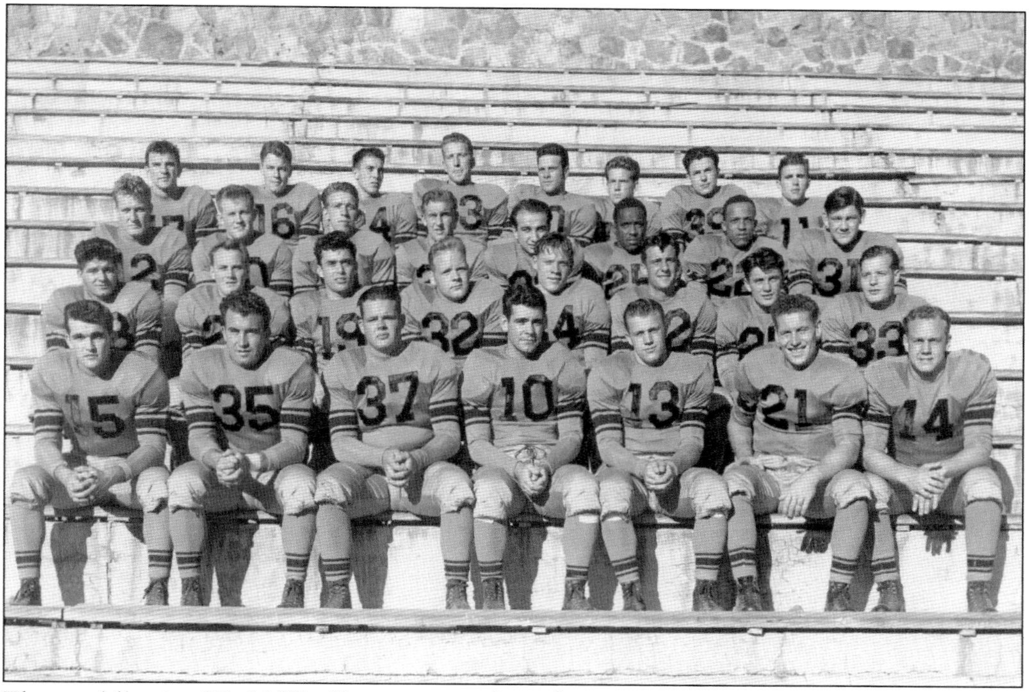

The era following World War II was among the richest in terms of sports history in Pocatello. The influx of veterans to Idaho State College can be seen in this photograph of the 1946 football squad. Jake LaRue (No. 22, third row, second from the right) would later be inducted into the Idaho State University Sports Hall of Fame for his achievements in football, baseball, and track from 1946 to 1949. (ISU.)

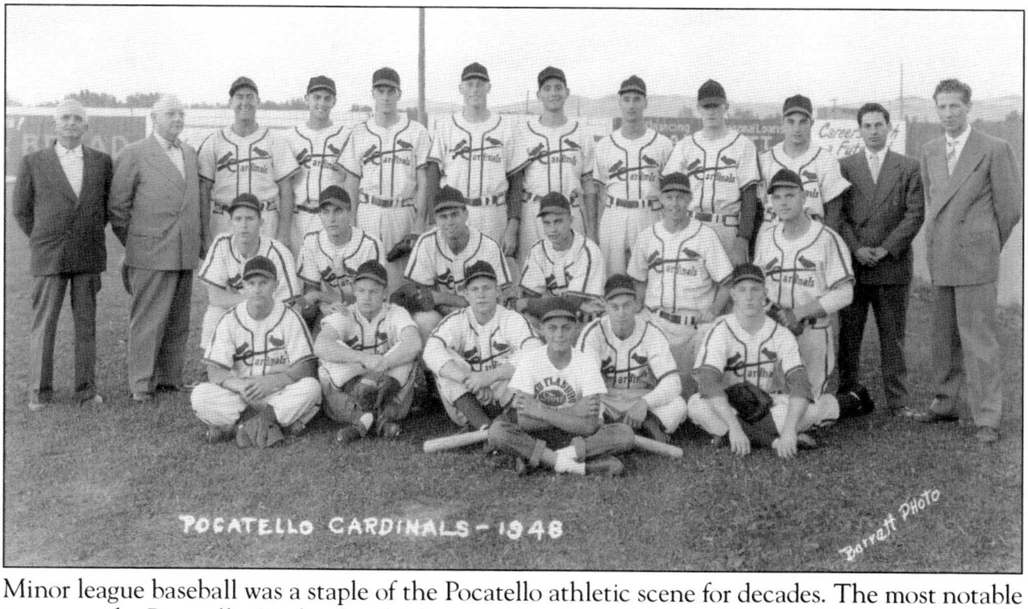

Minor league baseball was a staple of the Pocatello athletic scene for decades. The most notable team was the Pocatello Cardinals, which was a Class C (rookie league) team. This photograph of the 1948 Pocatello Cardinals squad shows batboy Kent Hadley, who would later become a standout player both at Pocatello High and the University of Southern California and later would play both in the major leagues and in Japan. (BCHS.)

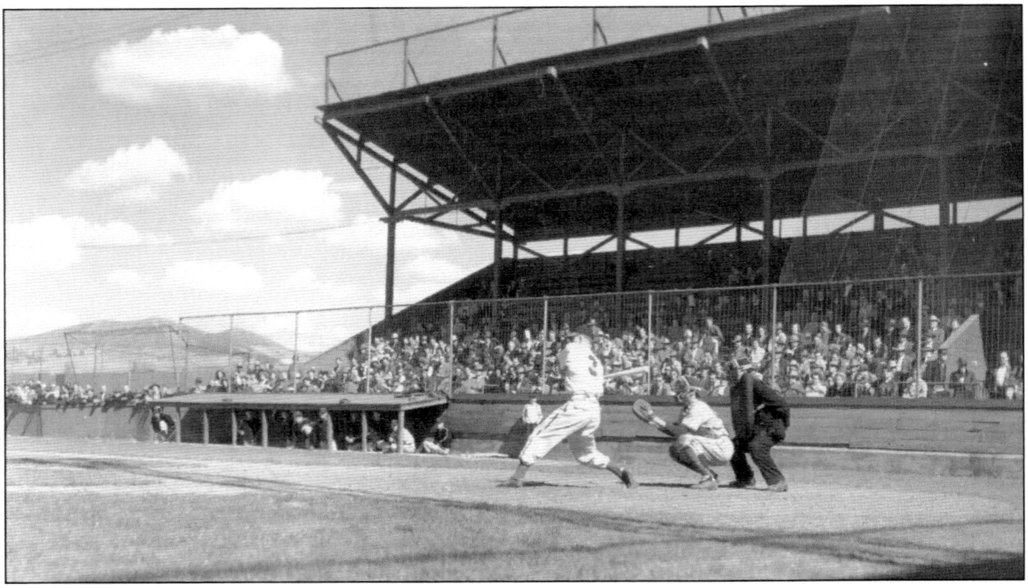

In this 1948 photograph of a Pocatello Cardinals game, the grandstands at Halliwell Park are visible. These grandstands would be a familiar sight to generations of baseball players and fans in Pocatello. (ISU.)

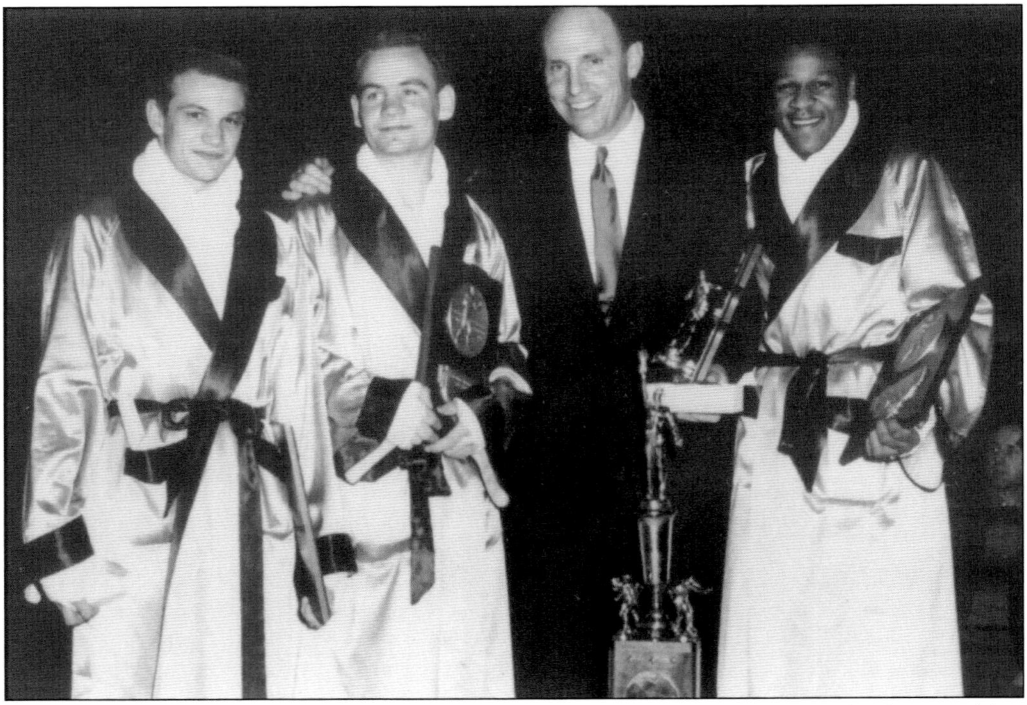

In the 1950s, the boxing program at Idaho State College, under the leadership of Milton "Dubby" Holt, featured championship-level squads, and many of the boxers on the teams went on to compete at the Olympics. In this 1953 photograph of the Idaho State College NCAA champions, Dubby Holt (second from right) is seen with (from left to right) Vic Kolle, Paddy Garver, and Ellsworth "Spider" Webb. "Spider" Webb went on to a professional boxing career as a middleweight fighter, where he won 34 bouts and lost 6. (ISU.)

Another famed boxer in the Idaho State College program was Ed Sanders, who played football as well during his time at the school. Sanders was drafted into the Navy in 1951, where he went on to join their boxing program and ultimately won a spot on the 1952 Olympic squad. Sanders won the gold medal that year, beating the later professional world champion Ingemar Johansson in the final. Sanders went on to a professional boxing career, where he died following injuries sustained in his ninth professional bout on December 14, 1954. (ISU.)

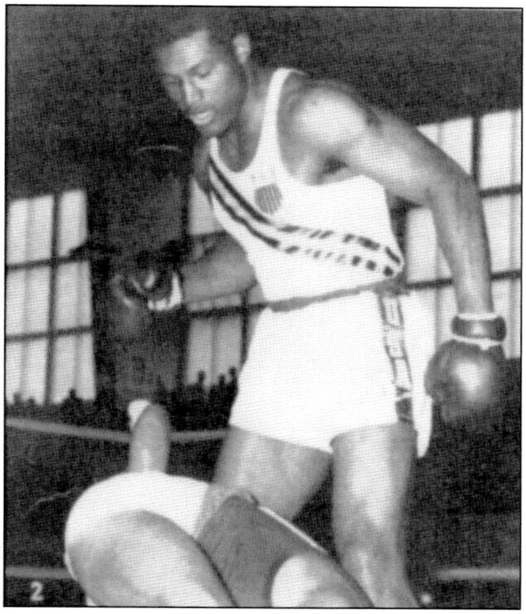

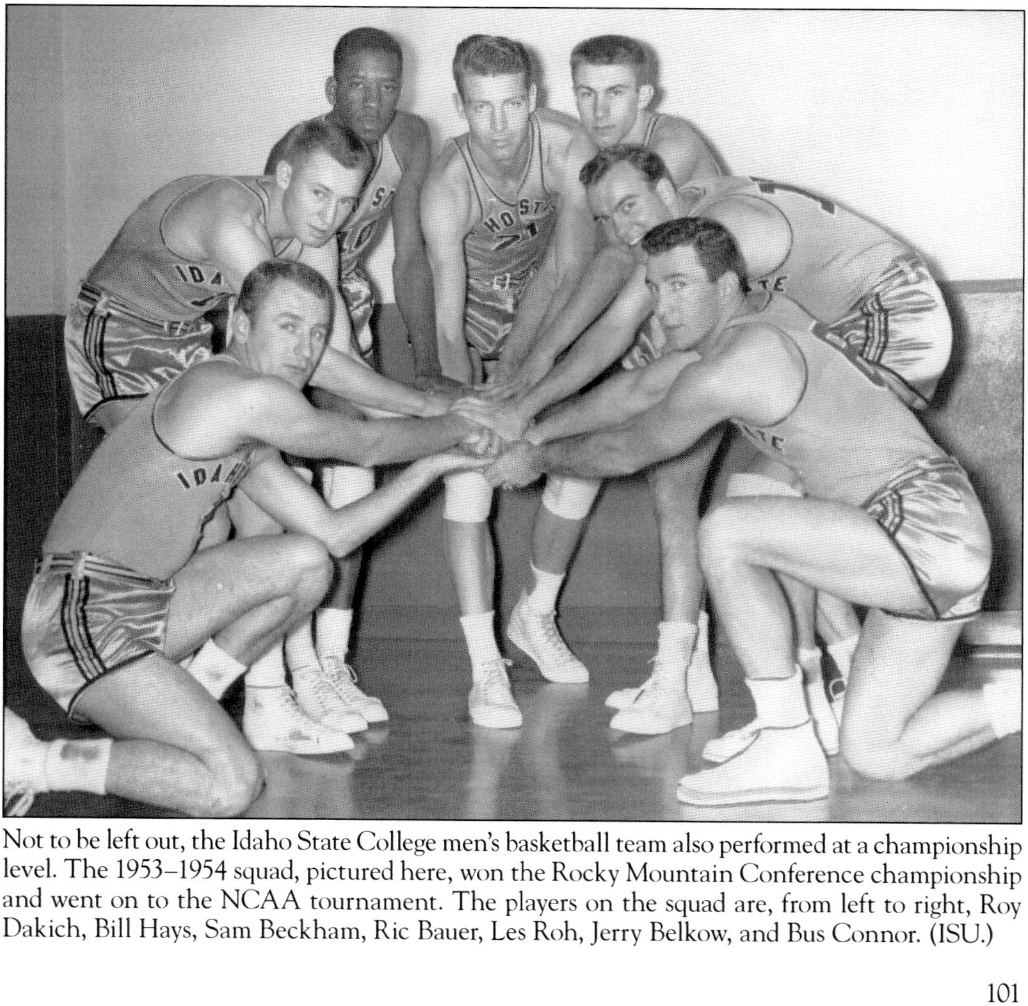

Not to be left out, the Idaho State College men's basketball team also performed at a championship level. The 1953–1954 squad, pictured here, won the Rocky Mountain Conference championship and went on to the NCAA tournament. The players on the squad are, from left to right, Roy Dakich, Bill Hays, Sam Beckham, Ric Bauer, Les Roh, Jerry Belkow, and Bus Connor. (ISU.)

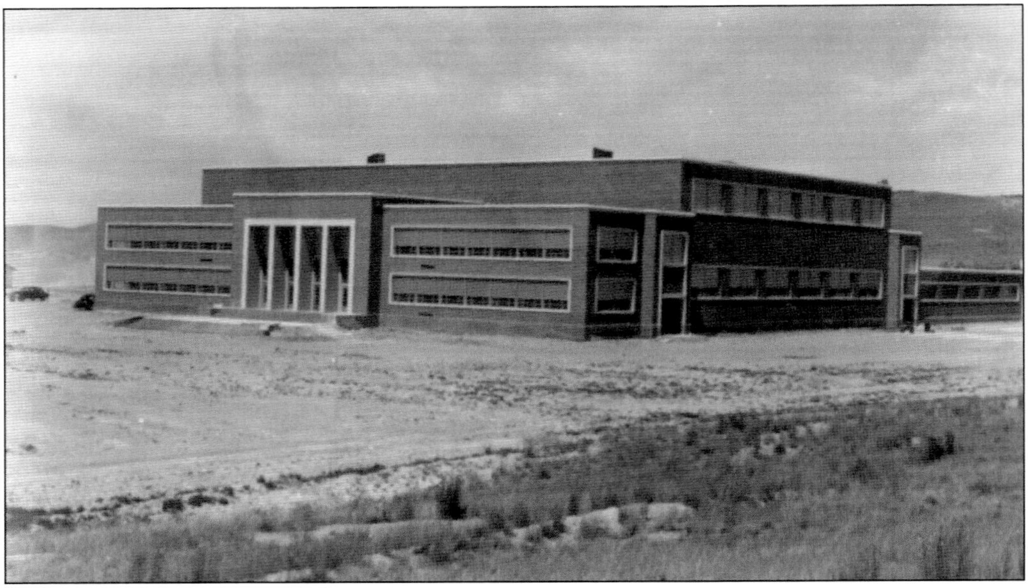

Pocatello athletics received a new home in 1951. Reed Gymnasium, meant as a replacement for the Reed Hall facility, featured a combination basketball and volleyball court, along with an indoor swimming pool and adjacent tennis courts. Reed Gym has hosted numerous basketball and volleyball competitions and was the home court for ISU basketball until the Minidome came into use in 1971. The facility is still in use to this day for various events. (ISU.)

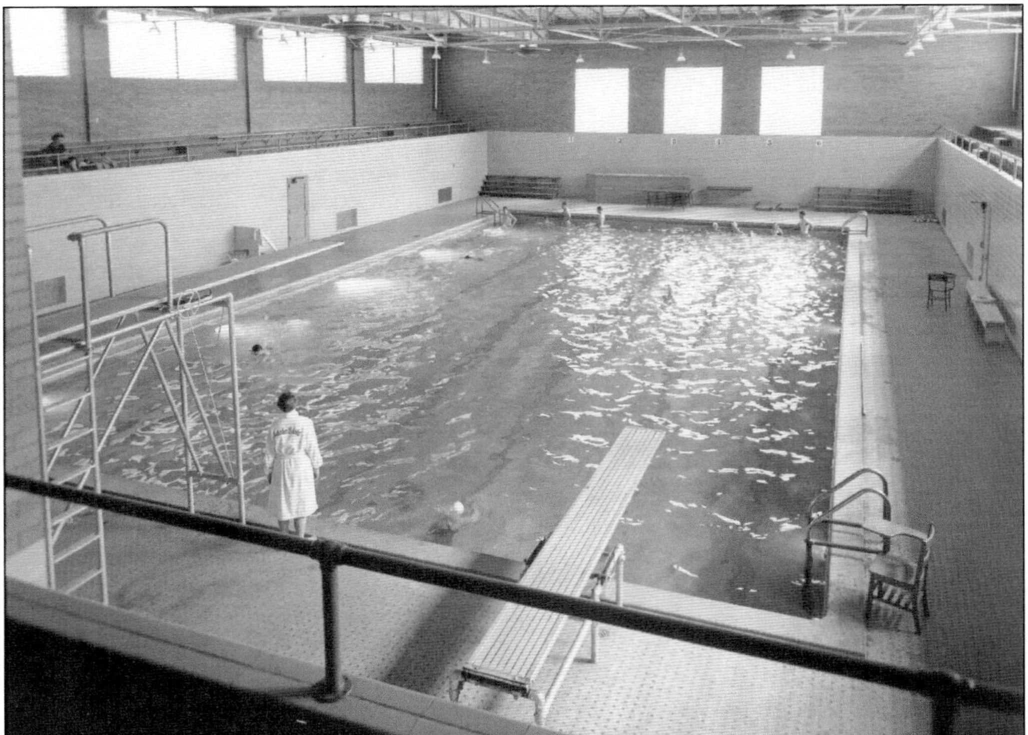

This photograph shows the indoor swimming pool at Reed Gym shortly after the facility opened in 1951. The pool is still in use today. (ISU.)

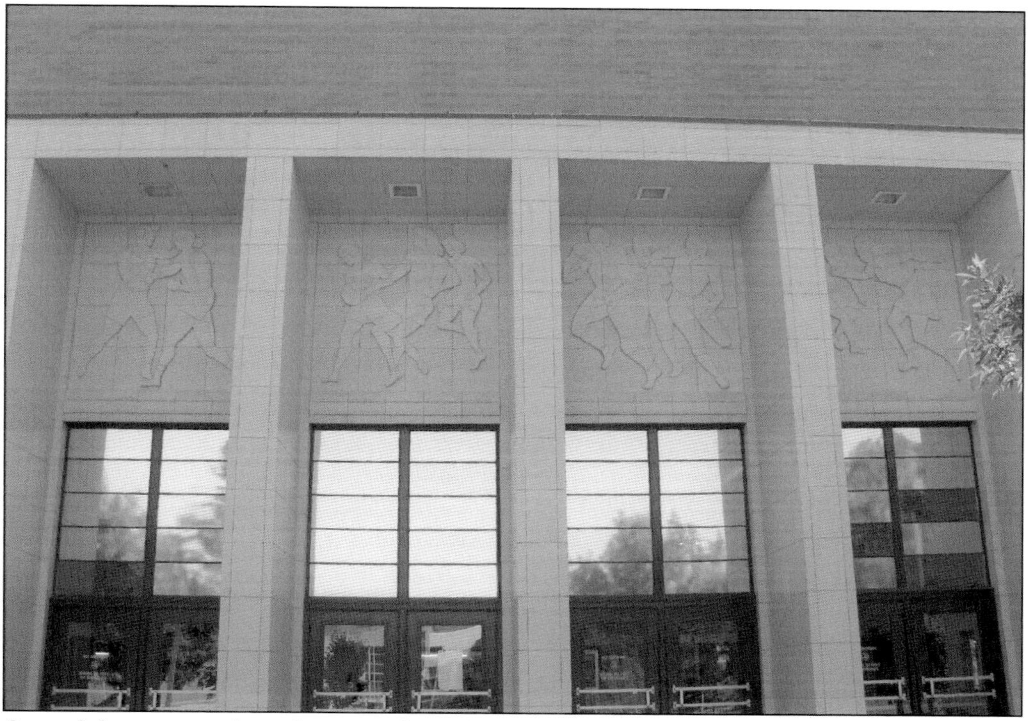

One of the most striking features of Reed Gym is this set of stone reliefs, placed above the entrance to the facility. These reliefs harken back to the days of the early history of Pocatello sports. (Walter Mallette.)

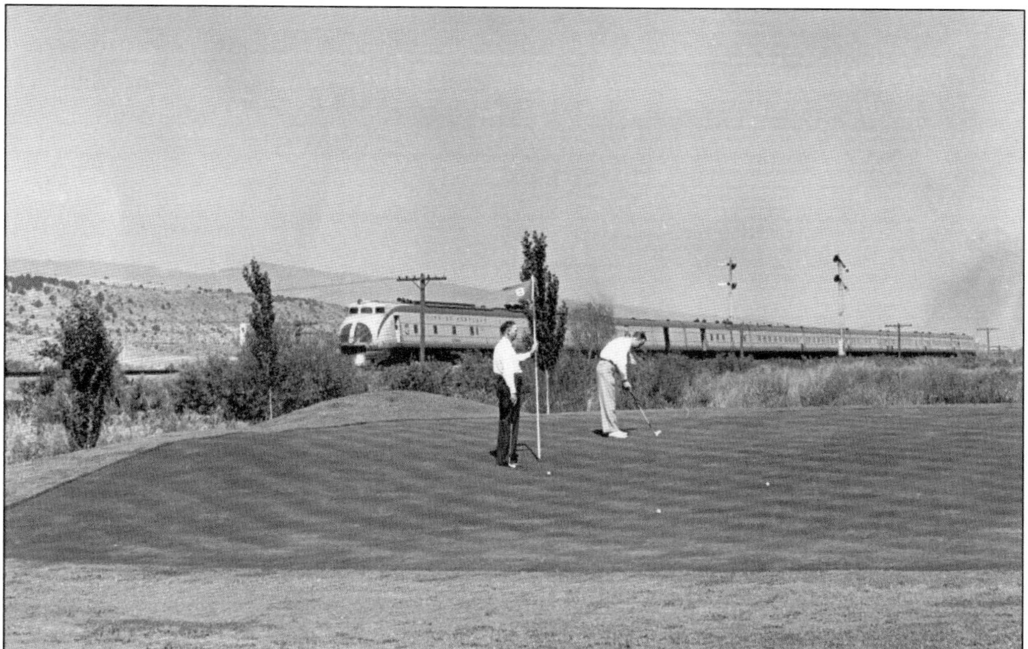

A number of sporting venues have been available to Pocatello residents. These two gentlemen are putting on the eighth green at Pocatello Municipal Golf Course in the 1950s, with the Union Pacific's *City of Portland* in the background. (ISU.)

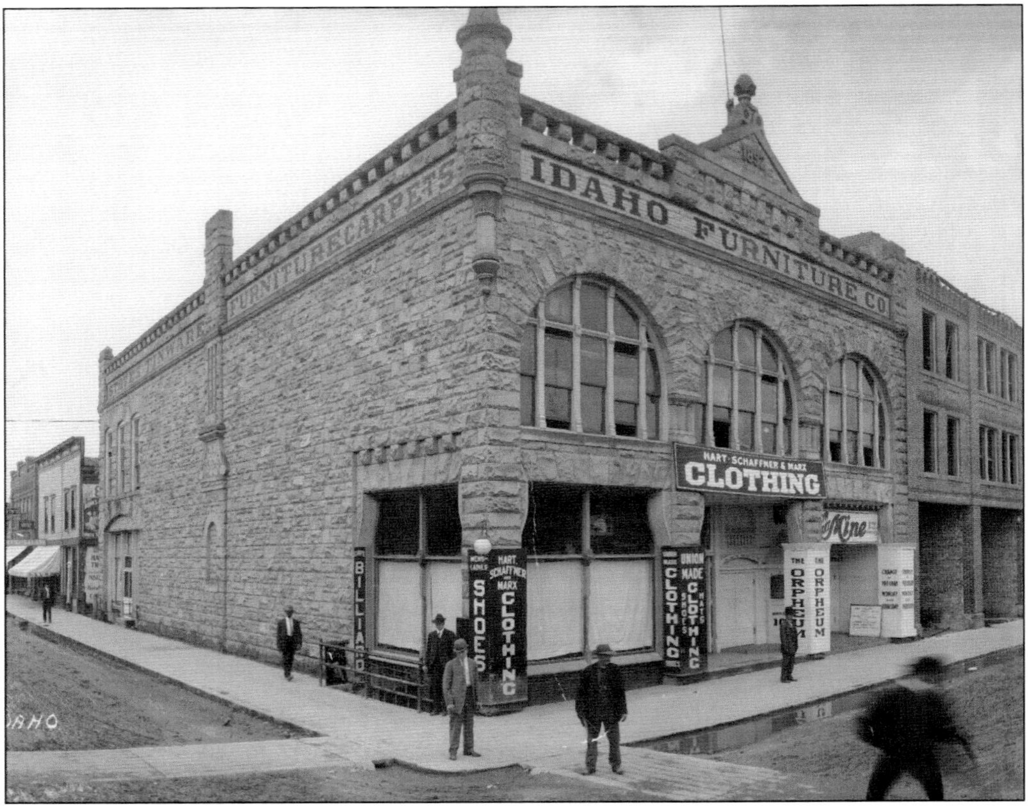

In the early days of Pocatello's history, entertainment venues were generally of the live theater variety. This 1909 photograph shows the Orpheum Theater, where *The Yellow Jacket Mine* was playing. (BCHS.)

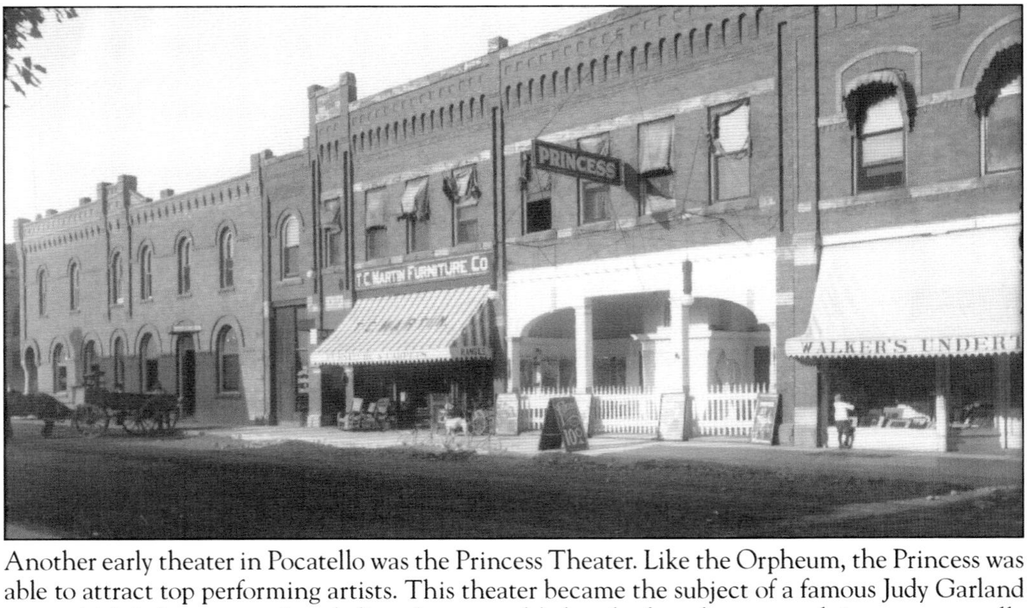

Another early theater in Pocatello was the Princess Theater. Like the Orpheum, the Princess was able to attract top performing artists. This theater became the subject of a famous Judy Garland song, which led many people to believe (erroneously) that the famed actress and singer was actually born in a trunk at the theater. (BCHS.)

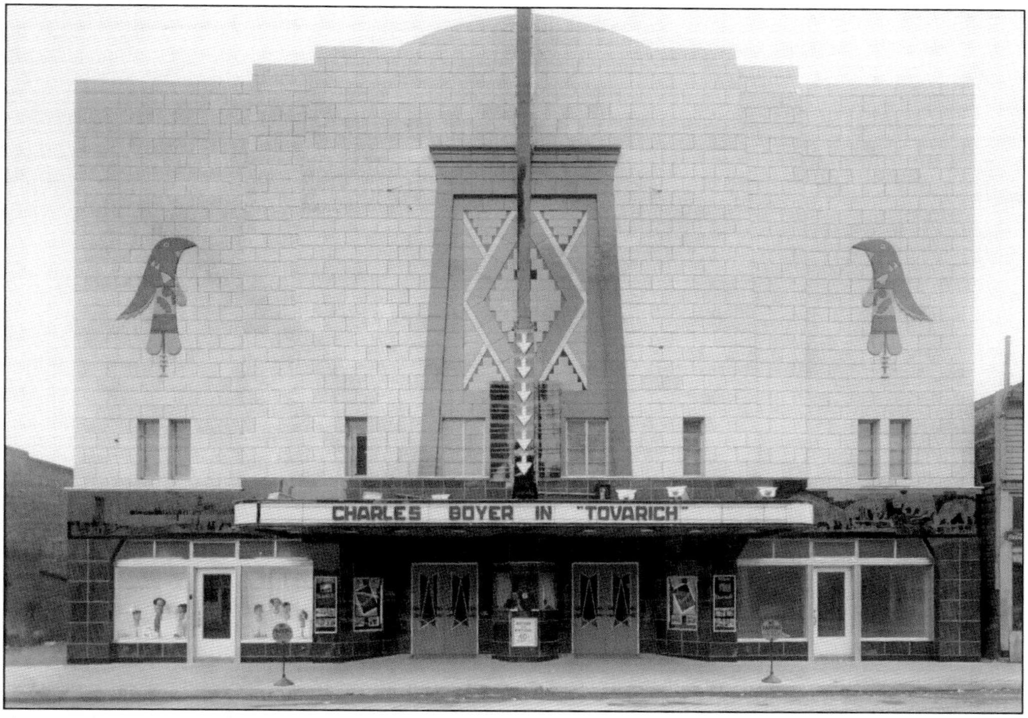

As was the case in other American towns and cities, movies were popular in Pocatello. The most spectacular cinema was The Chief, which opened on January 5, 1938. This movie theater featured a lavish interior with murals inspired by Pocatello history. (BCHS.)

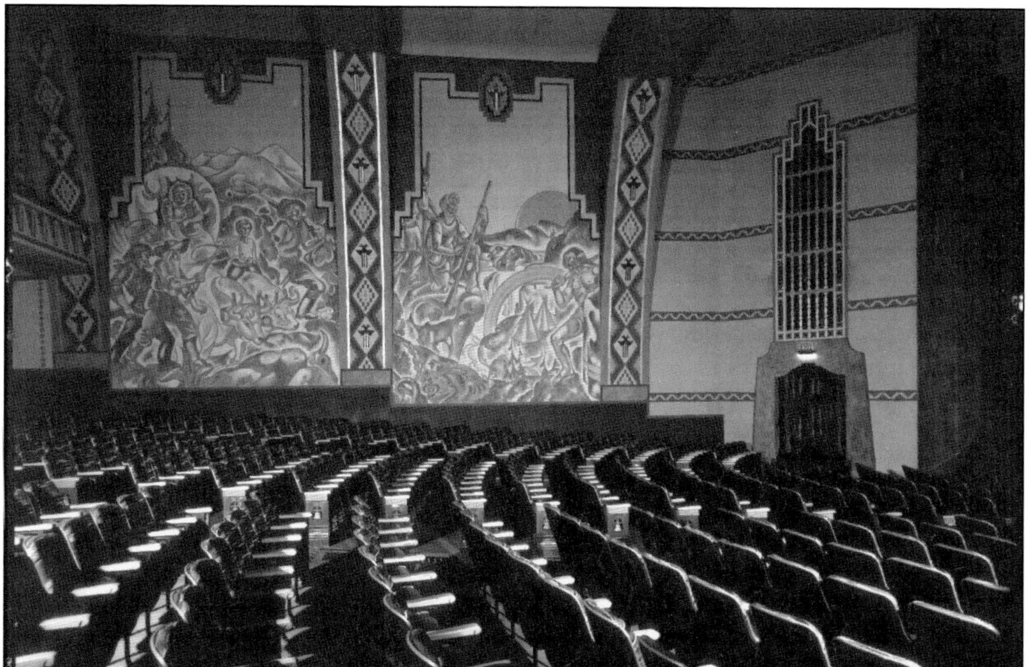

The interior of the Chief Theater is pictured here. Murals depict the immigration of non-native settlers to the region. (BCHS.)

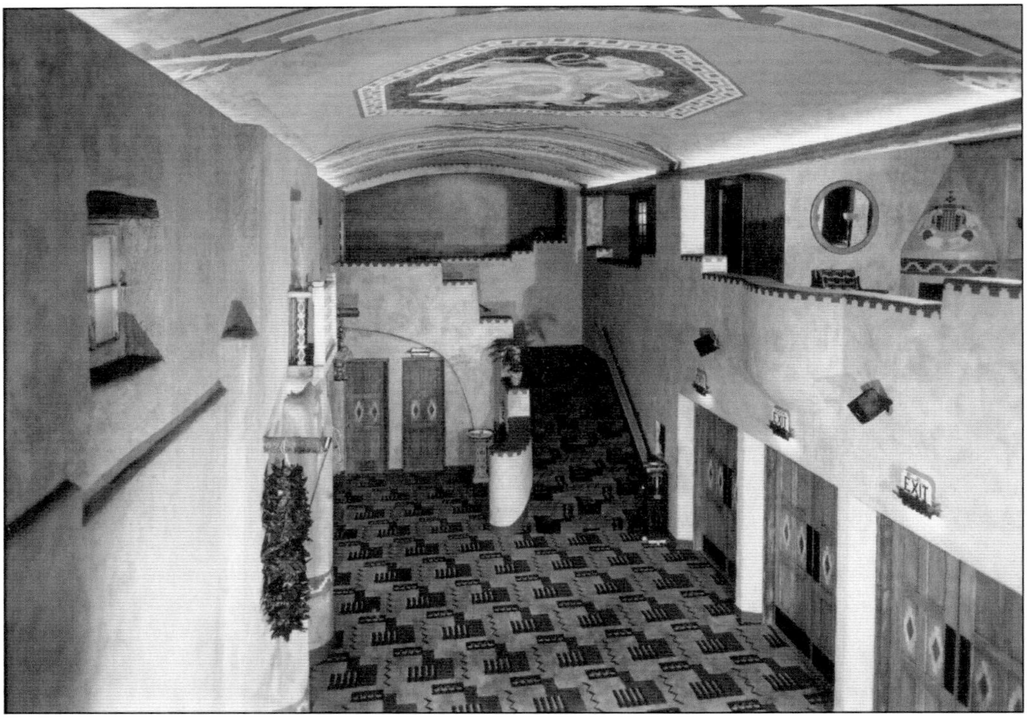

This photograph shows lavish decoration in the foyer of the Chief Theater. Sadly for Pocatello, the Chief burned down on March 20, 1993, and was subsequently demolished. (BCHS.)

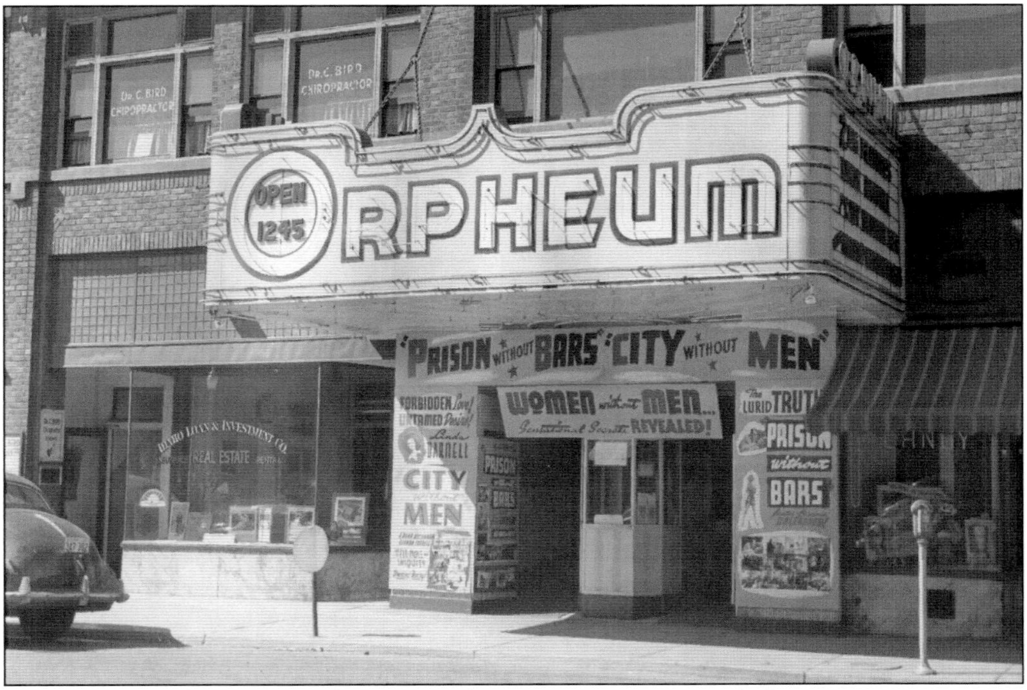

The Orpheum Theater, located at 147 South Main Street, is pictured after its conversion into a cinema. This photograph, possibly taken about 1943, shows an advertisement for *City Without Men*, starring Linda Darnell. (BCHS.)

Seven

Aiding the National Defense

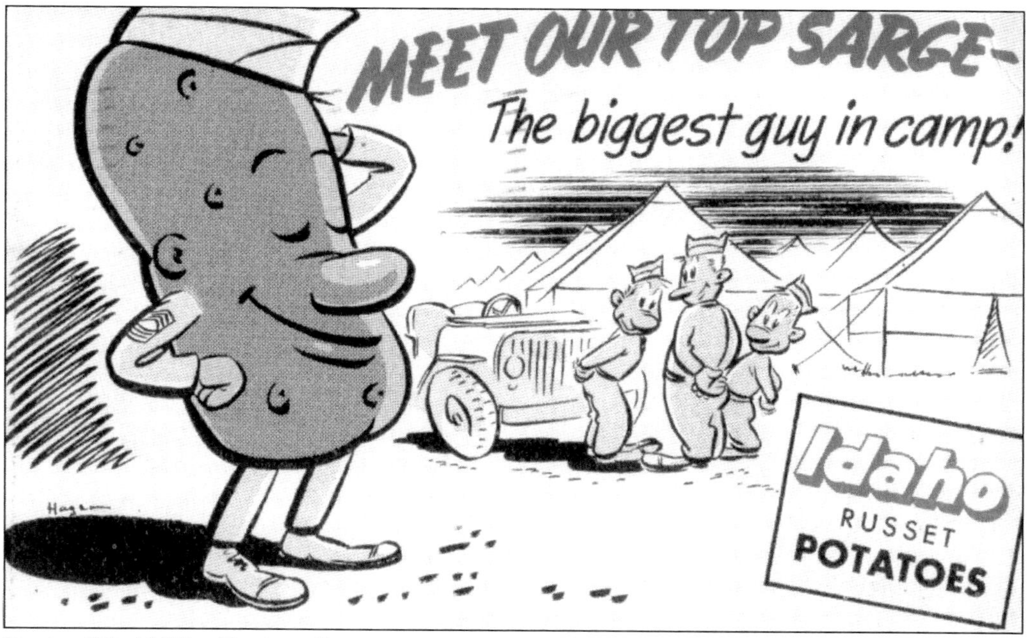

During World War II, virtually every consumer product was "enlisted" in the war effort. This postcard, distributed to members of the armed services at the Pocatello USO station, shows that Idaho potatoes were seen as a vital commodity in the war effort. This particular postcard was sent to a Mrs. M. Bennett in Ozone Park, New York, from her husband, Corporal John Bennett, who was en route to his unit in Oregon. In his note to his wife, Bennett commented on the "swell USO here in the station." (BCHS.)

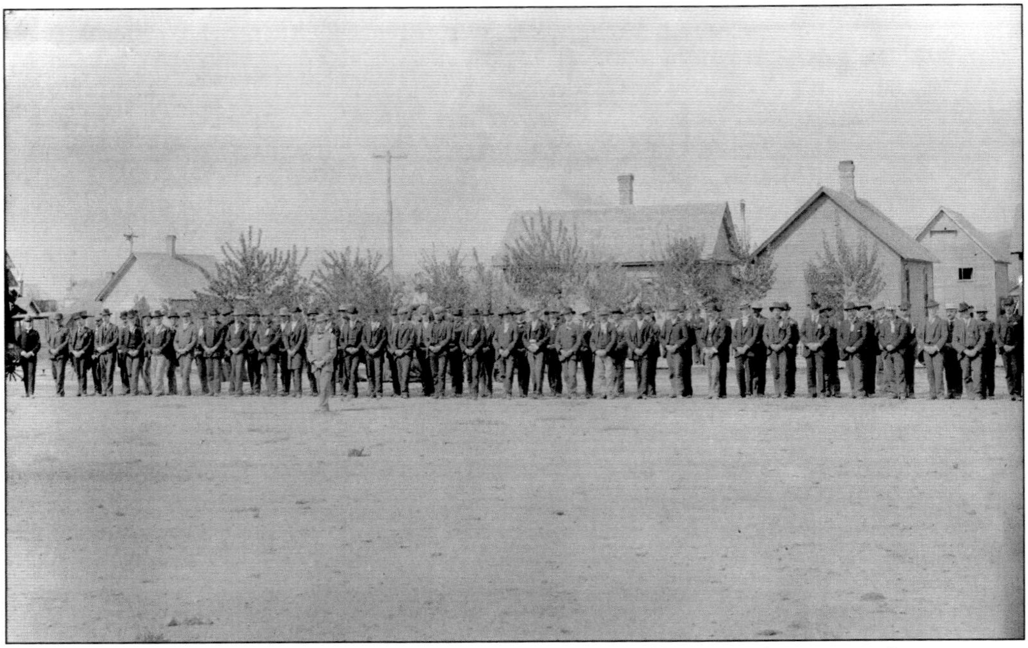

In its war with Spain, the United States was obligated to call upon volunteers to form units to fight the Spanish army, both in Cuba and the Philippines. In keeping with the national trend, Pocatello also provided volunteers to the armed forces. Here, the assembled volunteers are gathered on South Harrison Avenue, presumably to be inducted into the service of the First Idaho Volunteers. (BCHS.)

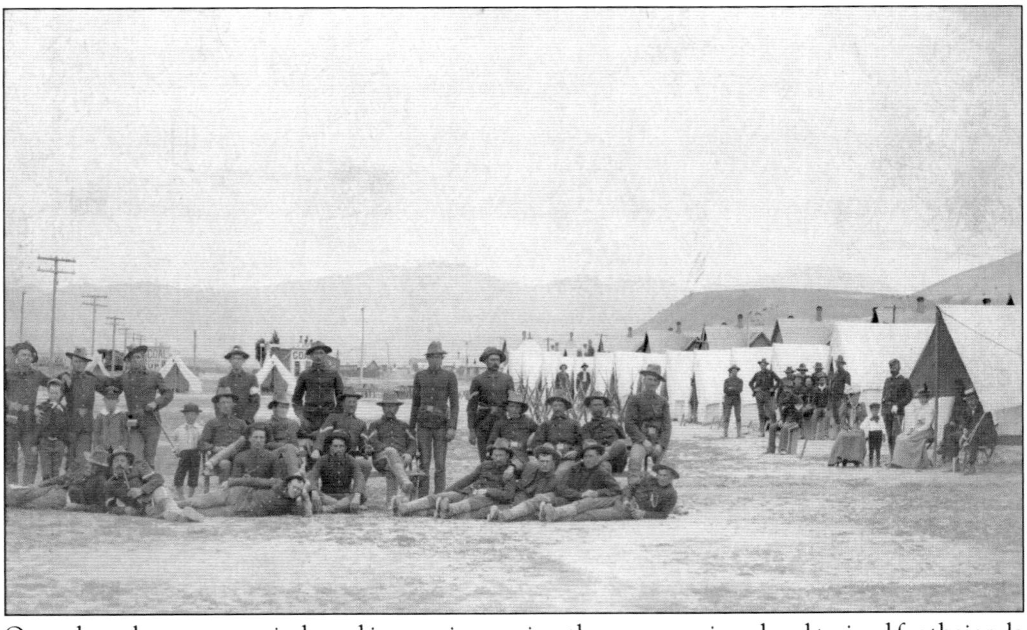

Once the volunteers were inducted into active service, they were equipped and trained for their role as combat infantry. In this Benedicte Wrensted photograph taken in the area of North Harrison Avenue near the railroad tracks, the uniformed volunteers are seen at their training site. Note the women and children; they may be family members of the volunteer soldiers. (BCHS.)

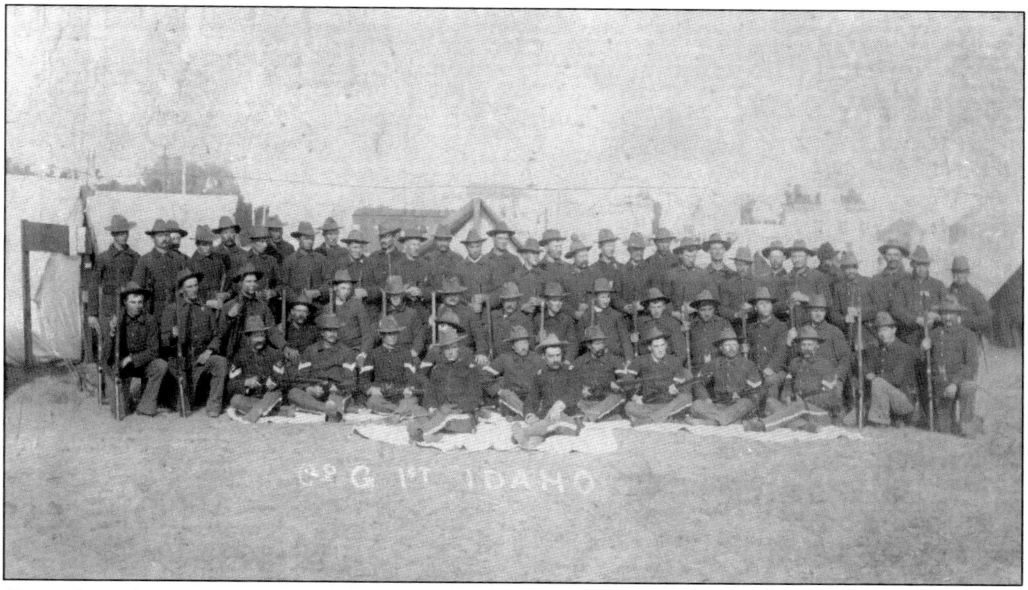

Once the volunteers were trained and equipped, individual units were assembled for embarkation to conflict areas. This photograph shows the volunteers of Company G, 1st Idaho Volunteers, presumably posing for a unit photograph prior to leaving for the Philippines. The contrast with the men gathered to volunteer in a previous photograph is striking. (BCHS.)

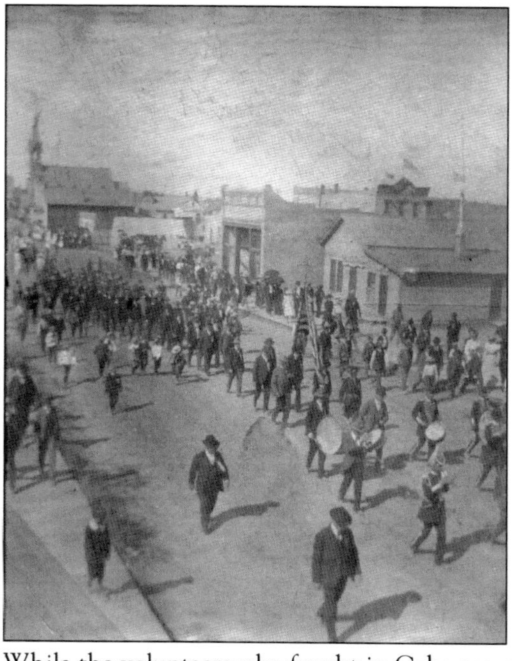

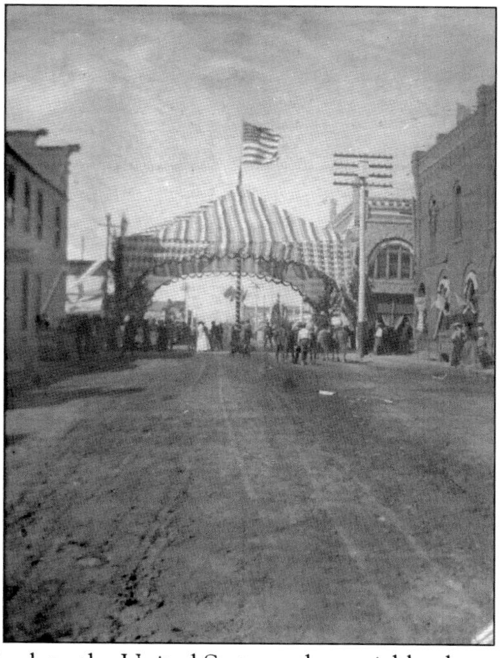

While the volunteers who fought in Cuba came back to the United States rather quickly, those who fought in the Philippines came back later due to the insurgency by Philippine independence movements that broke out shortly after the Spanish surrender in 1898. Due to this insurgency, US forces were obligated to stay in the Philippines until the following century. Company G of the 1st Idaho Volunteers was able to return to Pocatello only in September 1900. These photographs, taken by Benedicte Wrensted, show the volunteers returning to Pocatello and the tribute the city offered to the men who had served in combat. (BCHS.)

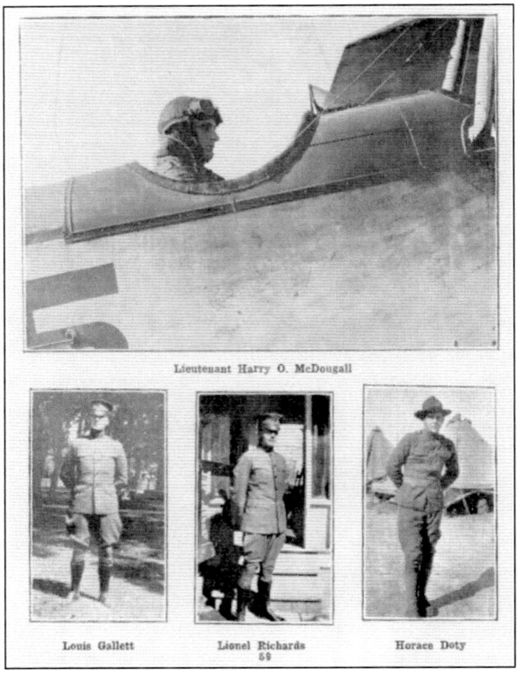

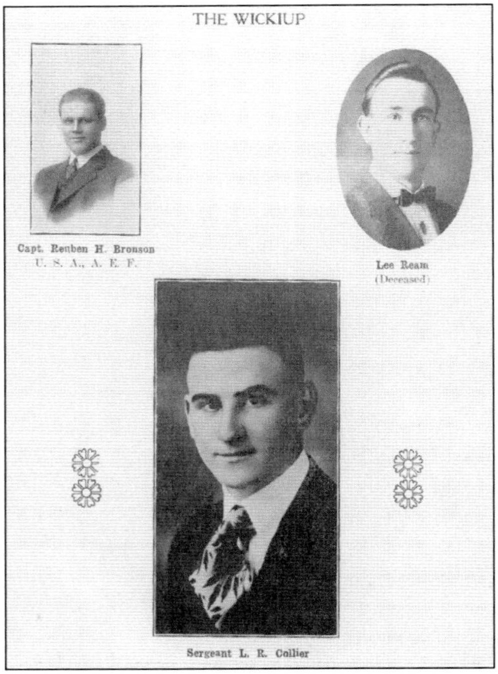

In World War I, the national effort concerned all segments of American society. Pocatello was no exception in this respect, as these pages from *The Wickiup*, the Idaho Technical Institute's yearbook, show in stark detail. Lee Ream, noted as deceased here, was one of five members of the Idaho Technical Institute who died in the service of their country. (ISU.)

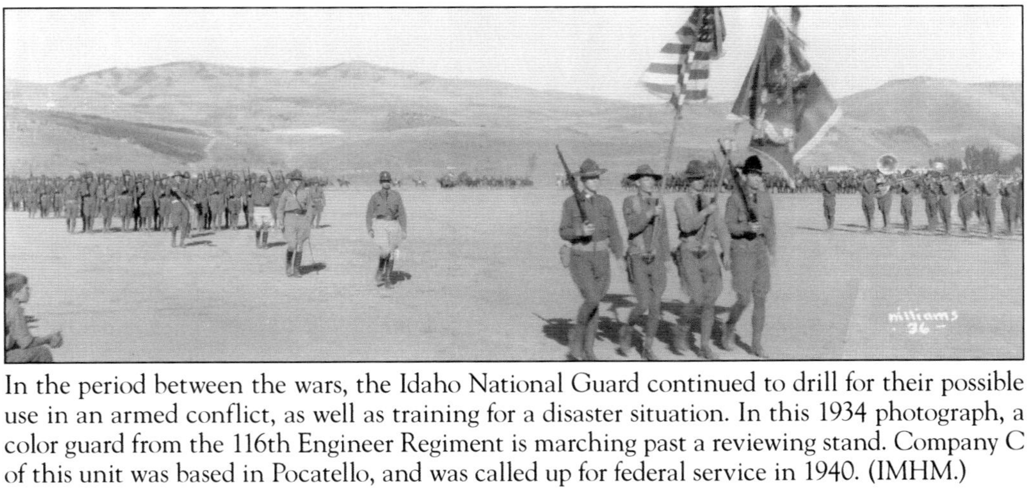

In the period between the wars, the Idaho National Guard continued to drill for their possible use in an armed conflict, as well as training for a disaster situation. In this 1934 photograph, a color guard from the 116th Engineer Regiment is marching past a reviewing stand. Company C of this unit was based in Pocatello, and was called up for federal service in 1940. (IMHM.)

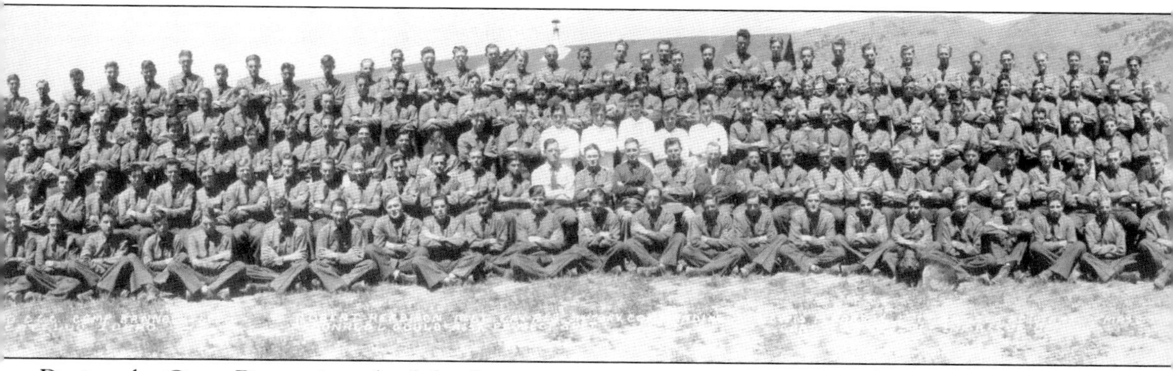

During the Great Depression, the federal government set up programs to employ young men in civic improvement projects across the country. One such program was the Civilian Conservation Corps, which was tasked with undertaking projects to repair damage to areas subject to erosion. This group photograph shows the members of the Camp Bannock CCC unit, based just outside of Pocatello. Pictured in 1939, this CCC camp was commanded by Army 1st Lt. Robert Herbison. CCC units were under the command of the Army, and Army officers were in charge of the camps. This unit was responsible for, among other things, the terracing of Red Hill just above the University of Idaho, Southern Branch campus. (BCHS.)

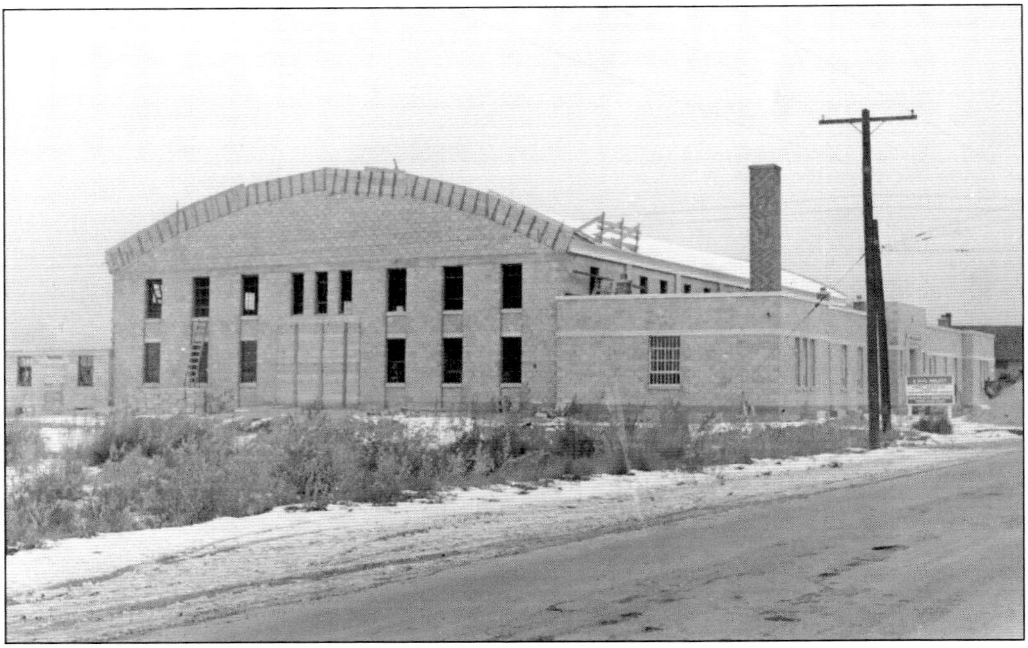

As with many other communities in the United States, the National Guard armory was a featured site in Pocatello. The new armory, sited along South Second Avenue, was built in the fall and winter of 1940–1941. The armory was turned over to Idaho State University in 1969 and now serves as the Diesel Mechanics Training Facility for the school. (BCHS.)

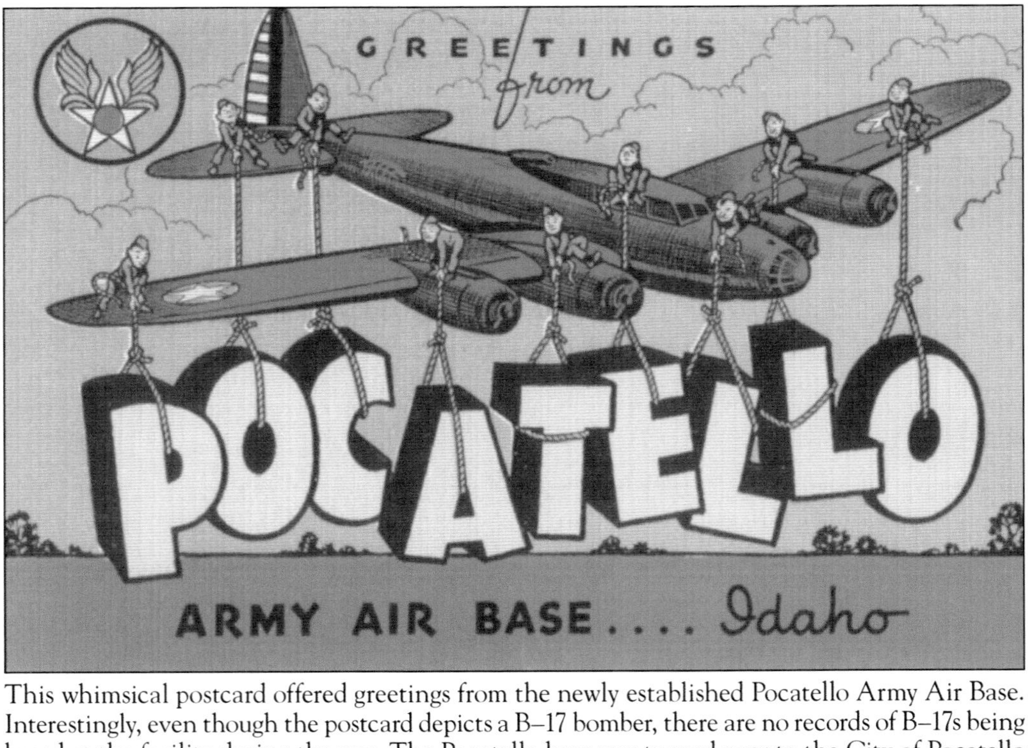

This whimsical postcard offered greetings from the newly established Pocatello Army Air Base. Interestingly, even though the postcard depicts a B–17 bomber, there are no records of B–17s being based at the facility during the war. The Pocatello base was turned over to the City of Pocatello in 1949, and continues to serve the community as Pocatello Municipal Airport. (IMHM.)

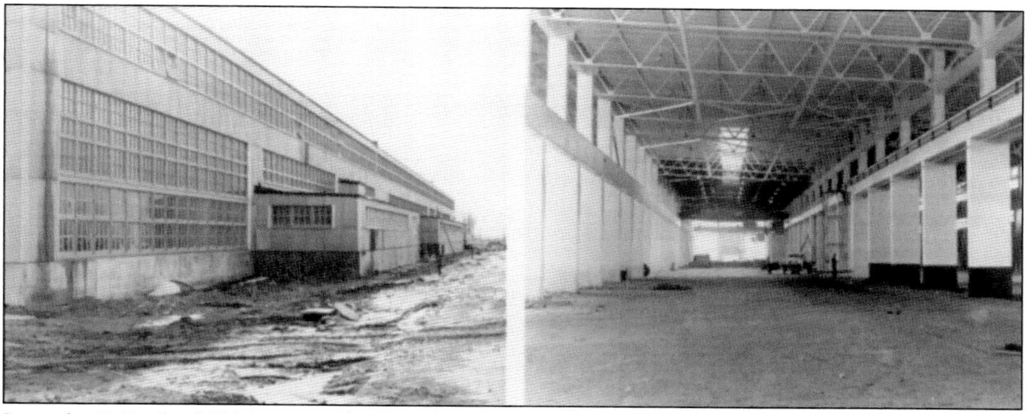

In early 1942, the US Navy sought sites for use as repair facilities for their weapons systems. One such site was identified at the Bannock County fairgrounds in Pocatello, close to what is now Yellowstone Avenue and Quinn Road. The Navy announced the establishment of the facility on March 19, 1942. During the fall and winter of 1942–1943, construction took place at the Bannock County fairgrounds for the new Naval Ordnance Plant (NOP). The scale of the work involved in building the facility is shown in this set of photographs, apparently for use in an official report. (BCHS.)

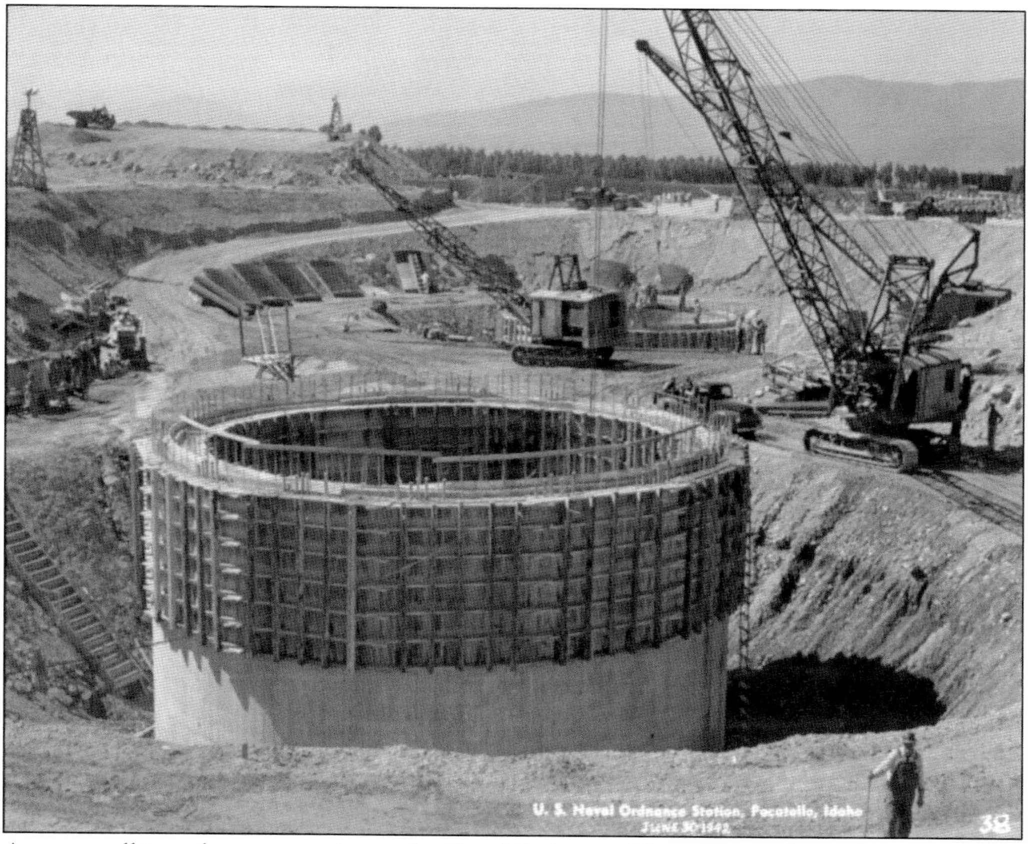

A water well is under construction at the Naval Ordnance Plant. This well was designed to cool down gun barrels that had been heated in reconditioning work. (BCHS.)

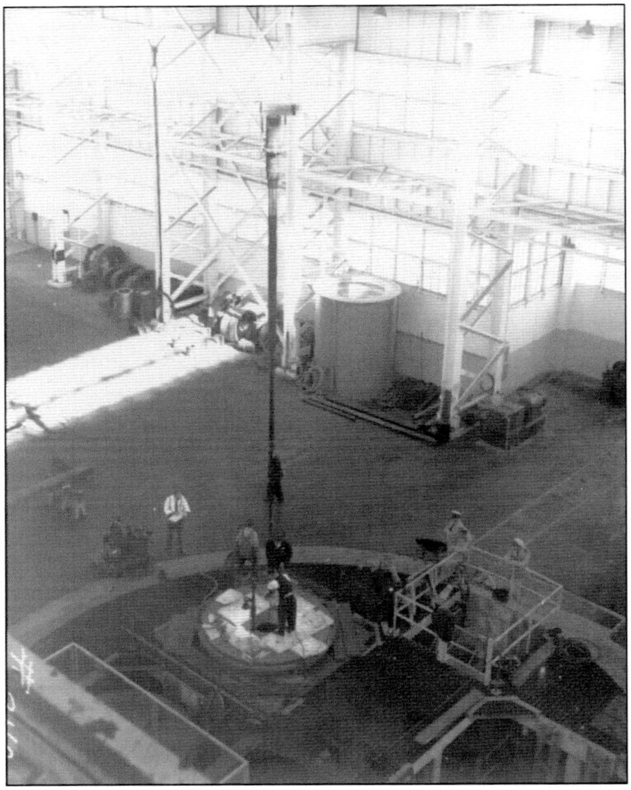

Once the NOP was completed on August 2, 1943, naval guns were sent to the facility to be refurbished for reuse in the war effort. This photograph shows a gun being lowered into the cooling well, where the barrel and a newly manufactured gun liner were melded together. Note the two dogs close to the water tank; they may be with their naval officer masters. (ISU.)

This photograph shows the first naval cannon that was refurbished by the new facility. Its size indicates that it was a 16-inch battleship cannon. The facility was initially decommissioned after World War II, but was reactivated during the Korean War and continued in operation until its final decommissioning on July 1, 1961. (ISU.)

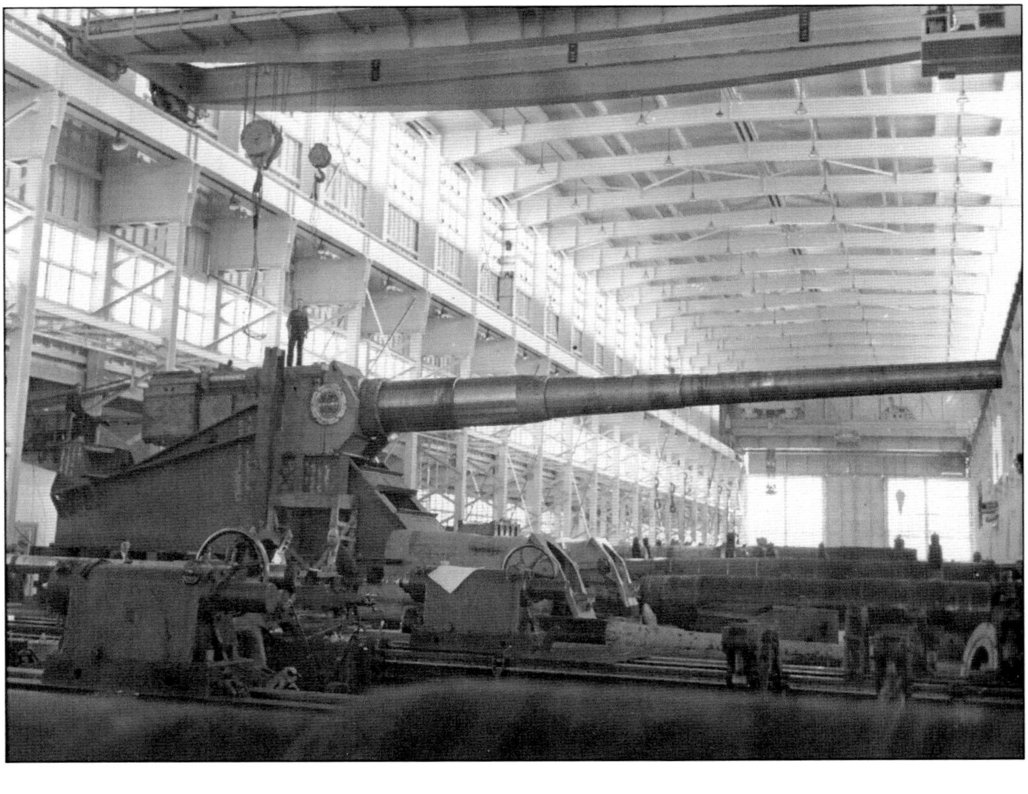

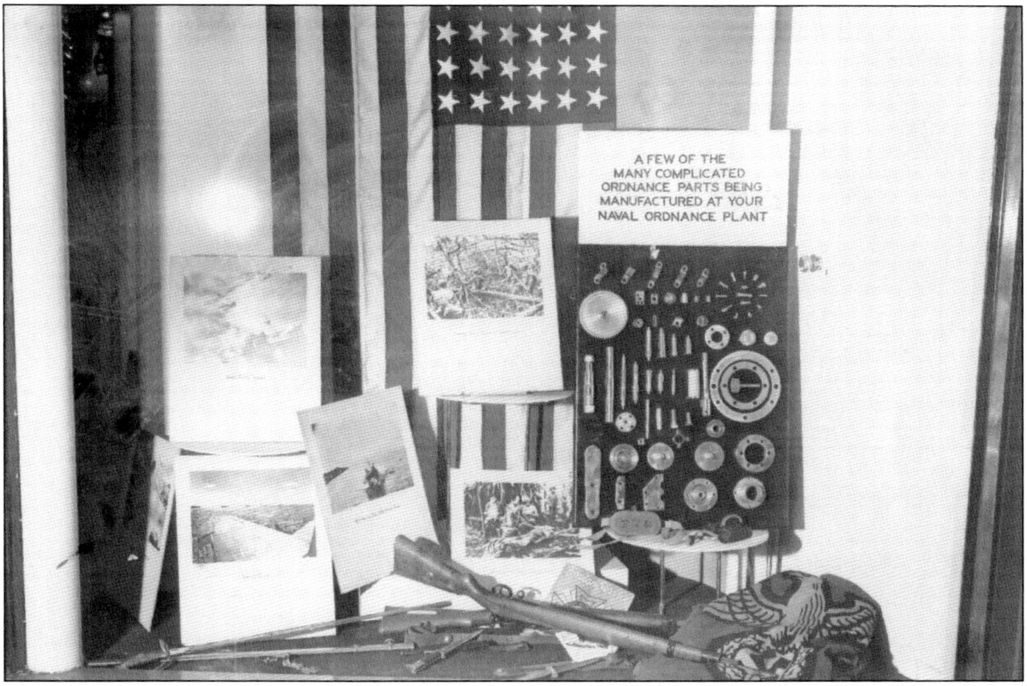

During the war, a continuing effort was made to inform the public about the work being done to supply the armed forces with necessary equipment. This display, apparently set up by the Pocatello Chamber of Commerce, shows a small but highly representative sample of the work that was done at the NOP. (ISU.)

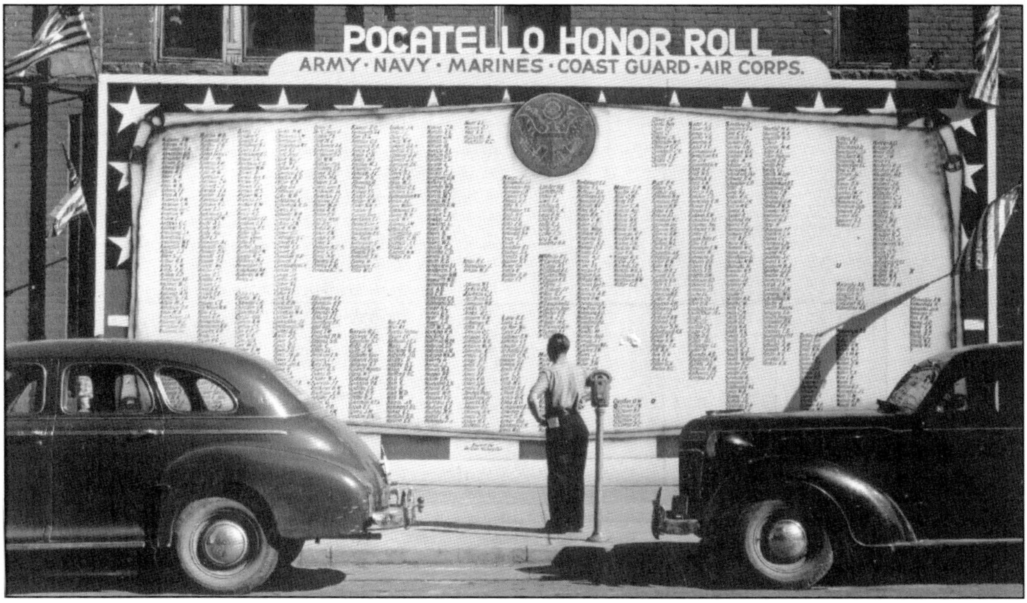

The period following the Japanese attack on Pearl Harbor saw a mobilization of men and material at a level never seen before in a conflict fought by the United States. Pocatello proved no exception to this trend, and many Pocatellans volunteered for service in the armed forces. This Honor Roll, at an unknown location in Pocatello, is presumably from early in the war, since many who would later serve are not listed here. (BCHS.)

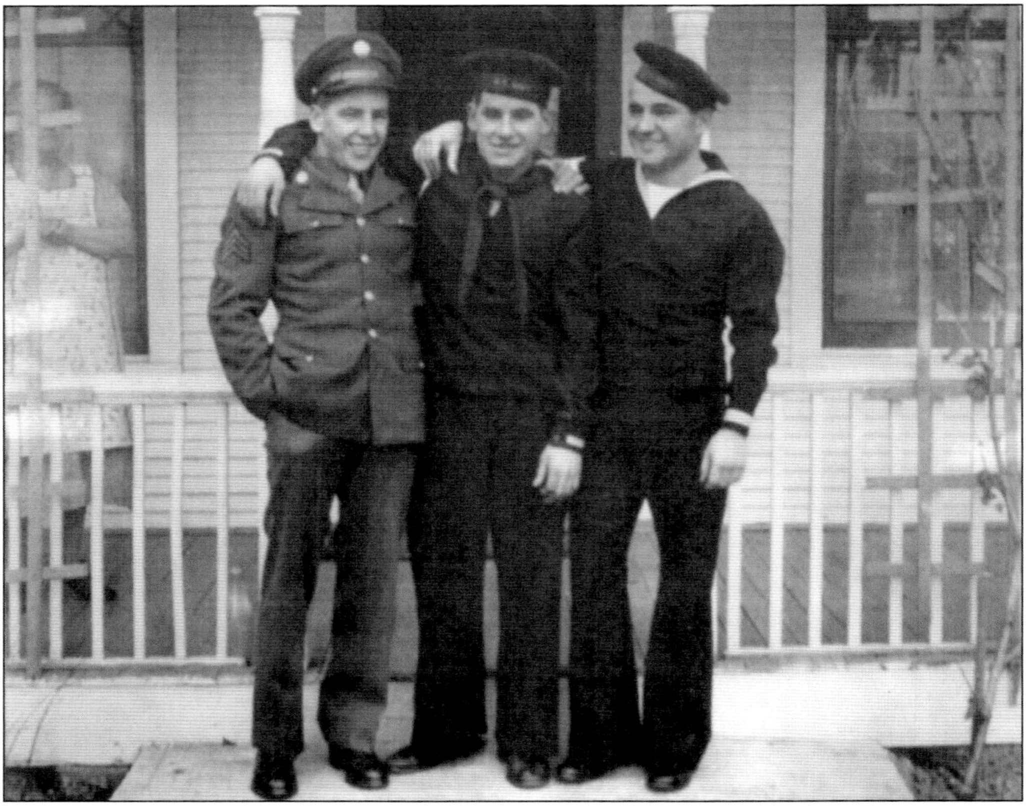

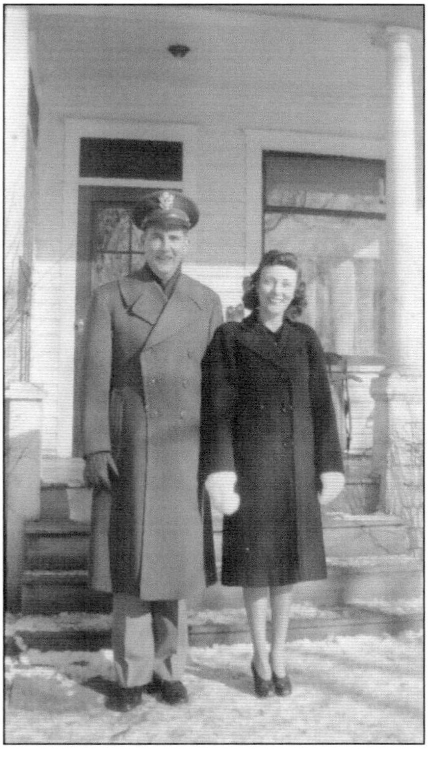

Many Pocatello residents served their country in uniform during World War II. As was the case across the United States, many families in Pocatello had more than one member in uniform at this time. Such was the case with the Peyron family: from left to right, Bob, Vern, and Maurie Peyron all served their country. (BCHS.)

While many Pocatello residents went overseas to serve their country, other US military personnel came to Pocatello to serve in the military facilities there. Such was the case with this anonymous US Army first lieutenant who was stationed at Pocatello Army Air Base. He is seen with his wife outside the Watlington House, where they rented a bedroom during their time in Pocatello. (BCHS.)

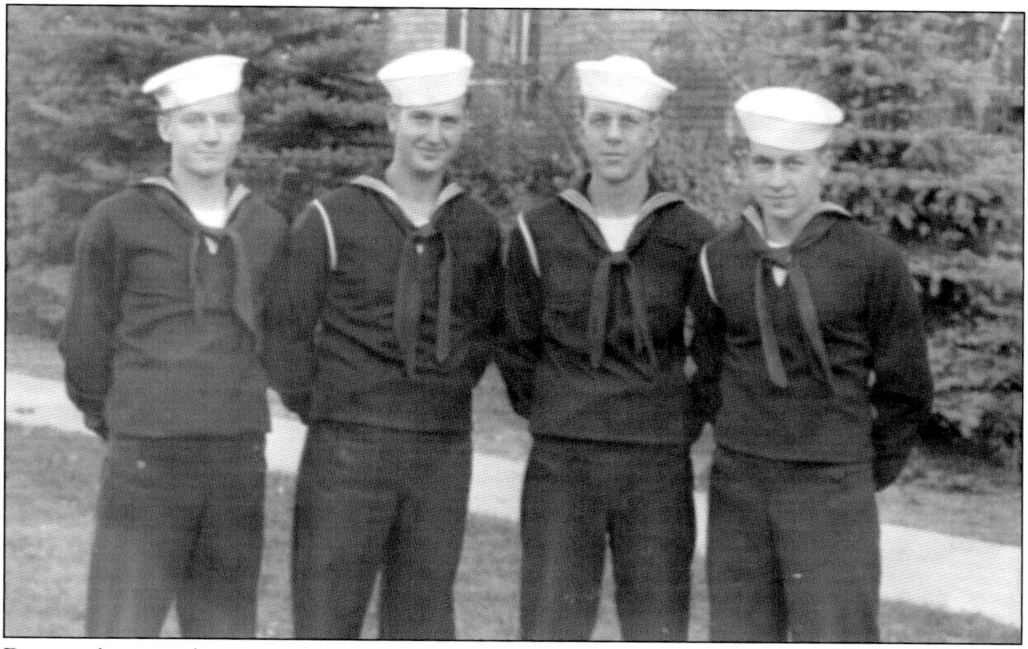

During the war, the University of Idaho, Southern Branch was the site of a US Navy training program for officer candidates. Initially known as the V-5 program, for the five months of instruction offered, the program later became known as the V-12, as it was 12 months long at that time. This 1944 photograph shows a group of prospective naval officers training at the V-12 program at the university. Note the candidate second from left. Known as Louis Weertz at this time, he would later gain fame as the pianist Roger Williams. (ISU.)

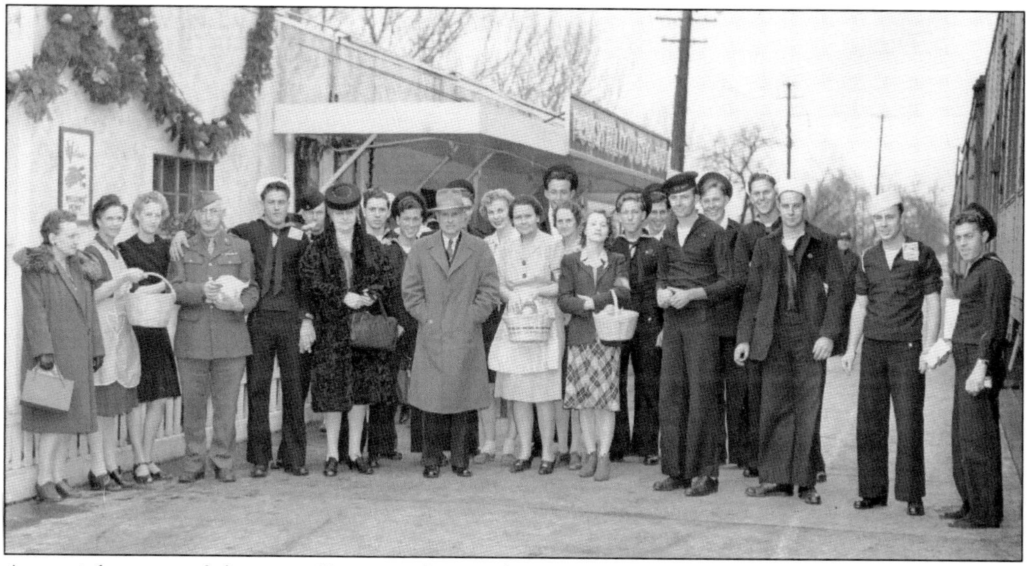

A crucial aspect of the war effort was the need to transport members of the armed forces both nationally and internationally. The United Service Organizations (USO) was an important component in these operations, providing refreshments and a friendly presence to men who were about to go off to combat. The USO facility in Pocatello, known also as the "Cookie Hut," was located just off the main Union Pacific Railroad facilities. As this photograph shows, the facility was frequented by members of all of the armed services. (BCHS.)

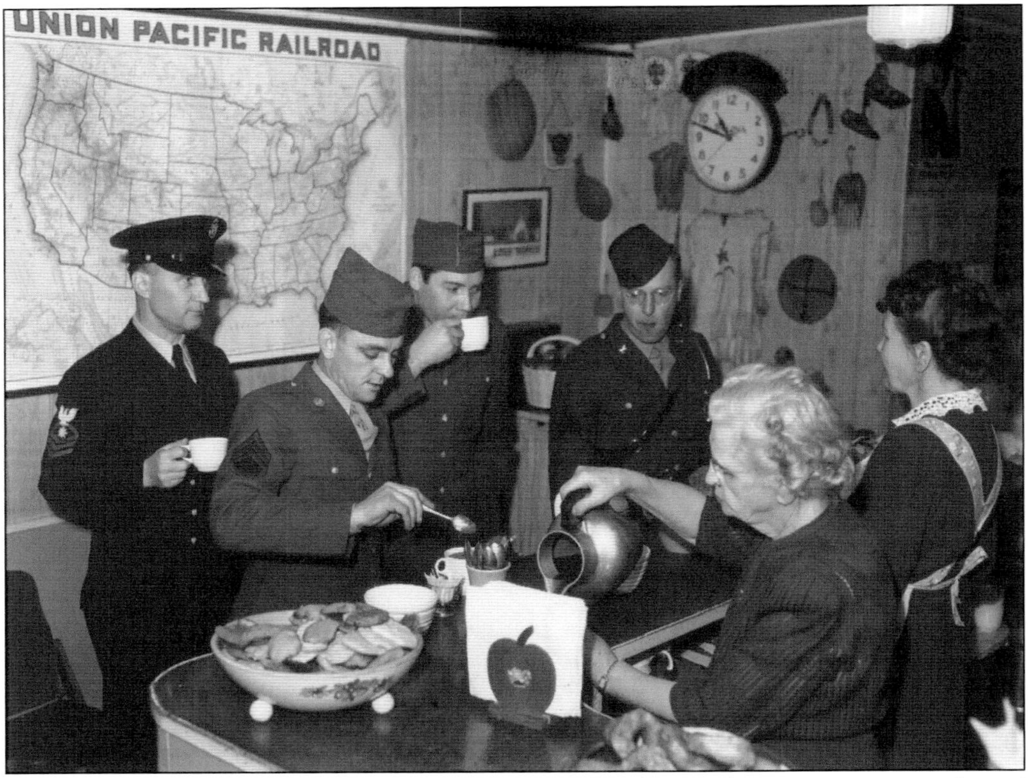

This January 1945 interior photograph of the USO facility shows volunteers serving members of the armed forces who have stopped along the way to their duty stations. An effort was made to make the facility as comfortable as possible. (BCHS.)

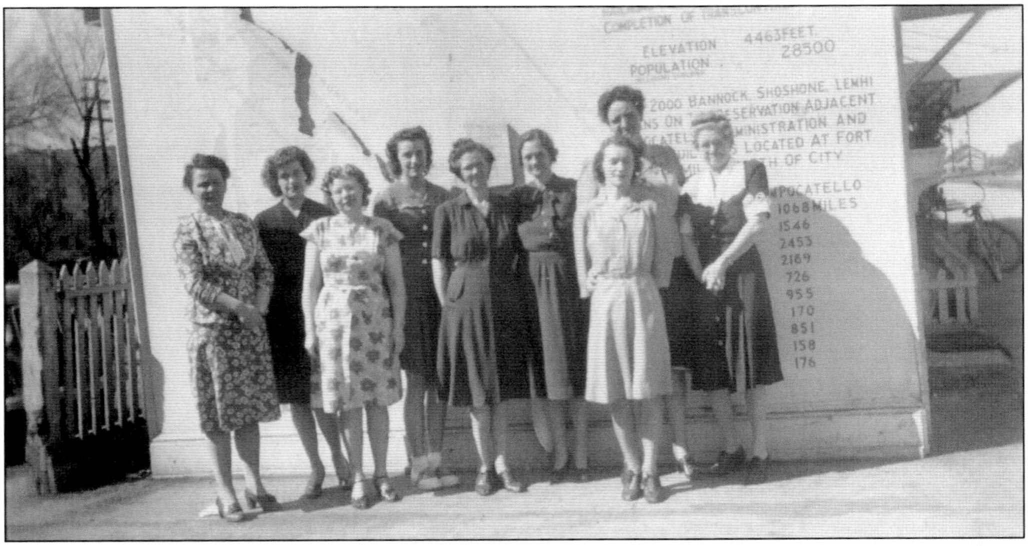

Some of the women volunteers who staffed the USO facility in Pocatello are seen here. These volunteers were remembered by the servicemen who frequented the USO hut as being unfailingly friendly and considerate in their efforts. Note the statistics posted on the side of the building listing the elevation and population of Pocatello as well as distances from certain cities in the United States. (BCHS.)

Eight

Pocatello Lives On

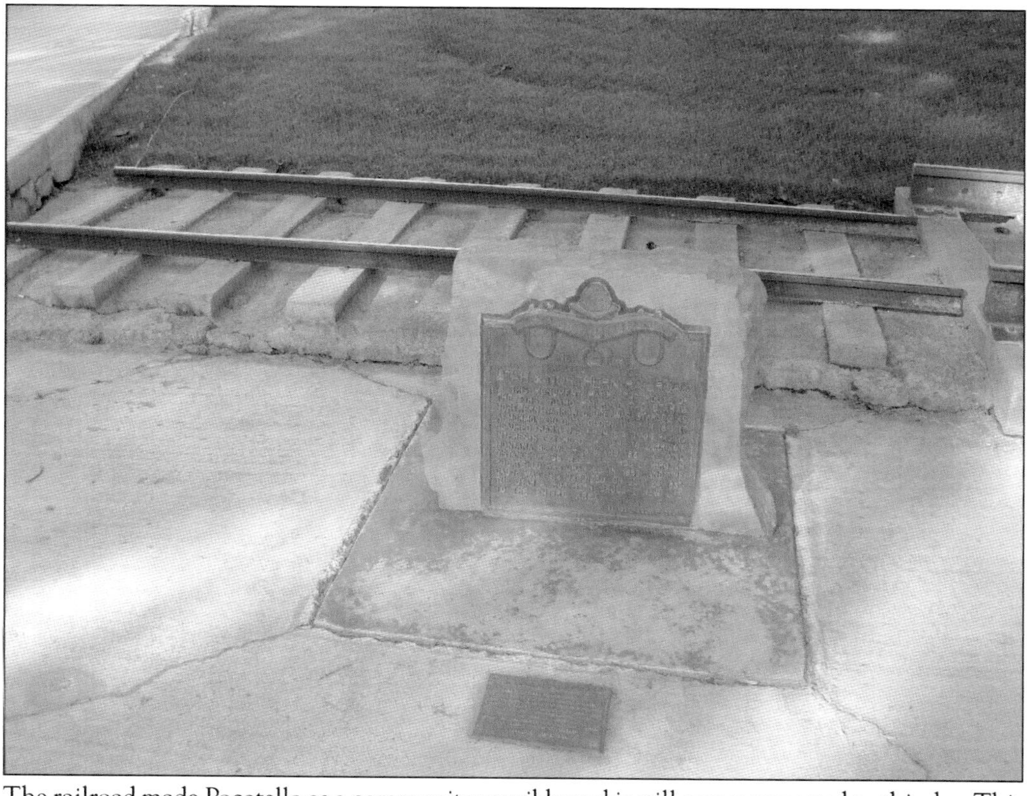

The railroad made Pocatello as a community possible and is still commemorated to this day. This memorial, located on the Idaho State University campus, marks where the Utah & Northern narrow-gauge rail system was located in Pocatello Junction, starting in 1877. In this way, the past is linked to the present in Pocatello. (Walter Mallette.)

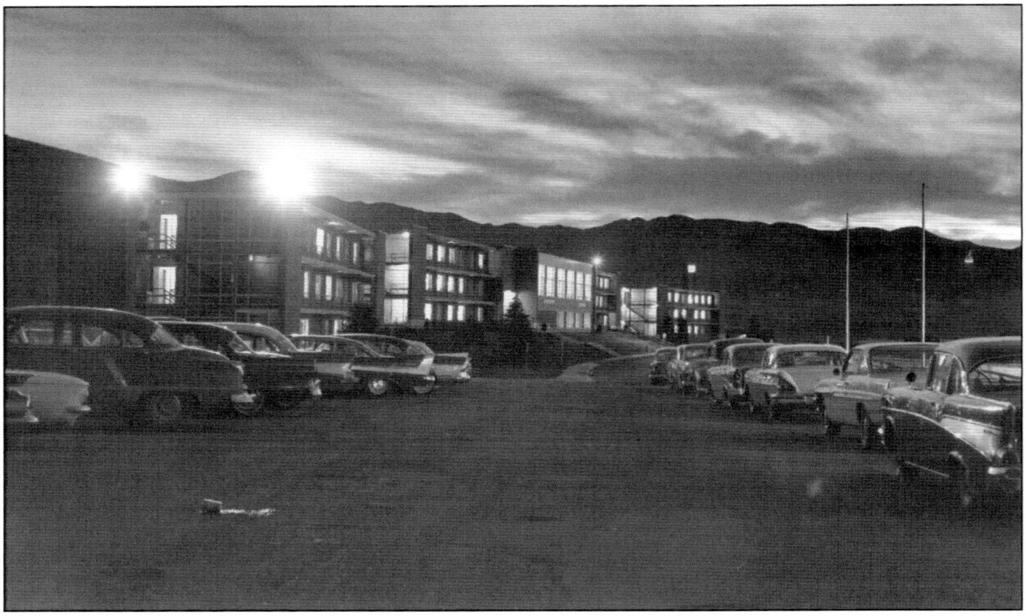

The expansion of the newly rechristened Idaho State University continued from the 1950s right thorough the 1960s, as the student population continued to increase. One need was for dormitory space for the student body, which was addressed by the newly constructed Nichols, Owen, and Redfield Halls on the north side of Red Hill. (BCHS.)

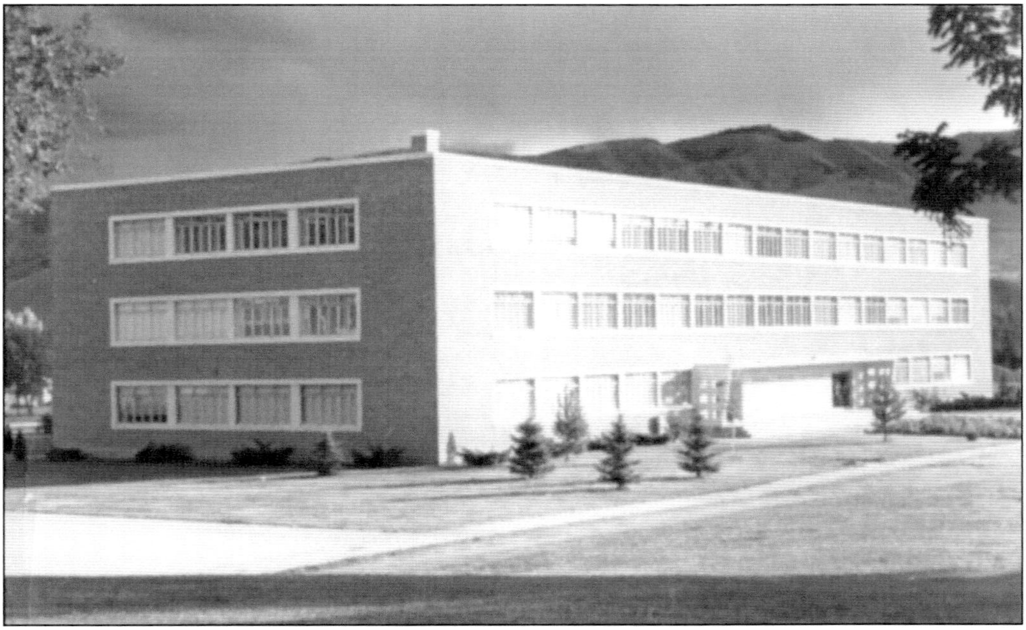

Another need for the expanding campus was for a larger library. This building, originally constructed to be the new library, was completed in 1954. It wasn't long before an even larger library was needed by the university. When a new library was completed in 1977, this building became the Museum Building, and houses the Idaho Museum of Natural History. (BCHS.)

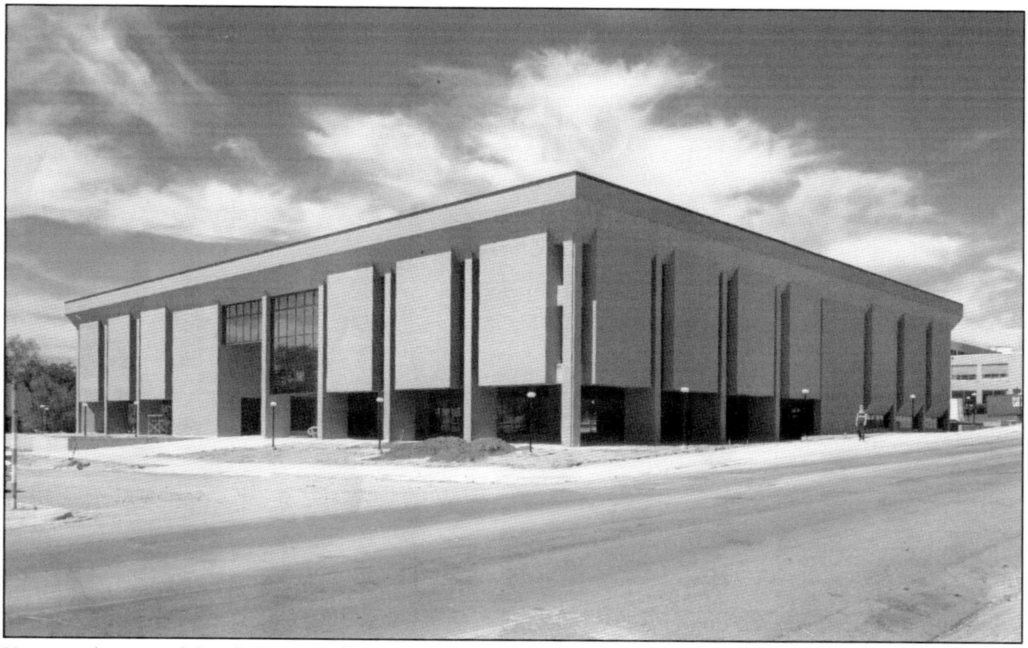

Yet another need for the expanding university was for a library facility that would accommodate the expanding volume of books, documents, and other media involved in conducting research in a university setting. The new library, completed in 1977, was later named in honor of Eli Oboler, the long-serving librarian at Idaho State University. (BCHS.)

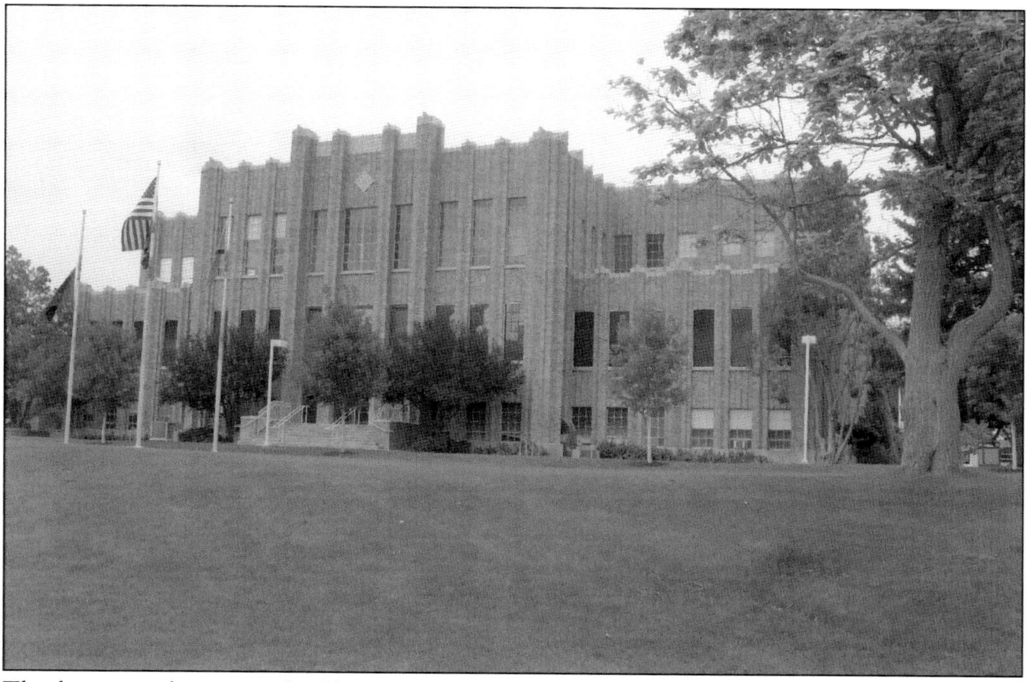

The former student union building on the Idaho State University campus continues to function as the main administration building for the university. While the interior has been completely transformed for this role, the exterior is remarkably unchanged from its original construction. (Walter Mallette.)

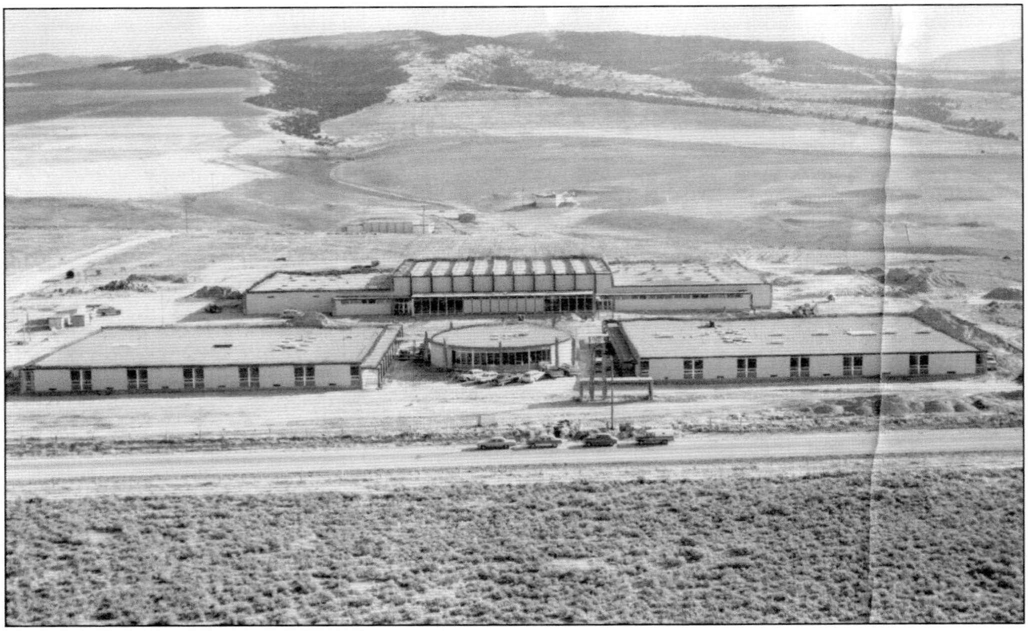

Pocatello ceased to be a single high school city in 1962 when Highland High School was opened. Located on Bench Road in the northeastern section of the city, Highland High soon gained a reputation as a fierce rival with cross-town Pocatello High, as well as being a presence in the state overall. This photograph shows the campus in the finishing stages of construction in 1962. The campus has since been converted to a one-building facility. (BCHS.)

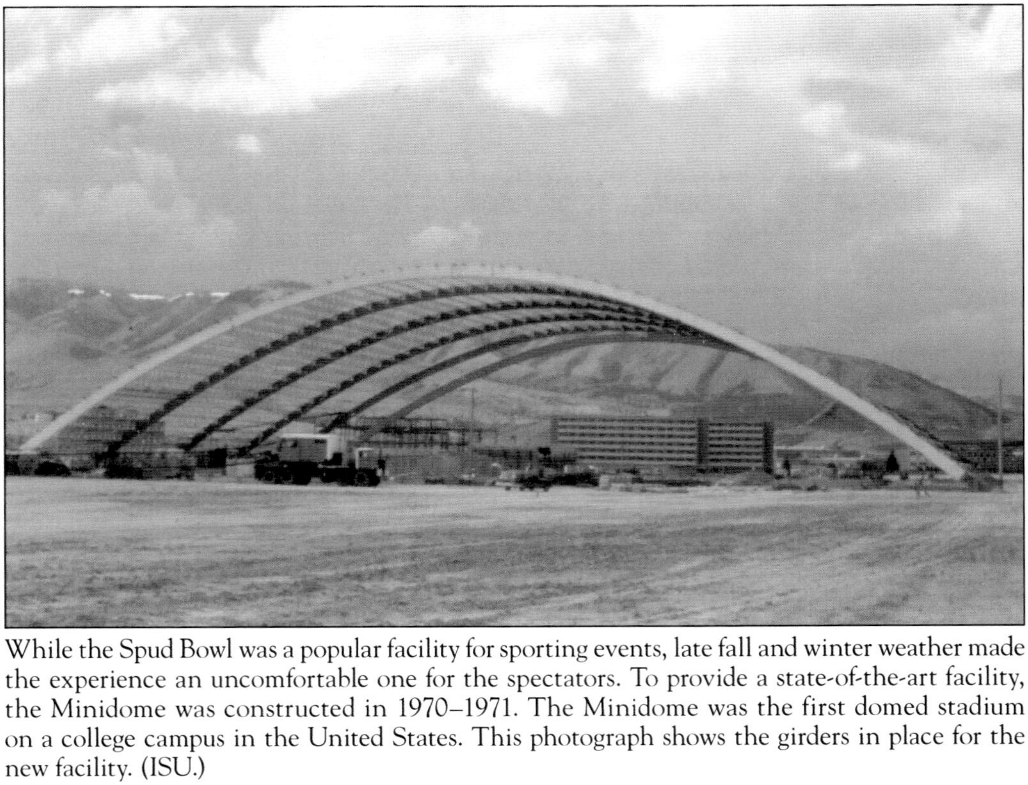

While the Spud Bowl was a popular facility for sporting events, late fall and winter weather made the experience an uncomfortable one for the spectators. To provide a state-of-the-art facility, the Minidome was constructed in 1970–1971. The Minidome was the first domed stadium on a college campus in the United States. This photograph shows the girders in place for the new facility. (ISU.)

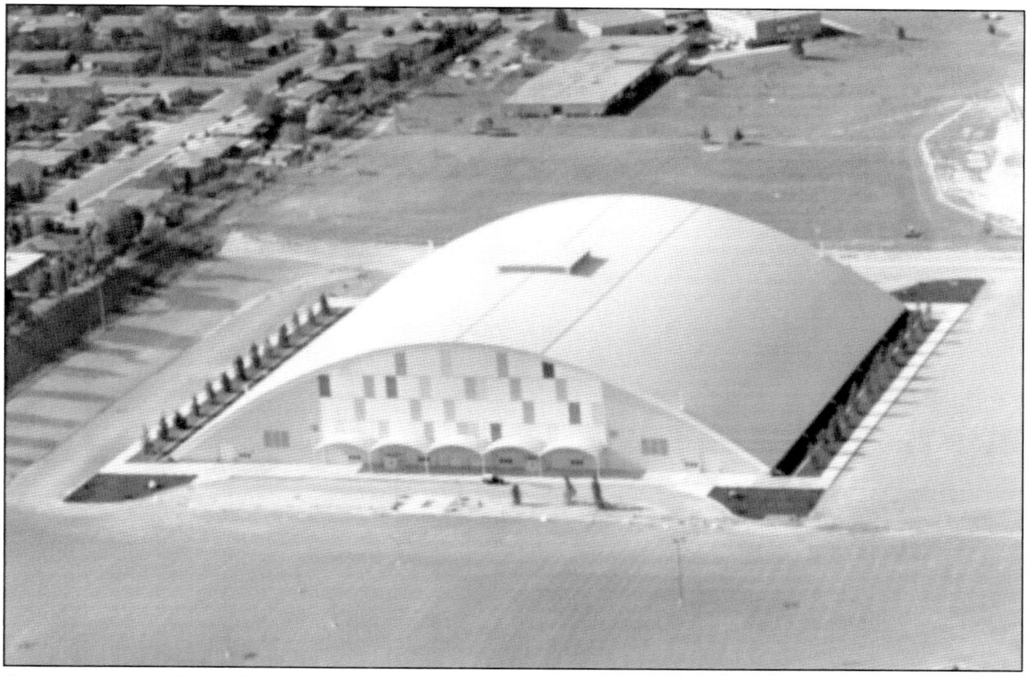

Once completed, the Minidome became a featured attraction of the Idaho State campus, and of Pocatello in general. The facility, since renamed Holt Arena (in honor of "Dubby" Holt), has featured numerous athletic events, as well as concerts, consumer shows, motorcross events, professional rodeos, and more. (ISU.)

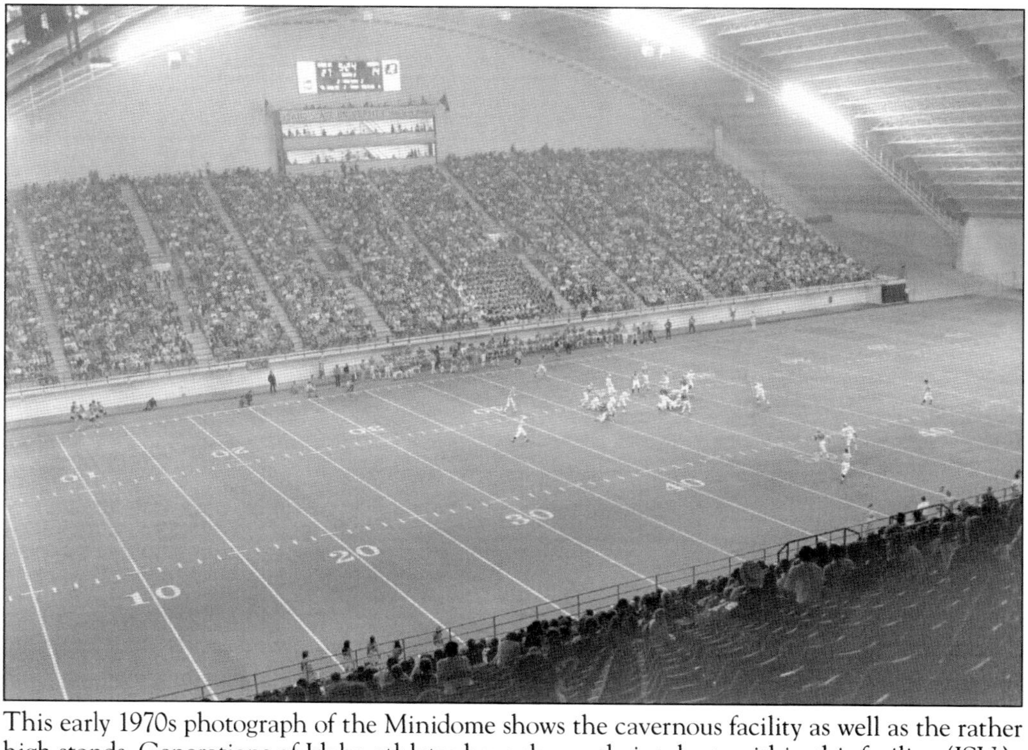

This early 1970s photograph of the Minidome shows the cavernous facility as well as the rather high stands. Generations of Idaho athletes have shown their talents within this facility. (ISU.)

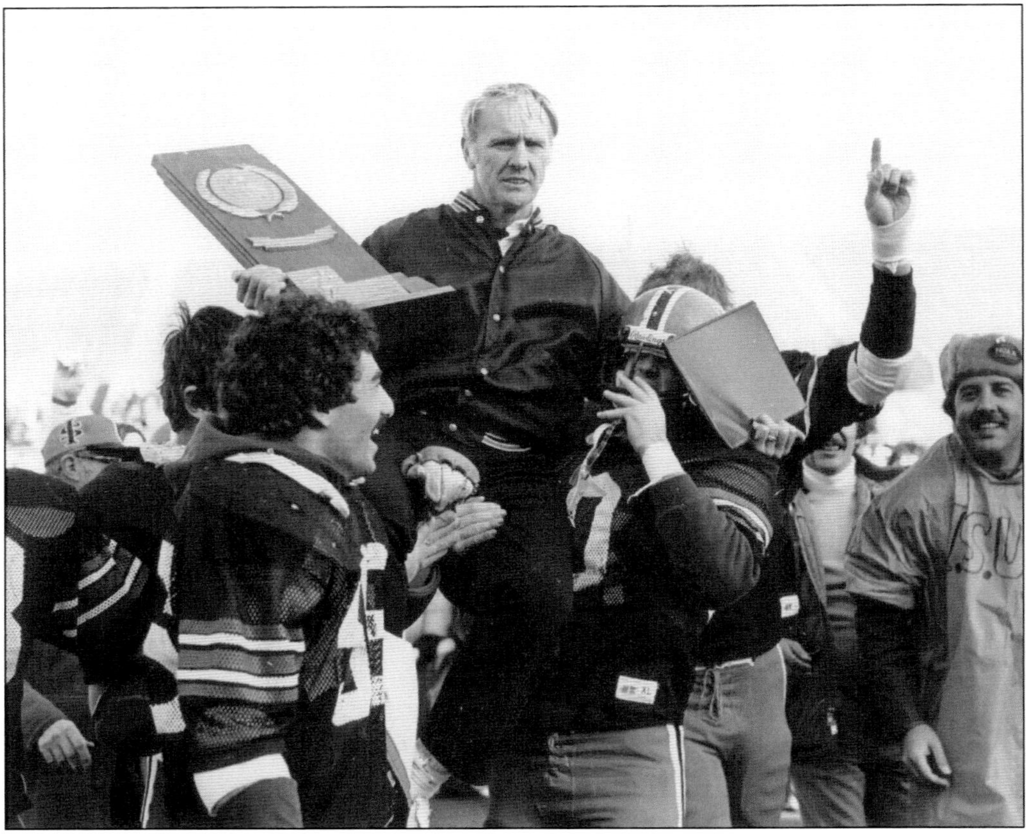

One significant highlight in the history of Idaho State athletics was the championship effort of the 1981 football team, which won the Division 1-AA national title. Led by coach Dave Kragthorpe, seen here being hoisted onto the shoulders of his players, the Bengals proved to be the best football team at their level in the country that year. (ISU.)

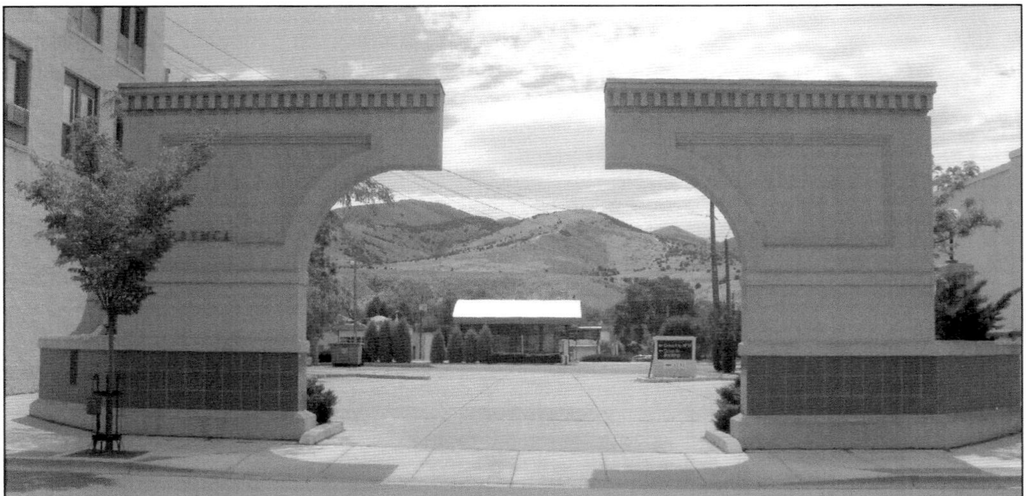

While the Railroad YMCA no longer exists, the structure continues to be commemorated in this memorial on Arthur Street. The arches pay homage to the arched entranceway of the original facility. (Walter Mallette.)

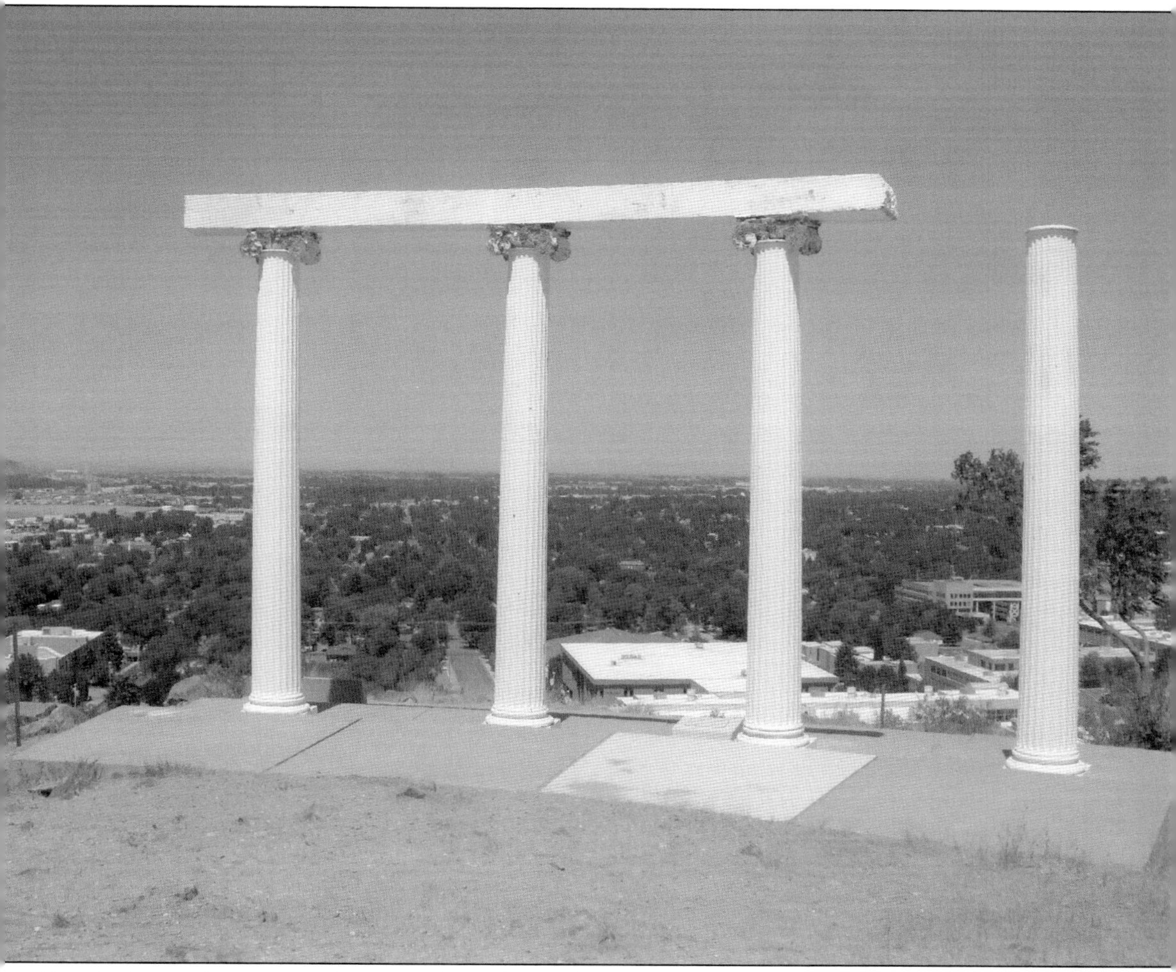

One highly visible landmark on the Pocatello skyline, these Doric columns were placed on the summit of Red Hill on the Idaho State University campus. The columns were formerly placed at the entrance to the McHan funeral home, and were donated to the university in 1962, when the facility was being demolished. This site remains a noted feature of the Idaho State University landscape and remains a popular hiking area. (Walter Mallette.)

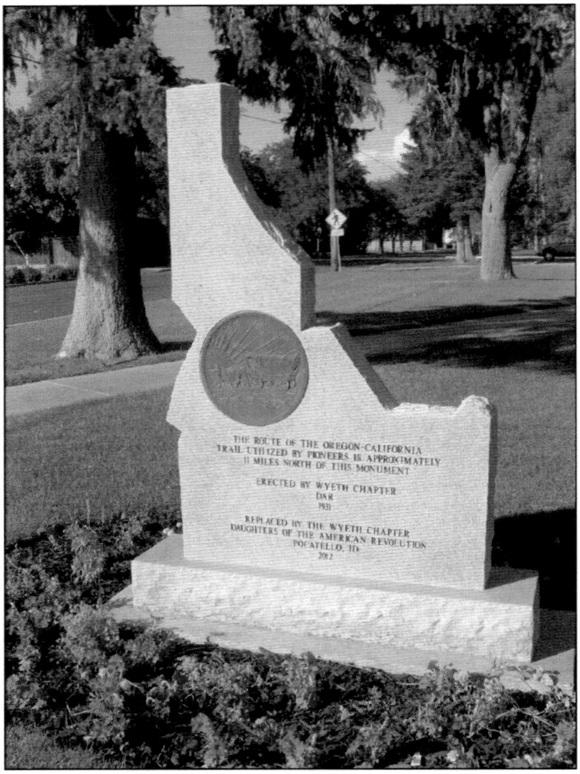

The route of the Oregon-California Trail, which went close to present-day Pocatello, is commemorated with this monument on the Idaho State University campus. This monument provides a link to the past for modern-day Pocatello. (Walter Mallette.)

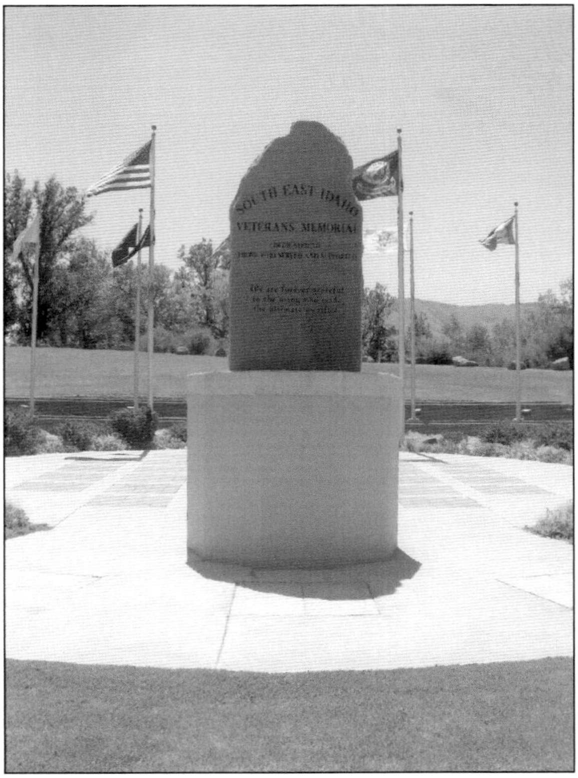

Today, the sacrifices that were made by residents of Pocatello, as well as residents of Southeastern Idaho, who served the United States, are commemorated at the South East Idaho Veterans Memorial. Located at the end of Fourth Avenue at the outskirts of Pocatello city limits, this memorial honors "the many who made the ultimate sacrifice." (Walter Mallette.)

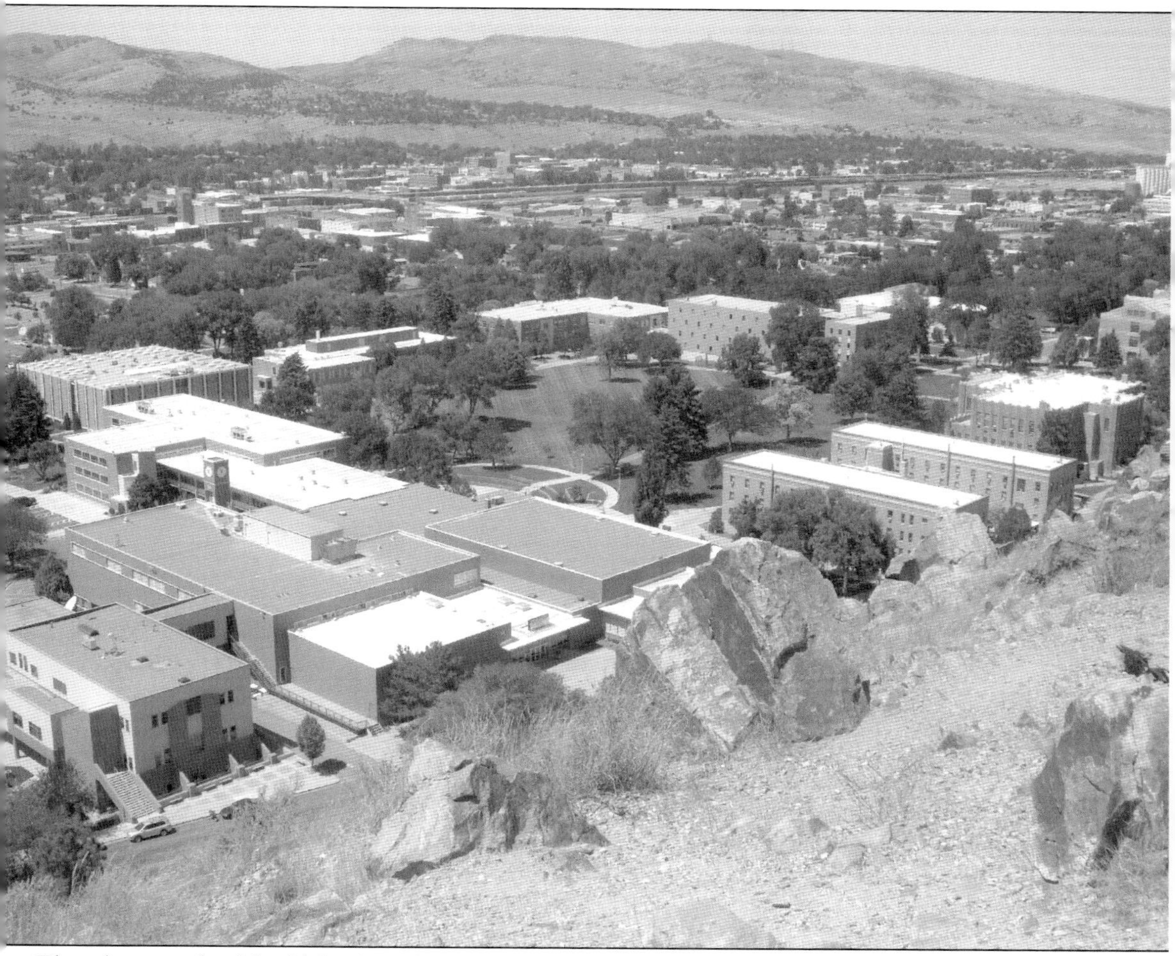

This photograph of the Idaho State University campus, taken from atop Red Hill, shows how the campus and the surrounding neighborhoods have expanded from the days when the Academy of Idaho started instructing students. The university continues its mission of education and research and remains a major presence in the city of Pocatello. (Walter Mallette.)

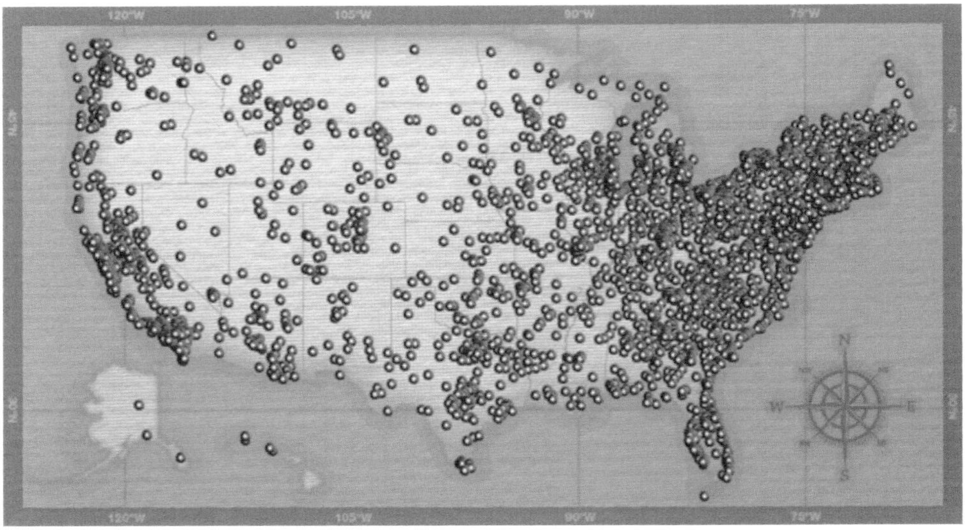